Art That Pays

On the cover:

The lingam *in the cover photo is a Hindu symbol of that which is invisible yet omnipresent, hence a visible symbol of that* Presence *that abides in all of Creation. Further, it is a* Shivalingam, *which denotes the primeval energy of the Creator, and it is said that at the end of Creation all of the different aspects of God will find a peaceful resting place in the lingam. Our hope is that in some small way we may offer to you, our readers, that same sense of peacefulness; that you may gain from this book the idea that you are not alone in your work of creating, that despite your fears you will be able to pay the rent; and, if you are true to your art and true to yourself and follow a few simple suggestions, it will all work out.*

Art That Pays

The Emerging Artist's
Guide to
Making a Living

by
Adele Slaughter
&
Jeff Kober

**A National Network for Artist Placement, NNAP,
Publication**

This book is based in part on material included in
For The Working Artist by Judith Luther.

Copyright © 1986 Judith Luther and
California Institute of the Arts
under title: *For The Working Artist* ISBN: 0-938683-00-4

Copyright © 1991 Judith Luther and
National Network for Artist Placement, NNAP
under title: *For The Working Artist* ISBN: 0-945941-01-3

Library of Congress Cataloguing in Publication Data.
Main entry under title: *Art That Pays*
ISBN 0-945941-14-5

cover design by Shirin Raban

photos of Matt Groening & Richard Jefferies
copyright © 2000, 2004 Mark Kirkland
photo of John Ritter and Jeff Kober copyright © 2000 Jenny Sullivan
photo of Shane Guffogg copyright © 2001 Shane Guffogg
photo of David Brown copyright © 2003 George Lange
photo of Tom Ormeny copyright © 2004 Tom Ormeny
photo of John Zorn copyright © 2004 John Zorn
cover photo & photo of Hubert Schmalix &
photo of Hubert Selby, Jr. copyright © 2004
Jeff Kober

For additional copies, contact:
National Network for Artist Placement, NNAP
935 West Avenue 37
Los Angeles, CA 90065
(323) 222-4035
www.artistplacement.com

printed in the United States of America

Dedication

John Ritter's passion for the theatre and for the craft of acting was second only to his passion for life and his family. He could make you laugh at will, and he loved doing it. He was a joy and an inspiration to anyone who knew him, and will be missed by everyone who ever had the privilege to work with him. Our book is dedicated to his memory.

∞

"…just as a guy who was interested in the golden thread that goes through me and you and…all the people out there…That's what an artist can do, or someone, anyone can do, if there's a willingness. Pluck that and either it makes you laugh or it makes you cry. It's that golden thread to humanity, and I'd like to be remembered as maybe a guy who plucked a few of those."

**John Ritter,
1948—2003**

Art That Pays

Table of Contents

Chapter 12
Music 139

Chapter 13
Visual Arts 159

Chapter 14
Writing

Appendices

Acknowledgements

Originally, this book was conceived through a series of workshops on how to survive as an artist, taught at CalArts back in the 80's. Warren Christensen, Stanley Fried and Judith Luther developed a curriculum to help students, once they left school, find their way through the maze that leads to becoming a working artist. They taught a variety of practical skills, like how to get jobs, do your finances, find apartments, buy health insurance, etc. The book that Judith Luther subsequently wrote was titled *For The Working Artist* and appeared originally in 1986 and was updated in 1991.

Recently, Warren Christensen, president of the National Network for Artist Placement, NNAP, asked me to rewrite the book and update the appendices that were over twelve years old. I brought Jeff Kober into the project because of his extensive experience as a working actor, his sassy writing style and his ability to understand and execute computer programs.

As we set about our task, we found much of Judith Luther's original information still to be quite pertinent and we incorporated what was applicable. As a matter of fact, when I contacted dancer Deborah Slater and asked her to read her quotes from the original book, she e-mailed me back the following:

> "(Sigh) – nothing much has changed. The extravaganzas are bigger but so is the workload. But obviously I still love it 'cause I'm still doing it."

So in the process of rewriting this book we took what we liked and added new information. For example, the chapter on the Internet is completely new since the Internet did not exist twelve years ago. We also interviewed some wonderful artists and expanded the general ideas of the book to include not only how to become a working artist, but how to become a successful artist as well. How indeed do you make art that pays? We wanted to know.

Many very successful artists shared their stories with us. We owe a special thanks to John Ritter, Matt Groening, Hubert Selby Jr., Dana Gioia, Richard Jefferies, James McManus, Murray Mednick, John Zorn, Craig Harris, David Brown, Connie Kupka, David Speltz, Tom Ormeny, Precious Chong, Shane Guffogg, Hubert Schmalix and Lula Washington.

We also preserved interviews and/or quotes from the original book from the following artists: Fred Strickler, Deborah Slater, Yen Lu Wong, Rebecca Wright, Donna Wood, Deborah Oliver, Carl Stone, Frans Von Rossum, Tim Miller, Kira Perov, Fionulla Flanagan, Peter Coyote, Barbara Bain, Bob Reidy, Bob Monaco, James Riordan, Larry Harris, Larry Stein and Kira Perov.

We thank Jenny Sullivan for letting us use the photograph of John Ritter and Jeff Kober, backstage at a production of her play, *J for J.* Thanks to Mark Kirkland for his photographs of Matt Groening and Richard Jefferies; and thanks to John Zorn for his self portrait, to Tom Ormeny for the use of his headshot and to George Lange for his photograph of David Brown.

We also give a round of applause to Judith Luther Wilder, Alexandra E. Liston and Dana Liston for their generous help editing and proofing this book. Finally, a warm acknowledgment goes to Warren Christensen for asking us to write this book in the first place.

We hope you find our book useful and we are grateful if we have been of service.

Adele Slaughter and Jeff Kober

Foreword

Art That Pays is a rewritten, updated version of *For The Working Artist,* a book I wrote for the California Institute of the Arts in 1986. The 2004 rewrite is uniquely the product of authors Adele Slaughter and Jeff Kober but still contains the words and wisdom of artists I interviewed almost two decades ago. It is reassuring that the spirit and vision of treasures such as Fred Strickler, Peter Coyote and Deborah Slater still inspire us today. Unfortunately, it is also alarming that so many of the barriers to success they faced in 1986 still prevent artists in a new millennium from enjoying the financial independence they deserve (which is why it is still important for today's generation of self-employed artists to follow their sage advice).

After reading the very first chapter of the new book, it was clear to me that the authors had produced a new book that was superior to *For The Working Artist.* New interviews with cartoonist Matt Groening, the late actor John Ritter, writers Hubert Selby, Jr. and Murray Mednick, actor Tom Ormeny and many others supplemented and enriched my own interviews with choreographers Fred Strickler and Deborah Slater, performance artist Tim Miller, curator Josine Ianco-Starrels, and photographer Kira Perov.

They not only updated chapters I had written about working overseas, financial management, taxes, acting, and living with visionaries and visual artists but wrote new and wonderfully useful chapters on grantsmanship, housing, the Internet, and the law.

Everything has changed since I wrote *For The Working Artist* in 1986. National boundaries have shifted, wars have been fought, and cures have been found for dozens of crippling diseases I grew up thinking had to be fatal. Thanks to a globalized economy, new technologies and networked markets, business in the United States and in the world will never be the same. And yet, because of a persistent lack of business capacity, artists have not kept pace with other industries that have been transformed by technology and contemporary business practices. This book simply encourages them to "catch up and keep up."

Artists will do themselves a favor if they heed this message. Cora Mirikitani, the CEO of the Japanese American Cultural and Community Center in Los Angeles and a long time program officer for philanthropic foundations such as the Pew Charitable Trust and The James Irvine Foundation, makes this point in a brochure she wrote for the Center for Cultural Innovation. She observes that "the many artists, writers, designers and educators who make up the new 'creative class' and continue to work in the nonprofit sector can do so in a way that generates satisfaction and money.

"By linking their natural creativity and tolerance for risk to the latest business tools and practices," she says, "artists can bring their work to the marketplace in a way that is both spiritually and financially fulfilling."

The authors of *Art That Pays* echo her sentiments, and successful artists like Groening and Ritter reinforce their views. Struggling artists in this country and abroad should pay attention. Beverly Sills says, "Art is the signature of civilizations." No one in the arts community would disagree with Sills, at least on this issue. However, in most industries, when you put your signature on the dotted line, you get paid. Artists should structure their careers so that they, too, are paid when they leave their marks on cities and civilizations. And they shouldn't be embarrassed when they prepare their tax returns in ways that legally and properly enable them to pay the IRS as little as possible or follow the other sound bits of advice Slaughter, Kober and their friends have provided in their book.

"Art is long. Life is short" has been attributed to everyone from Hippocrates to Madonna. The source doesn't concern me a great deal (although it might concern Hippocrates and Madonna) but I do think artists should get paid for the former and enjoy the latter. *Art That Pays* wisely encourages both; and if your daughter or son is an artist, if you are married to an artist, or best of all, if you are lucky enough to be an artist, I urge you to read this book.

Judith Luther Wilder
President, Center for Cultural Innovation

> *Ah! This is an* opportunity, *instead of an awkward transition!*
> **Precious Chong, actress**

Chapter 1

Choosing the Artist's Life

> *"Oh, God, did it terrify me, to think that I'd live however long I was going to live and look at my life and be forced to say, 'Cubby, you blew it.' And then I'd be snuffed. Pmmfft! Oh, it was terrifying. So I had to find some way of doing something with my life. I couldn't stand the idea of living and doing nothing with this thing."*
>
> **Hubert Selby, Jr., writer**

Many of my teachers told me that you do not choose to be an artist, you accept what you are—accept that you are someone who simply *has* to make art. You feel an urge, something inside that has to be born, and so you find a way and a place to create and to express that impulse. You throw paint, string together words, sing musical notes and choreograph steps in a dance. You do whatever it takes to make art. There is something driving you from within; there is a goal ahead of you, vague as it may be, but stretched out as you are between that urge and that goal, you use what is at hand— you use your body and mind and spirit in whatever way is necessary—to move forward. If you are an artist, this is what you do. How you do it is your business. Art is what feeds your soul, feeds your being, so art is what you do with your life. Are you willing to be who you are? Are you willing to be different, unique, perhaps a bit odd? Are you willing to be an artist?

You are reading this book because you already have sensed on some level that you are an artist. Perhaps you are trying to learn how to make your life as an artist better or you are trying to decide whether or not to do it at all. How can you take this vague idea of being an artist and make it pay?

First, you embrace the choice as a possibility. Rarely do people *choose* to face the unknown, and yet that is precisely where the artist must live. In order to make art that pays, in order to live in that unknown, the artist must have a vision. How do we create that vision? How do we commit to our art? So many times, we get married, pregnant, take out a mortgage, accept a job, and our life happens without a clear vision, without us ever *really* making a choice. Yet, those who embrace their choices are at peace with what is. They know exactly what they are getting into and then choose to do it anyway. A happy ending *is* actually possible if one makes informed decisions.

The List

Some sages suggest that when confronted with a decision, it is wise to make a list. Two lists, actually. Take a sheet of paper and divide it into two columns. On one side, you list one set of reasons under the heading, *Reasons to be with Joe,* and on the other side, *Reasons not to be with Joe*, or, *By Choosing to be with Joe, I Gain...?* and *By Choosing not to be with Joe, I Give Up...?*

If you've tried this before, you know that there may be twenty entries on one side and only one on the other, but the one is so compelling that, when seen in black and white, you must make the choice in that direction. Other times, you fill up pages and pages and still have no idea what to do.

You can make your own list about Joe. Here, we are going to list some reasons for being, or not being, an artist. For some, maybe the choice has already been made, but try it anyway. Find the point of clarity. Gaining insight is an ongoing process for an artist. Vagueness creates resentment, resentment creates distance, and distance creates divorce. Give yourself the opportunity to have a good, loving, long-term relationship with your art. When we have clarity, we can see our gains and we can accept our losses. We can determine whether or not the rewards outweigh the costs.

By choosing to become an artist, what do you gain?	*By choosing to become an artist, what do you give up?*
Satisfying that deep inner drive to create art.	Financial stability and security.
Making up your own schedule, freedom, unobstructed days, a broad horizon.	Conventional work environment, daily structure, routine.
Being your own boss.	Vacation pay, sick pay.
Seeing life as fresh and new at each moment; keeping yourself young and alive.	Security. Knowing what's coming next.
Living outside the norm, which means you actually get to find out who you are.	Corporate rewards for "toeing the line" and/or being a good soldier
Garnering fame and fortune; and more important, respect from a community of like-minded professionals	Ability to start a family in a timely and "usual" fashion.
Leaving behind something of value on this earth.	A company retirement plan.
Exuding sex appeal (at least in your own mind, and that's really where it starts, isn't it?).	Approval of society, parents and peers.
Creating original works of art that may stand the test of time.	Company health plan and social security benefits.
Making a connection to something greater than yourself.	A larger company and/or corporation that provides a feeling of safety, security and family.

In order to make art that pays it will benefit you to address some of the points on our list. In addition to helping you make your choice, this is a great exercise to exorcise those hidden self-limiting beliefs—those nasty shit-birds that sit on your shoulder and say, "You can't write, say, paint, act, sing, dance that shit."

Satisfaction/Security

An old friend has a habit of saying, "security is overrated." For him, it's true. But then, he's never had it. For most of us, giving up security and financial stability is a big nut to crack; perhaps even the biggest issue for anyone deciding whether or not to be an artist. The idea of little or no financial security can be extremely unsettling and flies in the face of nearly everything we are taught about how to live on this planet. However, if you have the good fortune to find a way to make a living at your art, it's worth all the canned soup and peanut butter you may eat and all the part-time jobs you have to take to keep yourself alive until you get to that place. You may never strike it rich as an artist, or you may be wildly successful, but you *will* find a way to pay the bills so you can continue to make art. Why? Because when you accept the responsibility of your choice to be an artist, you can embrace the decision and end the worrying. If you choose it, it's the right thing to do.

Freedom/Convention

Many artists scoff at the idea of a bourgeoisie routine. *Nine to Five* has been a song, a movie and a way of life and has been often denigrated, and perhaps rightly so. But clichés form because there is support for them in society, and there must be more than a few people in the world who want that kind of schedule, or it wouldn't exist. What is missed, though, by the detractors, and embraced, consciously or unconsciously, by those who are on that schedule, is the comfort that can come from knowing where you have to be tomorrow morning, and the morning after that, and knowing just how much you'll be paid for being there.

Scheduling is every bit as important for the artist, but in his case, things *must* be scheduled *by him*. You have to work on your art every day—*and* do the laundry *and* pay the bills *and* go to your 'B' job. It takes work just to make up a schedule that fits everything in. The upside, though, is that part of your job as an artist is also occasionally to rejuvenate your creative flow, which means that sometimes a mid-week matinee or a morning spent in bed can be part of the job description.

You're the Boss/Vacation & Sick Pay

Artist or not, each of us would like to be the boss, at least in theory. Until we are called before the Board of Directors and asked to explain the drop in production over the last quarter or we need to confront Charlie in accounting about his drinking. As an artist, though, being your own boss is a pretty big plus. You make your own hours; it's hard to get fired; there are no office politics. But as the boss, you'll have to earn enough on your own to be able to pay yourself to take a vacation.

Seeing Life Fresh/Knowing What's Next

Many artists see the world from an original point of view, like children. It's one of the necessities of the job, as well as one of the perks of the job. The need to see life as fresh and new at each moment can be a hell of a lot of work, but can also be meditative. Meditation has been shown to calm the nervous system and to promote a general sense of health and well being, and it is generally true that a happy man lives longer. (A study done at the University of Toronto found that actors who received an Oscar lived an average of four years longer than actors who had not won the coveted award. So you have *that* going for you.)

As for knowing what tomorrow will bring: yes, it certainly has its advantages (see above) but in the end, it's an illusion anyway. If we really knew what was going to happen, we'd all just go to the track.

Outside the Norm/Toeing the Line

Many of us want to be unique. We want to be seen as different and special and "other than;" and as artists we can fulfill that wish. (Actually, many of us overshoot the mark and end up as eccentrics.) But we do get to spend our lives searching for something in our work, and that something is always, in some form, the Self. Those of a spiritual bent would say there is nothing else in life that matters *but* that, and toeing the line and living *within* the norm makes that search much more difficult. However, a personal *"Eureka!"* moment, joyful as it may be, is not necessarily going to get you a promotion, though it will probably inspire more art.

Fame & Fortune/Family

Fame is often overrated and the desire for fame can never be the basis for choosing to be an artist. Most artists will say that after the movie they made, the book they published, or the screenplay they wrote, the thing that ached inside, that compelled the art to be created in the first place, was not satisfied by that accomplishment. If you're in it for recognition, you're in it for the wrong reason. Being recognized or acknowledged might be gratifying and fun for a moment, but ultimately it does not fill the well. Fame does not inspire, nor does it fuel, our desire to continue to create.

Please note, we are not saying that having a family is un-doable for the artist. But it does seem to be a given that financial pressures are going to be more pronounced in a household that does not have a steady, predictable income; and even though an artist/parent who works at home could conceivably take care of children *and* do his work (we speak from experience here), chances are good that one job or the other will suffer.

Leaving Something of Value/Retirement Plan

> *Retirement? No, I'm fucked. We're fucked. We're fucked! I've got Social Security. We have no savings. Pension plan from SAG will give me a few hundred dollars a month. I can starve on that.*
> **Tom Ormeny, actor/theatre owner/teacher**

Art provides the possibility of leaving behind on this earth something of value that is not necessarily measured by money or by the balance in our retirement accounts. We all want to find meaning in our lives. For some of us this urge is satisfied by having a family and children, and/or by building a business. For others of us, in addition to the desire for family, we want to matter in some other way, some way perhaps that we can't even articulate. We feel a need to see ourselves as more than just a brief collection of cells and electrical impulses, here for a moment and then gone; and we want to create something unique, special and divinely human to fulfill this need. We want respect and recognition for what we create and produce. We want to have an impact. And, as you shall see in our book, Tom Ormeny's quote aside, you can come up with your own retirement plan.

Sexier/Approval

> *The thing that kept me interested and kept me going all through the years is that I did what I wanted to do, and that was it. And I didn't give a fuck who thought what about it. I followed my particular muse, without any regard whatsoever to what people wanted me to do. And that keeps you young. I'm not going to use the word "happy" because that's really irrelevant to the whole thing. That's for fuckin' yuppies, you know? The American dream is just some distraction so the government can keep you under control.*
>
> **John Zorn, composer**

We think the above says all you need to know about the choice between being sexy and seeking approval. Zorn is a very sexy artist because like most successful people we know, he does not search for the approval of anyone else, but makes art because he wants to and that ability to follow an artistic vision is inherently sexy. Think of Picasso, Diego Rivera, Anne Sexton, Sylvia Plath, Ted Hughes, Brad Pitt, Anthony Hopkins and so on.

Creating Original Works of Art/Health Plan

The literature of the world, from Nietzsche to Ecclesiastes, tells us that, *"...there is no new thing under the sun."* That is undoubtedly true, but it doesn't mean you have to stop looking if looking is what gives you a reason to get out of bed. And, like the retirement plan mentioned above, you can have a health plan as an artist, too.

Connection to Something Greater/Corporate Umbrella

This, the final entry on our list, is perhaps the most personal of all our comparisons. It simply comes down to "what gives you a feeling of safety?" For some of us, it's the 401K and a company car, or the sense of belonging that comes with wearing the uniform of our company; and for some others it's being able to face ourselves in the mirror, knowing we've done everything in our power to connect with some sense of The Ineffable and to express it. Neither is better or worse, merely different. Thanks for playing along.

> *And this kid says 'What'll I do? I'd like to have a plan like my buddies have a plan....I said, 'Well that's a really good idea. You should have a plan, but it's not going to be the same kind of plan that a fireman has.*
> **Tom Ormeny, actor/theatre owner/teacher**

So the question remains, how does an artist make art that pays? What are the steps that you take to move from the idea of being a painter, a novelist, a poet, a musician, a sculptor, an actor or dancer? What do you do to become a paid professional? We believe that this book can help you by pointing you in the right direction. By pointing you to resources for the basics, ideas about jobs, how to manage your finances, get a lawyer, write a grant, find a community, market yourself on the Internet, work overseas, get an agent, join a union or make a resume you can begin to set up a life in which your art can make you money. This book can help you structure a plan for success that fits your needs and lifestyle. One of the most valuable things we offer in this book is the experience of other artists who have found success, and who have been gracious enough to pass on what worked for them.

Bottom line, as an artist you have an even greater need to make long term plans than other folks. Income will likely arrive at irregular intervals. You'll have to make a spending plan and save money when you can, maintain good credit and find the ways to do your art and get your work into the marketplace. The goal is to achieve a balanced life while still allowing you the freedom to create on a daily basis.

We aspire to give you workable ideas, practical, concrete suggestions and overall encouragement. The pursuit of art is noble— a fact not always acknowledged or supported in our society. And we want to remind you that as hard as it may be to achieve your dream, you can make it, and you can even have fun in the midst of the absurdity and wonder that is this life you have chosen. Enjoy.

∞

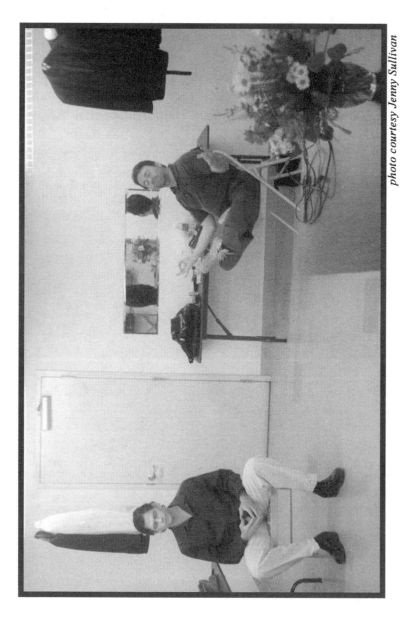

photo courtesy Jenny Sullivan

John Ritter with the author, backstage, Santa Fe, NM, 2000

John Ritter Interview

John Ritter, who first made celebrity status in 1977 on the sitcom Three's Company, *talked with us in between first-year episodes of his ABC series,* 8 Simple Rules for Dating My Teenage Daughter. *Several months later, three episodes into their second season and just as this book was about to go to press, John passed away. Joseph Fuqua, who directed John in* J for J, *an original play written by and starring Jenny Sullivan, one of John's oldest friends, tells this story:*

"One day after rehearsal I said to him, 'Hey, John. I really like that shirt. You always dress perfectly for John Ritter.' You know, it was that silk shirt with the coffee cups on it. And John started unbuttoning it, and he said, 'Here, I want you to have it,' and I said, 'No, John, I don't want your shirt,' but he wouldn't hear it. He insisted I take it. He said, 'No, I love this shirt, and I really want you to have it.' He took it off—he had a t-shirt underneath—and gave it to me, and that was the beginning of our running bit about, 'He gave me the shirt off his back.'

"We had lots of nice talks. We got to be pretty close. Then several months later, I hadn't seen him for a while, I was doing [the play] Dancing at Lughnasa, *and John and Amy [John's wife] came to see it. They waited around after the show, and when I came out, John said, 'Joe, I loved it. You were so great. The way you delivered that line, "Well, well, well!" It was wonderful.' And I said, 'Thanks, John. I love your jacket.' He was wearing this beautiful purple jacket. I didn't know it at the time, but it was a Versace; and John whipped it off and said, 'Here! Here! I want you to have it!' I said, 'No, John. I don't want your jacket.' He said, 'No, take it, take it!' We were actually wrestling with it. Finally I tried it on. It was too big for me, but John said I looked great. It gave him such pleasure to give someone [else] pleasure. He just beamed. And as always, we laughed a lot. So I kept the jacket. Of course when he was*

*leaving,climbing into his Cadillac, I said, 'John, I like your car,'
and he said, 'Okay, that's enough.'*

*Jenny Sullivan ads the kicker to the story: "The last time I saw
John, a bunch of us had gone to see Amanda McBroom. She was
singing at the John Anson Ford [Theatre]. I was settling in and
someone said they'd seen John down front. As I was going down to
say hello, I saw Joseph come in. So I found John. Je looked nervous.
He told me he was meeting his ex-wife and her parents there. It was
Amy's idea. We laughed. , I rubbed his back and said, 'It'll be fine.'
And then I said, 'Oh, Joseph's here! You should say hi!' and he said,
'Oh, Jesus, don't let him know I'm here. I don't have any more clothes
to give him!'"*

My first piece of advice is: see a play a week; and if you can't,
read a play a week. If you don't have money, go to the library. See
what the great authors are talking about. And if you want to be an
actor to make a whole bunch of money, forget it. Learn how to be
an agent. Because if you want to be an actor to get rich, you're in
the wrong business.

Go out on auditions and try to do little theatre. There's theatre
all around. Get *Backstage West* and see where the auditions are.
Hang out with actors, go to plays and go backstage and ask an actor,
'How did you do that?' The phone is not going to ring with a casting
director saying, 'We heard you were talented from your uncle Sid.
Can you be in our movie?' That's not ever going to happen.

When I was at college, we went on auditions between classes
for little plays, so I worked on this trilogy of anti-war plays at the
Pasadena Playhouse, and then I got on the Pasadena Freeway back
to USC and I was the curtain puller on *Imaginary Invalid* by Moliere.
I completely fell asleep one time and someone kicked me awake
wearing a mask. Scared the hell out of me.

I really love doing theatre. I did [the Neil Simon play] *The
Dinner Party* for about two years on and off, nine months in New
York, every night, eight shows a week. I think it was Anthony

Hopkins who once said, 'I think I've completed my relationship with the theatre.' Right now I am so happy going to work every day. I have to say I really enjoy doing the little play every Friday night in front of three hundred people, and having it beamed out in about three weeks to the country, and in the meantime I've done different plays with the same company, and that's a sitcom. But all in all I think I'd have to say doing plays is my favorite medium.

I think one of the things that really helped me, in comedy, was hearing the laughter [doing plays] and knowing what's funny to an audience and what's not, and what *you* do that can tag a joke line or make something funny. You try it one night, and that works, and you try it another night and it doesn't work—the experience you get in front of an audience as an actor for drama *and* comedy is invaluable. An audience can tell you so much about what's going on.

My problem with interviews—I would never, ever, ever, as an early actor, get a part doing an interview. I would come in, and they would say, 'Tell us about yourself,' and I would say, 'Well, there's not much to tell.' It was very hard for me to sell myself. Then I realized, later, when I had been on the other side of interviews, people really need you to come in and be in the moment and it doesn't really matter what you talk about. Don't try to own the room, but be assured of yourself—you know, people don't really have the time to take care of you, be your nursemaid. They want to see what you can bring. Also, if you get a chance to do it again, take their notes and show them something completely different. Then they know that you're not locked into one thing. You're trying to establish yourself—show off your wares. It's really tricky: you have to be real, then that's maybe not enough, so you have to be interesting, and then maybe you have to be funny on top of that, it can be tricky. But one of the things is, in an audition, you really have an audience, buying and selling, hiring and firing, so the more you are in front of an audience as an actor, the more comfortable you will be in an audition or when you're taping or filming something in front of a camera."

You've got to go out and work. And after a while, you'll either say, 'Well, nobody believes in me, but I believe in me,' and you'll keep going, or you'll say 'Nobody believes in me, maybe I'd better try this other profession.' Or maybe you'll say, 'I really like to work with the set designer,' or 'I can manage this theatre better than they can' and you'll get into the business side. Or you'll say, '*I think this fabric would be* much *better,* 'and you'll become a costume designer *[laughter]*. You'll be with people doing something that's bigger than you. You'll be with people dealing with ideas and communicating with an audience, and it's a vibrant way to live. But you still have to earn money. So don't be too proud to take a job to support yourself as an actor. There are so many different ways to come at acting; there are so many different success stories. But your story is your story and you can create your own path.

[John] Blankenship said to me in college, 'In order to be in the theatre, you have to be a fanatic about it.' You have to really, really love it. You have to feel that heat inside of you that makes you want to go out there and put yourself on the line. It's tough. And when you get rejected, it's not like they rejected what's in your briefcase, it's, 'We wanted to go a different way, we don't want you.' And you've got to be able to take that. And you've got to be able to handle success. It's a weird profession. We have to keep one foot planted in the real world and one foot planted in the play world.

One of the things I'm telling my son Jason, who is a young actor, is you somehow have to look yourself in the mirror, and I always put my word and my friendship out there, as opposed to what you think is the golden goose, if something better comes along, you know…it's sort of like dating: you promised you'd go out with Zelda, but then Naomi comes in and says I'm available, well, you've gotta go with Zelda to the dance, otherwise you're a rat. I remember I was doing a play at Bovard Auditorium and I got an offer to go and film a movie, but I was already working, so I remember having to do the play and feeling pretty good about it because I met some people I really liked, and it was a play that was a forerunner of how I felt about doing sitcoms.

Acting class? [Nina Foch] taught me something. We were trying to create a private moment, and I was holding a cat, and I was blowing in the cat's face—this really happened to me—and the cat looked at me, and about the fourth time I did it, it just raked my face with its claws, scratched my eye. It actually scratched my cornea, this cat I had. And so what I did, which I didn't do in real life but I did in the improv is, I just beat the shit out of the cat. I flung it around by its tail and smashed it into the walls and I just tore it up, and I was making the cat sounds and the kids in class were peeing themselves because it was so violent and funny and completely abnormal behavior, like a psychotic thing; and I had a thing with my mother calling me, and I said, "I'll just be a minute," and I'm just trying to get the catshit off the walls. Anyway, the audience was really laughing because it was so off the wall. And Nina said, 'That was really funny.' And I said, 'Oh thank you.' And she said, 'You know you're funny, right?' And I said, 'What?' And the class got really quiet, and she said, 'Do you know you're funny?' And I said, 'Well, sometimes.' And she said, 'Well, you are. But here's the deal: from now on in this class, I don't want you to do anything funny.' And I said, 'What do you mean?' And she said, 'Whenever I give you an improv, I want you to take a dark justification, not a light one. I want you to go away from [the comedy]. Don't try to make us laugh. Don't try to please us.' And when she said that, it was like she gave me freedom, because everybody heard that. And no one had ever called me on that before. It was like, 'Don't take the easy way out. Go to the pain. Go to the dark side.' Because what she saw in that [improv] was fury and anger. And

I could show it in a joke, but not for real. So it really changed everything when she said that.

I've encouraged [my kids]. They all have natural ability, including my four year old, Stella. She said, 'Dad, I'm a magician *and* an entertainer.' She'll hold up a tooth brush and she'll do knock-knock jokes, and if you don't laugh, she'll tap the tooth brush and say, 'Is this thing on?' But my son Tyler, he's still a senior in high school; he's doing an Oscar Wilde play, *The Ideal Husband*. He's the butler. And people come up to me and say, 'Have you seen your son in the play? He steals the show, he's so [......] funny!'

The secret of life is your kids. If someone asks you, which is more important: your work or your kids? No one ever died thinking, 'Gee, I wish I'd spent more time in the office.' So that's very clear. And then the joy of your family helps feed you as an actor. And when you're fulfilled as an artist you can come home and be cool with your family. But you're always seeking. It's never done. There's always something not finished. There's a room that's not picked up or something that's not quite ready. It's all sort of a work in progress and I think that's how it still is with me. And that's sort of thrilling too, that it's always sort of refining itself, you're always uncovering something. I'm never quite satisfied. I always think I could have done that one thing a little better, maybe if I just took a little bit from that night, and a bit from this night. But I'm not tormented about it [anymore]. I can let it go.

John Ritter, 1948 - 2003

∞

Chapter 2

'A' Job/'B' Job

> *How have I always survived? Precariously. I just had all kinds of jobs.*
>
> **Hubert Selby, Jr., writer**

In this book we characterize your ideal job—your artistic career—as your "A" job. The "A" job is the ultimate goal as you define it. Your "B" job is the job (or jobs) that you will need to work in order to survive until your "A" job can become a consistent, financially stable reality. This chapter discusses what types of work constitute the best "B" jobs, and allow you still to have the time and energy to pursue your artistic vision.

There's an old joke in L.A. that there are no real waiters, they are all unemployed actors and that even the bagger at the supermarket has at least one script hidden under his apron. Odd jobs are what we do to survive. We have worked more than a dozen different odd jobs such as assistant to a producer, teacher/professor, and assistant director for a non-profit, temp paralegal, taxi driver, limo driver, waiter, bartender, and caterer. We have worked for our mechanic and run a fashion line designed by a former spouse. Why? Because the landlord wants the rent and the acting jobs or writing jobs happen at irregular intervals. For most artists, finances can get pretty scary in between job, and 'in between jobs'can be a long time.

No one becomes an artist in any field and immediately starts to make a living. "What about that 12-year-old girl who paints like Picasso?" you may say. "She's doing a lot better than just making a living!" True, but unless you're a brilliant 12-year-old girl who paints like Picasso, get over it. You have to have a fallback. You have to have a way to eat, to keep a roof over your head, to be able to afford all those things you need to be the artist. What kind of job should you get?

> *I worked as a clerk, as a secretary...any old thing. It took me about six years to finish my first book. I came home every night from work and just wrote. It took me six years.*
> **Hubert Selby, Jr., writer**

Wallace Stevens was an insurance executive. Raymond Chandler sold life insurance. Novelist Jerry Stahl wrote for *Alf*. Ken Kesey worked nights in an asylum, and wrote there. J.D. Salinger wrote short stories for the New Yorker. (Salinger may be an exception to the "no one immediately starts to make a living" theory.) T.S. Eliot was, famously, an accountant. William Carlos Williams was a doctor who made house calls and scribbled poems on scraps of paper. Charles Ives was another insurance executive. Tom Waits worked as a doorman at a rock club and got up and played between acts. Katey Sagal sang back-up for Bette Midler. Michael Keaton was a bartender at Café Figaro in L.A.[1] Everyone in the business knows the story of Harrison Ford, who worked for years as a carpenter.

---

[1] I worked there later on, 1984-'85. By this time, of course, Michael Keaton was somewhat legendary among the underemployed actors, singers, writers, directors with whom I shared bartending duties, owing to his success after *Night Shift*. "That could happen to you, kid," said the manager at one point. I seem to remember it as being more caustic than supportive, but then he was, himself, a rock bass player who probably never got past playing along with records in his living room. But for the rest of us, though each of us believed to at least some degree in our chances for success in our chosen fields, there was something awe-inspiring, refreshing, reassuring and also unbelievable that Keaton had been right back here throwing drinks like the rest of us, and he had made it out. Since then, one of the waiters has become a show runner on a major network, another a somewhat successful filmmaker. One is a working actor. A waitress sings with a world-class choir. A few have moved away to become grade school teachers or therapists. And at least a couple–Seth the actor and Joey the painter–are dead of AIDS. (JK)

> *I wonder: if I didn't have to spend so much physical energy on that [job], if I'd have had another six books. I don't know. Maybe not. I really don't know. To work—it just takes a lot out of you.*
>
> **Hubert Selby, Jr., writer**

This book will discuss and establish how to create a spending plan. As you continue along you will discover which jobs are the most conducive to the skills you possess. We will talk about how to create an ideal schedule that includes making art and earning money. Your goal will be to define and obtain the job that pays you the most amount of money for the least amount of work. Find the job that does not suck your soul right out of your body. A job that leaves you with enough juice left over to be able to come home and do your work. A "B" job.

So, what kind of job for you? If you can make money in your area of interest, even if the job itself is not exactly what you want to be doing, it could be beneficial to your artistic career. Working in your field of interest can provide you with invaluable experience, contacts and exposure to an otherwise competitive field. Rather than seeing yourself as "selling out," you might think of yourself as a student of your own business.

If you're a writer, for instance, and can get a job writing ad copy or articles about make-up for an on-line fashion magazine, take it. You can work as a freelance writer, script reader, grants writer, writer-in-residence, teach as an adjunct or substitute, or even do office temp work. Many writers and actors we know have made ends meet as legal secretaries. As a visual artist you can illustrate fliers for others, help design web sites, work at an art store, or teach art to children. As an actor, put together a voice-over tape and find a voice-over agent. You can get work as a production assistant or personal assistant. Modeling and commercial work, regardless of your shape or look, can be very lucrative. At least you'll be working with a camera and maybe you can barter to get someone to take a good headshot of you. Dancers and choreographers can broaden their expertise and make money by working at a theatre tech job, such as lighting design or costuming, or teach classes in aerobics, dance, yoga or Pilates. The holistic arts, such as acupressure or massage therapy, are ideal jobs in that your schedule can be your own. Musicians can get part-time work at a nightclub, studio or radio station.

Yen Lu Wong, formerly a choreographer whom we hear more about and from in the chapter on dancers, in an interview seventeen years ago with Judith Luther, had this to say (and it still holds true) about employment: "In California there are many new immigrants willing to do good work for very little money. Dancers can't compete in the unskilled labor market. If you're going to be a waitress, don't go to Marie Callender's. Go to the most expensive restaurants and get a job as a hostess or a hat checker until a waitress job opens up. If you type, don't just go to any office and type for minimum wage; type for studios that use Teleprompters. The money is better and your schedule will be flexible. Instead of teaching aerobics for $10 an hour, learn to do Shiatsu and earn four times that amount."

Such is the common wisdom: do what you can to do what you do. If you can eke out a living in some way that keeps you connected to your art or your craft, do it. If you cannot, then find another type of job that allows you to be free when you need to be free to get to auditions, rehearsals and classes without driving a boss crazy. Find a job that gives you the amount of money you need to survive; that doesn't require so much time and energy that you have none left over for your art; and, if you're lucky, that allows you to have some sense of life and purpose even when you are not working in your chosen field.

"There are services that people want you to do," says actor/theatre owner Tom Ormeny. "I mean, I know people that do dog walking, I know people that clean houses, I know people that work half the night in a legal office because they're pretty good at computer work and make a lot of money. So as an actor you have got to have a skill that will let you survive, because there's no guarantee that you're going to walk into this town and make money."

Still, the best "B" job is the one that moves you toward your "A" job. Often it shapes your art and sometimes it provides you with stepping stones or opportunities you may not otherwise have. If you can, find a job that is specific to your artistic skills. If you can't, find the job that takes you the least away from your life as an artist, yet pays you enough to support yourself and your art. Set yourself the task of finding a job that works for you rather than a job you work for. In the following chapters the working artists we interviewed discuss how they survived before their art became profitable.

∞

photo courtesy of Mark Kirland

Matt Groening at the Hollywood Walk of Fame
Star Dedication Ceremony, January 14, 2000

Matt Groening Interview

Cartoonist Matt Groening is perhaps one of America's most powerful subversive satirists. He began his career in 1977 with the now-syndicated comic strip, Life in Hell, *and he is most widely known for creating* The Simpsons, *which first aired on Fox in 1987. Groening doesn't want or need any more publicity than he already has. He granted us this interview precisely because he wanted to be of service and to give back to the working artist. He remains a pleasant combination of humility and self-effacing charm. One would never assume he's one of the most powerful men in Hollywood. We couldn't help but feel that Groening was one of those people who said to himself when he was a kid, 'I'll never forget what it's like to be broke and wondering how I got stuck in this life in hell.' He generously told the story of the beginnings of his career and offered up some sound advice to the young artist. All he asked of us was that we clean up his grammar, something we didn't have to do at all. Groening is articulate and insightful and we hope you enjoy his palaver as much as we did .*

I went to a little liberal arts college in Olympia, Washington, a state school called Evergreen. Evergreen was started after all the cultural uproar in the 1960's about progressive education. It was one of the few colleges that started and flourished during those times. We didn't have to take any required courses and there were no grades. You were encouraged to follow your enthusiasm. In 1977, when I graduated, I drove my crummy little lime green Datsun down to LA. Within 24 hours of arriving, the car broke down. Luckily, I had a place to stay. I didn't know exactly what I wanted to do; I had some vague idea about writing for a living. I was drawing cartoons, and I was drawing for the college newspaper, but no one ever said, "Drawing is your ticket to success." I knew that I was going to draw cartoons on my own, but I just never thought I was going to get paid for it

I had a few friends who tried to point me in the right direction as far as getting a job. I remember cold calling for jobs and being so shy that I didn't even get past the [first] phone call. These were things like working for advertising agencies and I had nothing to offer. I was a new college grad with no experience. I applied for a job at the *Los Angeles Free Press,* but when I walked in to apply for the job the receptionist was sobbing and said, "Don't work for these bastards," so I didn't. The paper shut down a couple of weeks later anyway.

I used to sneak into the UCLA Employment Center and read the jobs offered on the bulletin boards but nothing came of that. Finally I looked in the *Los Angeles Times* want adds and naively looked under 'Wanted: writer.' There was an ad for a 'Wanted writer/ chauffeur' and I called up this eighty-eight year old guy who had been a movie director. The last movie he worked on was probably in the late 1930's. He hired me to drive him around during the day and listen to his stories. In the evening I was supposed to work on his autobiography. The manuscript was already a foot tall from his previous drivers. I used to drive him all up through Beverly Hills and Bel Air and the Hollywood Hills. He would take cheap Polaroids of houses because he had a side business of scouting locations for film. I also took him to the Chalet Gourmet and he spent more money on meat than I made in a day. I would push his shopping cart for him.

You know what? He was the original Mr. Burns! *(laughter)* This never occurred to me. He was Mr. Burns, and I guess that made me Smithers. I never thought of that before. And he looked like Mr. Burns, now that I think of it. The topper was it was all about his mother. He lived with her until she was like a hundred. And every single page of the manuscript had some reference to her. He would write, "At the age of 90, Mother began to lose control of her bowels, which meant frequent stops whenever we went on road trips." It was just awful. Horrifying. The whole thing felt to me like a weird version of the movie *Sunset Boulevard.* I was like William Holden with this old guy telling me stories about the past, and not only did he have nothing to say of merit, his stories were completely contradictory.

The point is, that is what I did to pay the rent and I quit, finally, when I realized that everything I did seemed to anger this guy. He was one of those kinds of guys who would say, 'Get me a glass of water and carry out the garbage.' And no matter what I did first, it would be the wrong thing. It was a very LA, Hollywood kind of experience.

I got even more discouraged. After that I got a job at a copy place. I thought it was pushing me one step closer to writing, because I was Xeroxing all these manuscripts. I got to read a lot of stuff after people dropped off their screenplays and I learned that there is a lot of bad stuff out there. On the other hand, I got to meet the rock critic, Richard Meltzer, who came in and had me Xerox his autobiography. Plus, I helped Hubert Selby, the author of *Last Exit To Brooklyn*. He was probably the person I was most excited to wait on, although I did get to Xerox something for Twiggy *[laughter]*.

I got more and more depressed. I hated my situation. I had no money. My roommates were getting more bugged with me for not being able to pay the rent. I made a comic book for myself, called *Life in Hell*, and Xeroxed twenty-five copies for myself the first time and gave them all away. I quit the Xerox place and I got a job on Sunset at Licorice Pizza, the record store right across from the Whiskey a Go Go, and that was great. It was during the heyday of punk and disco. Those two cultures didn't fit together, but they certainly mingled. I sold drug paraphernalia to all the drug fiends and my comic book with all the punk 'zines. I really wanted to be creative and do something creative but had a whole series of jobs that had nothing to do with what I wanted to do.

My friends were all in the same boat, working miserable jobs, and we all sat around whining about how unlucky we were and how other people didn't have the disadvantages we had and I got *really* depressed. I did that for a couple of years, working at these crummy jobs. Then in 1979, both the *LA Reader* and the *LA Weekly*, two alternative newspapers, started publication. I got a job delivering newspapers for the *LA Reader* after having written an article for them. I called them up from the record store and the editor said, "Well, we're looking for articles. Got any ideas?" and I said, "Yeah," and I looked out the window and there was this billboard and I said, "I'd like to do an article about how billboards are painted on Sunset Boulevard." And he said, "Great." That's how I got my first writing gig.

The article got printed. It was the cover story and they misspelled my name. I went down to the office in downtown LA where they hired me to be publications director. There were three people in the office. I answered the phones, typed up the classifieds, answered all the mail and on Thursdays I went to the printer in Glendale. I delivered 28,000 papers to stores from Glendale to Santa Monica. After a while I started to deliver them as far as Malibu so I could end my day in Malibu and pull over to the coast to go swimming in the ocean.

I got through this by considering that every form of writing, even typing up a classified, was a piece of writing, and I tried to make it as good as I could. Then I realized that complaining to my friends was not doing anything but was pulling me down into a malaise of unhappiness and I wasn't getting anything done. All my creative friends had a thousand really good reasons for not making it: bad parents, no money, the wrong time in history, people don't appreciate good art and so on. I said to myself, "Those are all good reasons but I am going to make a decision that I will not give myself any excuses." I was trying to approach my stagnating situation from the other direction. I knew that I would do whatever it took. I began drawing *Life in Hell* and they gave me space in the back of the paper.

There was nobody to tell me what I was doing was great; in fact, I got negative reinforcement. My girlfriend at the time thought my cartoons were a waste of time. I think my parents were worried about me, although they gave me no money. They gave me a book about depression, which was really depressing. I was writing for this paper, I was writing about music, and I became an editor.

Although I wasn't making a great living, I could pay the rent. I would write until I made the rent and then I would work on my own stuff. I hardly ever got ahead that way. The problem with being a freelancer, as I saw it, was that I always felt guilty knowing I could be working to better myself. The only time the guilt would alleviate was when I went to the movies. I would feel guilty all the way up to and through buying the ticket, but as soon as I gave the ticket to the ticket taker, the guilt would vanish. So I went to a lot of movies.

The misery of not getting recognition or acknowledgement was so discouraging that I almost gave up. The only reason I didn't was there was something inside me that was going to do what I was doing whether I got paid or not. I could be working in a tire warehouse and I'd be drawing pictures of the boss and putting them up on the bulletin board.

If I had advice to give people about being creative, I'd say wherever you are in your life you need to finish the work that you're doing and it needs to reach an audience. If it's a poem, give it away; if it's a comic book, it has to be Xeroxed and give it away. Your work has to be seen by someone at every level. With luck and hope you can actually get paid for your work.

I assembled a bunch of comic books and went to a local press, called Peace Press. I went to them because I liked the name. I made a deal with them and printed 3,000 and made them the size of an album cover because I figured I could sell them in record stores and they could go right in the bins. I was able to sell those books and I attracted the attention of a real publisher.

I decided that I was going to be a commercial artist. One of the excuses of friends who weren't making it was that their art was so refined that the world wasn't ready for it. I decided that one of the ways I could value what I did was whether or not I got paid for it. So I decided that whatever I did would pay me back.

Let's say you want to be a fine artist and you want to be hanging in a museum. You don't have the materials to make that kind of work, but you can still make something. You want to get to Z and you're at A. I think a lot of creative people can't see that B, C, D, E is progress. They want Z. I have a friend who worshipped Bertolucci and he said, 'I will not make a movie until I can make one as good as Bertolucci.' And guess what, he's not making any films. You have to do the things that may not have much perceptible value, but really are progress.

There is a term in animation called 'pencil mileage,' which is the amount of miles that your pencil marks in the course of making an animated cartoon. I think that term can apply to writers, painters and other creative types as well, in that at the end of a thousand pencil miles you will be a different person whether or not you've sold your stuff to a big gallery. You are a different person after you've done ten paintings, and after you've done a thousand paintings. I'm a big advocate of sketchbooks and journals, anything to keep you going, because it all helps your art. There is a lot of stuff that I've done that represents artistic dead ends but I had to do it to get it out of my system. I have some stuff that is just so awful that even I can't believe it. The thing is, if you do a thousand drawings it's easier to throw away or set aside the bad ones. But if you're only working on one masterpiece you're not likely to throw it away.

Also, find like-minded, ambitious people who can encourage you and with whom you can pace yourself. I used to sit with my friend Gary Panter and we used to kid about sneaking into pop culture. We decided to see how far we could sneak into modern pop culture. Gary went on to design *PeeWee's Playhouse*. He got to do what he loved to do: design toys and sets. I was watching from the sidelines with my mouth hanging open. And then, I got to do *The Simpsons*.

∞

Chapter 3
The Basics
Housing

> *I was very frugal. Back in those days, I found a place to live for twenty dollars a month. I just went to this building, I went to the super and I said, "Do you mind if I live in the basement next to the boiler?" and I just swept this little space out and I gave this guy twenty bucks a month cash.*
>
> **John Zorn, composer**

For an artist, choosing an ideal place to live may be a challenging task. Finding affordable housing is tough, unless you live outside a major urban area. Most artists, however, gravitate to expensive metropolitan areas where art thrives on a grand scale—cities like New York, Los Angeles, Chicago or Houston. It's hard to get a part in an off-Broadway production, a show in a SoHo gallery or first chair viola in the LA Philharmonic if you live in the mid-West. Once in the city, artists generally choose to live on the edge of things, on the fringes where the lifestyle of the artist is acceptable, even appreciated, and where everything is less expensive. Perhaps living there makes better art and perhaps it's where artists belong, with those others who shout the lines of *Streetcar Named Desire* to each other on the street or practice their piano scales at midnight.

During the 1970's, New York artists changed the commercial zoning laws by squatting in lofts in SoHo, and as more and more people followed suit, the artists moved to Tribeca and across the bridge to Greenpoint, Brooklyn. Those buildings they moved into were soon designated AIR (Artists In Residence) buildings. Artists changed the face of New York. Ten years to fifteen years ago in Los Angeles, Silver Lake was *the* place to live if you were a beginning to mid-level artist. The whole area, from the Hollywood Freeway up to and into Atwater Village, west of Los Feliz and east of Echo Park, was filled with actors, musicians and painters sharing the coffee shops and markets with a heady mix of gay couples, leather boys and Central American émigrés. It was one of the few neighborhoods in Los Angeles where cultures actually mixed and intermingled, and at a place like the Tropical Bakery young artists discussed the latest *whatever* over Cuban café con leche at a sidewalk table next to one of the local street people as an AA meeting went on in the back room. Young artists are drawn to areas like this because of the affordable housing available and because they tend not to care so much about societal conventions. And as more and more of the artists move in forming a community of their own within the community at large, the more courageous or foolhardy business owners follow to open up the coffee shops and bookstores and antique shops that the young and trendy may want. This of course leads to more people visiting the neighborhood to see a play or an opening at a gallery or to buy gift candles; and before you know it, old apartment buildings are being refurbished and the rents have started to rise and eventually the artists have to find somewhere else to live. In New York, they moved out to Jersey. In LA, they picked up and moved further east, and as of this writing, Echo Park is what Silverlake was.

Finding an apartment in any city can be an arduous and even competitive task. For artists who require large space at a low price, sharing living quarters is the most practical and affordable option. As with any shared space, your choice of roommate can be critical. Aside from all the usual issues, such as smoking, overnight guests and pets, you will want to make sure you are compatible since you and your roommate(s), as artists, may be spending a lot of time at home. Does your roommate stay up all night composing music when you have a 6 am call? Don't be afraid to interview many potential roommates before making a decision.

Whether you choose to share or go it alone, the best resources are the usual ones: word of mouth, newspapers, weekly's, rental and roommate services, many of which are listed in our appendix. Tell everyone you know and everyone you meet that you are looking. Check the bulletin boards at schools, bookstores, studios, coffee shops, theatres or any venue that may possibly cater to people of an artistic persuasion.

Although a roommate service will charge a fee, they will offer a selection of roommates, many of whom already have very nice homes or apartments. There are also resident houses, hotels and government housing projects. New York has a plethora of resident houses, but they generally have long waiting lists. The Internet is a good source for information on government housing projects for artists. The rent for such apartments is scaled according to income, so even though it can actually take years for your application to be processed, the time and effort spent could eventually pay off. (See appendix for information about government-subsidized, artist-owned and private housing projects.)

Home Office

> *...a woman must have money and a room of her own if she is to write fiction; and that, as you will see, leaves the great problem of the nature of women and the nature of fiction unsolved.*
> **Virginia Woolf, *A Room of One's Own***

Most artists need a place of their own. Painters and sculptors need a large space to make their works of art, actors and dancers need a stage on which they can perform and writers need a desk, ideally in a quiet environment free from distraction.

Creating an actual place in which to work is vital and akin to creating a sacred space within. It is the practical, profane, actual place in which you do the work. Make your space sacred if you must, but make space to make art. Some writers say they find it effective to write in the same place every day, to keep that place as one keeps an altar and to use it for nothing else. Most writers need at least to have a place where they can be comfortable and able to concentrate. On some level, the outer space reflects the inner sacred space where art happens, so the "where" of our work is not something to be left to chance. At the very least it is true that if you make a place to work and show up and do the work each day, day after day, you will make art; and eventually you may be one of those who find a way to make money at your art. It happened that way for most of the artists we interviewed to write this book. And it can happen for you.

Now in more practical terms a home office allows you to deduct part of your rent or mortgage right from taxes—a very nice plus for the self-employed artist—while helping to substantially minimize overhead expenses. What constitutes a home office? A room in which you take care of the business side of your art or in which you generate work that pays; where you can send out photos, packets and other marketing tools; where you can keep your expense files, rewrites, photo negs or headshots. Many successful writers rent an office to work in, but the tax break of having an office in the home can be substantial if you itemize and follow IRS instructions. (We are writing this book in our garage/office, along with paying our bills and reading our email, and that is working just fine.)

Telephones—Can you hear me now?

Telephones: the boon and the bane of our existence. Performing artists must have one, or at the very least an answering service. Actors, writers, dancers, musicians, and even painters may find it helpful to use a pager. Finding the best plan and solution since the breakup of AT&T is challenging, at best. Plans and prices vary widely. Investigate your phone options thoroughly, consult with your friends, and watch for promotions.

1. Cell Phone. For many performers waiting for an audition or journalists waiting to get the next interview, a cell phone is a must. There are excellent plans for flat rates depending on the number of minutes you plan to use your phone. Be realistic when coming up with a figure though because the extra minutes are very expensive.

Since you'll be charged for incoming calls as well, it's a good idea to give out your cell number only to agents, managers or directors—those people who *really* need to reach you when they really need to reach you—and wait until you get home to return calls of a more personal nature. These days no one pays for long distance on their cell phone, and no one has to pay for roaming charges (though be careful if a job takes you over the border into Canada). Be smart. It requires some research, but check out a number of plans, do your research and get a plan that works for you. Suggest that they give you free cell phone to cell phone minutes. That way calls to your own number to pick up your messages will be covered. Always remember to turn off the cell phone in important meetings or auditions. (Also, please, just for us, in bookstores.)

2. Business Listings in the phone book cost more that **Residential Listings**, but can be tax-deductible if you itemize. Depending on what business you're in, a business listing may be worth the extra cost.

3. Local Phone Company Options. You can sign up for an answering service, call waiting, caller ID and call forwarding with your local phone company. Most working artists depend on the efficiency of their phone system for regular work. The telephone is an artist's lifeline to incoming jobs and new opportunities, so you will want to take advantage of any options that can help you stay in touch.

4. Phone Company Answering Service, aka Voice Mail. This is a great option. For many of us, the days of home answering machines are over. There is a monthly fee and you cannot save messages indefinitely; nor can you screen calls. However, with the service provided by your local Bell, you can talk uninterrupted while another caller leaves a message and then return it (or not) right after you finish. Also, phone company systems rarely, if ever, break down.

5. Call Waiting allows you to put someone on hold while answering an incoming call.

6. Call Forwarding enables your incoming calls to be forwarded to wherever you are. This is less important with the advent of cell phones, but if you choose not to have a cell it's a good feature, particularly for artists, particularly actors, who need to be readily accessible to their agents.

7. Pager. The bare essential, a pager allows you to be in touch with your business representatives every bit as much as any of the other systems. Obviously, though, it does have its drawbacks. In order to return calls, you will have to either borrow someone's phone (which is often times less than convenient), find a pay phone or have a cell phone, and then why have a pager? Also, with the proliferation of cell phones, you may have noticed there are far fewer pay phones available. Many of them do not allow incoming calls, so you cannot get someone to call you back after they have checked on something, or to save money. And pagers are more expensive than ever.

Transportation

Every city has its advantages and disadvantages. In New York you don't need a car, while in LA it's almost impossible to get around without one. (Actually, we know a handful of people who use the buses in LA, but it's a sad, time-consuming option.) If good public transportation is not available in your city, then a car may be a worthwhile, even necessary investment, despite the expense. There are plenty of used cars for sale—get a good one and change the oil every 3,000 miles. If truly strapped for cash, you may consider the option of sharing a car with a friend and working out a week on/ week off schedule with trade-offs available for off-week auditions, etc. It can be a royal pain, but might be worth your while.

Also, find a good, honest mechanic. (Remember the old Steve Martin joke? "How to be a Millionaire: First, get a million dollars…"). Once again, ask around, talk to your friends.

Health Insurance

If you are one of the younger readers of our book, please read this section. Though at the moment you may be, for all intents and purposes, immortal, unshakeable, invulnerable, this will not always be the case and a costly mishap can put you in debt for years. Regardless of how healthy you are, good medical coverage is essential. Every person is well-advised to have insurance. If you can get coverage from your spouse or your parents, do so. If you do not have that option and cannot afford a standard policy, contact an insurance agent to find a modification of that policy which you can afford and pay for it yourself. Basic emergency coverage is available and affordable. Many arts service organizations offer group health insurance plans and many of them work through **Support Services Alliance (SSA)**, a good source for affordable medical coverage, though it's only available in New York. SSA is an organization that pools the resources of small businesses and the self-employed in order to offer programs and services to those who might otherwise find them economically out of reach. Services offered include group term life insurance, dental and vision insurance, surgical and major medical and short-term disability coverage.

Policies offered by the unions and guilds are the best, but you do not automatically qualify for them by becoming a member. For the **Screen Actors Guild/AFTRA**, eligibility is based on your income for four consecutive three-month periods. For Plan I, if you are just starting out, you need to earn $20,000 over the four quarters, going up to $21,000 in January of 2004. This initial eligibility establishes the "base period" upon which all future eligibility is calculated. Coverage begins three months after the earning of eligibility. For Plan II, the amount is $9,000 in 2003 (going up $500 each succeeding year) or sixty-one days of employment with a SAG signatory producer. Plan I is the better plan, but Plan II offers very good coverage with slightly higher deductible and requires the use of solely network providers in California. Under both plans, all dependents are covered to the same extent as the participant. There are also self-pay options available to participants when eligibility expires.

In **Actors Equity**, the insurance offered by The Equity League is comparable to that of SAG, though eligibility and coverage differ. Equity eligibility is based upon an actor working for ten weeks over the period of one year (four quarters) and qualifies the participant for one year of coverage. There is no waiting period. Coverage begins the day eligibility is earned. Coverage for dependents (both children and domestic partners), however, must be applied for and paid for by the participant.

Writers Guild of America offers a popular supplemental health plan option to Guild members. These programs offer an affordable option for members who do not qualify for coverage under the primary Guild plan and need to purchase other health insurance privately.

The first option for writers who had health coverage under the Guild plan, of course, is to self-pay to continue the benefits. For cases where that choice does not make sense or does not apply, the Guild has "Writers Care." This program, available through a private insurance provider, offers affordable HMO health coverage to members of the Guild. Call the Guild for more information at (323) 782-4568. In addition, the Guild refers members to the Good & Welfare Fund or other industry and public agencies for writers in need of financial assistance.

Members of the **Graphic Artists Guild** are able to buy medical insurance through Union Privilege, a plan developed in 1986 by the AFL-CIO to use the buying power of unions to offer low-cost coverage to union members.

Finally, some people purchase catastrophic health care. You can save money by opting for a health plan that does not cover doctor's visits, medical tests, and pharmaceutical costs. A catastrophic plan has a high deductible, say $2000 to $5000. Some people want this kind of coverage in case they're in a car accident or have a life threatening illness, while other people want comprehensive health insurance. It's your choice.

If you are unable to pay for health insurance at all, get information about your local free clinics *before* you have an injury or illness. Most cities provide free hospitalization and medical care for patients who can document unemployment and a lack of resources and assets. In Los Angeles, the LA Free Clinic offers medical care, dental care, mental health care, prenatal care, family planning, integrative medicine (acupuncture, yoga, chiropractic) and legal services to all comers, regardless of income (or any other variable, for that matter). The Health Consumer Alliance can help you to find alternatives dependent upon your circumstances. USC/County General Hospital is available for emergency, trauma and hospitalization. In New York, Bellevue Hospital, a teaching hospital like USC/County General, offers excellent care to its patients. You will spend hours (if not days) in waiting rooms, but the medical care is excellent and if you are truly broke, their services will be provided at no cost.

Unemployment Insurance

Unemployment insurance is financed by employers through payroll taxes and is run out of an agency called the **Employment Development Department (EDD).** Benefits are paid to the unemployed through an industry tax and theoretically are paid only to job seekers who are unemployed through no fault of their own and who are ready, willing and able to work.

In order to qualify for unemployment benefits, you must have worked at least twenty weeks during the fifty-week period that ended with your layoff and your employer must have covered you by paying payroll taxes. The twenty weeks work need not have been consecutive or with only one employer. If you qualify, your weekly benefits will equal approximately half of your average weekly salary during the time you were working, up to the current maximum. Benefits last for twenty-six weeks, although it's often possible to apply for and receive an extension.

You are not required to take a job outside your classification. You can therefore use your time between acting jobs to study and train, thus increasing your employability. You should familiarize yourself with Unemployment Insurance regulations so that you can use the program to benefit you during those frequent periods between jobs. Pick up a handbook outlining the entire *Do's* and *Don'ts* governing Unemployment Insurance at your nearest Unemployment Insurance office.

Actors' Fund of America

The Actors' Fund of America, founded in 1882, is the oldest theatrical charity in the world. The Fund is a national organization with offices in New York, Los Angeles, and Chicago. Its services are not restricted to actors, but are available to all bona fide professionals working in any capacity in the entertainment business, including: designers, writers, sound technicians, musicians, dancers, administrators, directors, film editors, stagehands, electricians—as well as actors. In addition to providing emergency grants for essentials such as food, rent and medical care, The Actors' Fund provides counseling, substance abuse and mental health services, senior and disabled care, nursing home and assisted living care, an AIDS Initiative, The Actors' Work Program, the Phyllis Newman Women's Health Initiative, the Artists' Health Insurance Resource Center, and supportive housing on both coasts.

In 2000, The Actors' Fund budget was over $17 million, and they served over 6,200 people nationwide, disbursing nearly $2.7 million in confidential financial assistance grants. A full listing of services they offer is provided in the appendix.

∞

Chapter 4

Finances

As a freelance artist you will give up traditional security, standard retirement plans and the 401K provided by a full-time employer. Not everyone can manage their time well, stay upbeat and productive in the confines of their own studio and keep to their self-made schedule. The freelance life is not for everyone. The prototype of "the starving artist" does not exist because it is essential for one's development or for one's art. It exists because this can be a really difficult way to make a living. True, being an artist offers the "possibility of fame and fortune," but as others and we say elsewhere in this book, if fame is the only reason you are choosing to be an artist, walk away now. If recognition is your sole motivation—no moral judgment here—the work involved, the things given up, the sacrifices made are too great and you will eventually find yourself moving on anyway. That said...

You can start your own savings retirement plan, what is called an IRA or Individual Retirement Plan, even if you don't have an employer who will set up a 401K for you. Even if you work forever—many artists never stop making art—it would be nice not to have to worry about money as you grow older.So if you are self-employed, look into establishing an IRA and building an investment portfolio.

> *It is better to have a permanent income than to be fascinating.*
> **Oscar Wilde, *The Model Millionaire***

What is an IRA?

Today most Americans will not be able to retire on Social Security alone. There is even some talk about abolishing our national retirement plan altogether. Nonetheless, artists who have an employer who provides a 401k are ahead of the game. For everyone else, there is something called an IRA. IRAs offer a retirement plan for people without an employer. Anyone can set up an IRA, no matter if they earned $100 or $100,000 in a given year. In a traditional IRA, as long as you are under the age of 70, you can contribute as much money to your IRA account as you would like and the IRS will allow a tax deduction for up to $3,000 per year that you contribute, $4,000 for 2005 through 2007 and $5,000 for 2008. Individuals over 50 will be able to contribute additional money as well. After 2008 there may be adjustments to these amounts based on the rate of inflation.

A Roth IRA allows you to contribute after-tax dollars into an account and, although there are no immediate tax savings, there are fewer restrictions on when you can withdraw money from the plan.

Balancing Your Checkbook

One of the hardest aspects of making a life as an artist is the management of our finances. When you have a fairly secure and fixed income, it is rather easy to develop a spending plan. Barring catastrophic occurrences, the flow of money into and out of your life is pretty much a given quantity. For those artists who work at making a living with their art, their finances are ever fluctuating and often unpredictable. Will you sell enough paintings at your show to be able to continue renting your studio? Will your TV pilot be picked-up? Can you afford to get your script copied to send it out to agents? How can you plan financially when your income seems to ebb and flow on the whim of a god who has yet to introduce Herself?

When you have little or no money, what do you do? What bills should be paid right away and which can slide for a moment? When you *have* money, what do you do? How do you keep records? How do you balance a checkbook? What about taxes? Do you need an accountant? Should you incorporate? And when? If you went to art school or music school or theatre school, you probably missed the class that taught you the answers to all these questions. As self-employed artists, we all have to work at keeping financial clarity. Here are some guidelines to get you started:

Keeping Records

We keep records for only two reasons:

- To know how much your business is making or losing.
- To let the IRS know how much your business is making or losing (more on this later...).

The best bookkeeping system is the one that works for you, meaning that it is clear and understandable to you, and its requirements are do-able by you on a continuing basis. If you're spending more than a few hours of your time per week on it, then it's too complicated.

One simple yet effective system is described in *Starting and Succeeding in Your Own Photography Business* by the photographer, Jeanne Thwaites. She suggests a bookkeeping system involving three ledgers and a Spike (a weighted base with a metal spike sticking upwards). Ledger I should be used to record money paid to you. Ledger II is used to maintain records on money owed to you. Ledger III is used to record your expenses.

QuickBooks Basic for a small business and *Quicken* for your personal accounts are excellent record keeping software programs for both Mac and PC. These programs are recommended by all our business-savvy friends, many of whom are also successful artists. They help save time on bookkeeping and paperwork and get us back to the business of making art. This software can simplify your accounting tasks such as paying bills, invoicing customers and tracking expenses. You can get rid of all the little scraps of paper and have all your financial information in one place. These programs generate reports instantly, including budgets in a spreadsheet format. *Quicken* and *Quickbooks* are very easy to learn and, contrary to what many people with limited resources think, the more you budget and the more clarity you have, the more money and time you will have.

For those who choose not to use computer programs, there are simple but complete systems for record keeping that will allow you to track your business expenditures and income. One is made by *Safeguard Business Systems*, which includes business checks and forms, an accounting board and journal sheets and the instructions for their use, and business envelopes and accessories. See appendix for contact information.

A check register is also a great help in record keeping. Always note on a check what the payment was for. Some check ledgers provide a box to mark if the payment is a legitimate business expense. Your cancelled check can be used in lieu of a receipt for the IRS.

Credit cards can also be helpful record-keeping tools because you are given an itemized list of expenditures which can be used to discern business expenses from non-business expenses, and which also are accepted by the IRS. One cautionary note: using credit cards requires you to have or to develop the ability not to go into debt. As a credit card user you must be willing and able to pay the balance in full at the end of each month or you will run up a debt, however slowly. One way to ensure you do this is to use an American Express card (*only* for business expenses) that requires you to pay it off each month.

However you keep your records, it is best that you stay current with your bills. Living the life of a freelance artist can be very stressful with regard to money, but the more you know about where you really are financially, the less it will stress you. And when you get some money, use it wisely.

> *I know that as a musician the best thing you can have is a place to stay. I worked on a Broadway show with Lena Horne for about four years at a time when housing was very afford-able. So when I had money, I bought a brownstone in Harlem. Being an artist is about ups and downs. Hopefully as you go along and mature in life, there'll be more ups than downs.*
> **Craig Harris, composer, trombonist**

Create a Spending Plan

We think the language we use is important and can influence our lives and attitudes toward life. The idea of creating a spending plan suggests prosperity, helping us to plan how we will spend the money we make. The word "budget" has come to mean scrimping or being close-fisted with our limited resources. A budget can be like tying a rock around your ankle and trying to swim, whereas a spending plan is moving with the flow.

Most small businesses fail because of cash flow problems. To alleviate the danger of this in your art business, pay attention to your expenditures and know what it costs you to create a work of art and/or how much it costs to keep yourself fresh and alive in your work with classes, workouts and so on. By overspending on items that don't contribute to your art, you may deprive yourself in ways that will eventually force you out of business. Good planning will allow you to continue as an artist and help you to know where you're going and how much cash you'll need to get there.

Word to the wise: we tend to manifest what we envision. However you choose to do your monthly spending plan, add a category for *Fun Money* or *Prosperity* in order to leave yourself open to the success and abundance that is just around the corner.

Here are some suggestions on how to handle your money: Keep a daily record of your spending. This helps you see where you spend your money and how much you spend, which in turn tells you how much you need to earn. Make a monthly spending plan. Include everything coming in and going out. We suggest you keep track of what you *expect* to bring in, as well as what you *actually* earn in a given month.

Also, make a monthly spending plan in which you can include your actual spending, your current plan and, after you have seen our comprehensive list, your new plan. Health insurance, savings and even wardrobe costs may not seem like essential expenditures, and thereby may fall by the wayside when the first of the month looms ahead, but with a realistic and proper spending plan we find it possible to keep a sense of continuity in these areas, even if you only save five dollars a month. The following charts might be of some assistance.

Income Chart

Income Source	Monthly Estimate	Monthly Actual
Wages	$	$
Wages, 'B' Job	$	$
Commissions	$	$
Residuals, Licensing, Publishing	$	$
Gifts	$	$
Refunds	$	$
Dividends	$	$
Interest	$	$
Investments	$	$
Alimony/ child support	$	$
TOTAL	$	$
Difference, estimate/actual: $		

Each of the categories below can have multiple entries. Everyone's spending plan will differ; however for most people, everything will fit into the following categories.

Spending Plan

Spending Plan:	Actual	Current Plan	New Plan
Shelter, includes:			
rent			
utilities			
telephone			
Food			
Transportation, includes:			
gasoline			
car repair			
car insurance			
Clothing			
Personal care			
Health Care			
Dependent Care			
Entertainment			
Education			
Vacation			
Personal Business			
Gifts			
Investments			
Taxes			
Debt Repayment			
Artist Business			
Fun Money			
TOTAL$	$	$	$
+ or (-) Cash flow	$	$	$

Tax Preparation

While it is both realistic and desirable for you to do your own bookkeeping, it is very important to hire an accountant to prepare your tax returns. Tax laws change so quickly you will be hard-pressed to keep abreast of them. If you insist on playing accountant, you may cheat yourself out of many profitable and legitimate deductions. If you can't afford to hire an accountant, you may be able to locate one who will work free of charge or at a greatly reduced fee.

Accountants for the Public Interest (API) is a national nonprofit organization whose purpose is to encourage accountants to volunteer their time and expertise to nonprofits, small businesses and individuals who need, but cannot afford, professional accounting services. API has 22 affiliates who recruit volunteer accountants, screen requests for help and match the two. While all of the affiliates work with nonprofits, each is autonomous and offers a unique mix of programs to their communities, such as small business assistance and help for individuals and families with low incomes. API can help you to:

- prepare your taxes
- prepare for an audit
- establish a record keeping system
- form a budget or cash flow forecast
- apply for a loan

Each affiliate offers specialized services and uses its own set of eligibility criteria to determine a match between an applicant and a volunteer. These criteria are generally based on the organization's annual budget and/or an inability to pay for accounting services. The service that the volunteer provides is free, though in some cases the applicant may be charged a small administrative fee. See financial appendix for contact information.

Doing Your Own Taxes

If you choose to do your own taxes, keep detailed records of your income and expenses. In the early years of a career an artist often invests more in his work than he gets back in income. With proper documentation you can legitimately place yourself in a bracket that pays no taxes. This involves keeping a diary, simple ledgers, and holding onto a lot of receipts for parking, classes, postage, office supplies and special clothing and equipment. Also, each discipline has its own unique set of expenditures that may be written off to some extent. An actor may write off video rentals (research) and trade publications (looking for work); a painter, the film for his camera and periodicals (the gathering of images); a writer, all books and newspapers. Whether or not you intend to do your own taxes, learn what can and cannot be written off and keep track of it all, regardless of how seemingly petty an expense it may be. Every little bit helps, and at the end of the year when you've saved yourself $500 you'll thank yourself for all those little piles of receipts and cancelled checks. Some other expenses that as of the date of publication can legitimately be deducted from your income in order to reduce your taxes:

- Travel expenses
- Offices and offices in the home
- Commissions to agents and managers
- Equipment used in your trade or business
- Auto insurance or repairs
- Supplies and inventories
- Special clothing worn solely for your work
- Legal and accounting fees
- Studio rent
- Entertainment related to your business
- Booking fees
- Dues and fees for business related workshops, seminars, classes, or memberships; uniion dues
- Research materials (books, films, plays, music, etc.)

These are only a few examples of expenses that can be deducted. Although tax laws may treat artists as both individual income earners and sole proprietorships, they also provide special benefits not offered to the population as a whole. Find an honest accountant who has worked with other artists to explain what some of those benefits are.

Simply proving you are, indeed, a professional artist can be a major problem if your major source of income is derived from driving a taxi or from tips you make as a waitress. Keeping records and saving receipts which document meetings with gallery owners, casting agents or publishers will not only help establish your identity as an artist but will also bring your net profit or taxable income down so that you pay the government as little as possible.

Good records from the lean years will also help you when you need to reduce your tax rate through income averaging. When your annual income suddenly skyrockets through the sale of a piece of sculpture or the commission of a piece of music, you will want good records to document that you lived on cat food and Kool-Aid the preceding four years. There are certain requirements to be met in order for income averaging to be applicable, but in concept, the process will level out the current year's (high) taxable income with the average (low) taxable income from the prior four years. The tax savings can be appreciable for anyone whose year to year income fluctuates widely.

∞

Chapter 5
The Internet

The Internet has changed the way we communicate—entirely—and access to it is perhaps one of the best tools for any artist to make her way in today's amazing marketplace. The Internet is a burgeoning universe and can be an excellent tool for you. Its perfection is in its imperfection. It is a place where anarchy reigns and we hope it stays that way. We include a brief history of the Internet here because it is a tale that informs our lives as artists who function similarly to the Internet—outside the norms of society.

The Internet began a little more than thirty years ago when the RAND Corporation sought to design a paranoid system of communication in the event our nation was besieged by enemy forces. The system was intended to be all but indestructible, able to withstand even a nuclear war. The network was designed to operate in such a way that even if whole parts of it were blown away, all the remaining intact communication units, called "nodes," would still be able to communicate. It was not like the telephone system; it was designed to be more durable. Out of this paranoid notion, ARPANET evolved. The first four nodes were established in 1969 and gave way to fifteen nodes in 1971, which grew into thirty-seven by the following year. The Cold War think tank authorities could never have predicted what happened next. Researchers used ARPANET to collaborate and to trade ideas, which was the original purpose of the system, but they also did what we humans do best: they socialized. In fact, the first e-mail mailing list was a newsletter for science fiction fans.

By 1993 there were tens of thousands of nodes in the Internet across forty-two countries with three to four million people using this computer network. As it turns out, no one person actually owns the Internet. It belongs to everyone and to no one. It is that rarest of events—a functional anarchy.

During the 1990's the Internet's growth was astounding. At times it grew at the rate of twenty percent per month. In 2000 there were approximately four hundred million people logging onto the Internet worldwide, and today there are almost seven hundred million users; which means about one in every ten or so people has access to the Web. This means that there are a lot of people logging onto the "anarchistic" Web, and that makes it the perfect place to sell your wares.

So how can you put this system to good use? In basically four ways: e-mail, discussion groups, long-distance computing and websites.

E-mail

This quick and efficient way of sending a letter has, in some ways, surpassed the U.S. Mail, which we "Outlook Express" users have fondly dubbed, "snail mail." With e-mail we can communicate faster, cheaper and more effectively. Over the weekend you can e-mail a quick pitch to someone in New York from Los Angeles and they can respond when they first clock in Monday morning. E-mails can help you maintain contact with agents, lawyers, managers, clients and gallery owners much more easily than in the past. A phone call takes up precious work time. E-missives are brief, to the point and move your business along much, much faster. Companies like Yahoo and Hotmail, among many others, offer free e-mail accounts which can be useful especially if you're on a budget or traveling overseas. You can access your e-mail from any server anywhere in the world and today there are Internet cafés in remote places like Bangalore, India. For home e-mail we prefer Outlook Express because you can keep all the e-mail messages you receive and never have to dump any because of lack of space.[1]

[1] I, however, tend to save things I don't need and being made to throw things away can be a good thing, implementing the principle of "getting rid of the old to make room for the new." (AS)

There are some elementary e-mail manners that are important to adhere to when writing potential clients, editors, gallery owners, etc. Because the Internet is a place where anarchy reigns, there is a loosening of standard etiquette; however, it is important to make a distinction between schmoozing and business. Be business-like when e-mailing the gallery owner or editor. Some things to think about include the following:

• **To:** When making an inquiry about a job or agent, it is best to address your e-mail to the correct person. Do your research. (Use the books in the appendix to get a name of the editor, gallery owner, dance company founder, etc.) Find out the name of who you need to write to and get his or her e-mail address, not the company info e-mail box.

• **From:** Avoid the cute tags many people use online. You wouldn't sign a formal business letter "Lunar Eclipse." Avoid nicknames. We suggest you set up a business e-mail account that has a professional e-mail address and operate your business out of that account. *Windsong@hotmail.com* can be for your online chatting with friends, but *HCooper@pacbell.net* is a more responsible, professional personality and one which editors, agents, educators, managers and gallery owners will be much more likely to respond to.

• **Subject:** Never leave the subject line blank. Let your recipient know what they're about to read and ideally why they will want to read it. Don't be cute or overly stuffy. Subject lines that read something like "You have to hear this," look like spam and very likely will go unread and be deleted on the spot. Be clear and concise.

• **The Content**: As it turns out, we read on a computer screen about twenty-five percent slower than on the written page. This is why so much content on the Internet is in short blocks. Additionally, many characters, such as long dashes or apostrophes, don't translate, making the content of your e-mail difficult to read. To avoid sending e-mails that are filled with errant characters, here are some basic principles to adhere to in your business e-mails:

- Keep your paragraphs short. Long blocks of text are very difficult to read.
- Single-space the content. Double-space between paragraphs. Don't indent.
- Keep it simple. No bullets, italics, bold, underlines or smiley faces such as: :-) (Called emoticons); no keyboard commands such as an m-dash (—). Rather, use two hyphens (--).
- There is no need to use HTML, to insert graphics or to use colored fonts or a background color.
- Use a readable font of either 10 or 12 pt. New Times Roman, Ariel or Courier are good choices. Outlook Express is set to use Verdana, which is also an easily readable font. Because you cannot tell how your e-mail will appear at the other end, e-mail a friend and have them print a copy of your e-mail message so you can see how your messages appear to the world outside your computer.

- **Signature:** One of the beauties of e-mail is that you can program a standard signature for the end of each e-mail. Again, make it professional. You might include a high point from your credits, as well as your e-mail address, a phone number, fax number and your mailing address. In Outlook Express you can have a variety of different signatures for different occasions.

Adele Slaughter
Writer, *What The Body Remembers* (Story Line Press, 1994)

2020 Pleasant Avenue
Studio City, California 91604
818-888-5555 phone
818-777-1234 fax
aslaughter@att.net

• **Attachments:** Unless an attachment has been requested, don't send one. There are so many viruses infecting computers that most unwanted attachments will be deleted. Most of what you have to say is best written in the body of the e-mail. If and when you do send attachments, be sure that you are sending a document that the editor, gallery owner or agent can open. *WinZip* is a common attachment program that can be downloaded from their website.

Other Than E-mail

The Internet is one large world-community of people taking a walking tour through our backyards all having as many kinds of conversations as you can imagine. There are at least four other ways that people communicate on the net and they include:

• *E-mail lists:* Using e-mail, a group of people might e-mail each other about a common subject. Everyone on the list receives each e-message that the individual member sends. Always use "bcc" so as to protect the privacy of the recipients.

• *Chat rooms:* These virtual rooms are places where people chat about specific subjects in real time.

• *Bulletin boards*: On the same model as a real world bulletin board, you post a thought or idea, someone responds to your thought and someone else responds to her thought, and so on.

• *Instant Messaging or IMing:* This is by far the most personal, quickest way to speak to another person on the net. It is immediate, and can be a good way to touch base with people on a daily basis.

As a working artist, you can use the Internet to create a community of people interested in your work; and it is an inexpensive, often free way to market yourself and expose your work to your target audience.

Long-distance computing

Having access to information worldwide was the original reason ARPANET was created. Programmers can work on powerful computers in another state and scientists can get information from supercomputers in another country. Students can access extensive electronic card catalogs from universities and libraries from around the world for research purposes. The Internet provides a vast array of tools and information. There are sites that offer free software to Internet users. There is an amazing amount of information you can download off reliable sites. Much of it is free, some of it is unreliable, but there are gems within the dross. Through trial and error and a few reputable foundations and organizations you'll be able to find accurate information.

Building a website to market your art

"Do androids dream of electric sheep?" asked Philip K. Dick in his prophetic story of the same name (which, of course, became the movie, *Bladerunner*). This begs the question, "How close to human intelligence can virtual/techno-computer-generated 'intelligence' become? *The Matrix* notwithstanding, the jury is still out. However, practically speaking computers need to be programmed and their programming needs to be periodically updated; they don't think on their own.

The intrinsic nature of business remains the same: customer service is the backbone of any moneymaking enterprise. Never forget the simple fundamentals: your customer base is human—people with the same needs, considerations and questions as you. The Internet and all its supporting apparatus simply facilitate greater market potential and ease of access. Any business, artistic or retail, large or small, needs continually to be evolving in order to maximize full market potential.

But, you might ask, how can I even begin to build a website? Doesn't it take a lot of cash to do that? Do you have to be a computer geek? No and no. Here is how to begin to create a website in four easy steps.

Step One: Make a Plan

What is the purpose of your site? What are your goals? Do you want to display your art? Develop a fan base? Sell your art?

The Internet has changed selling. You can market and advertise using e-mail and an artistic website. You can earn money on the Web if you are able to market your art properly. You can create a 'brand' identity. All this might seem antithetical to the artistic process, but only if your feet are stuck in the last century. Brainstorm. Create your site one page at a time. Make a map. And remember, keep it simple.

Step Two: Assemble the Parts

Design your site. Go on the Web and look at a lot of sites and take the ideas you like and integrate those ideas into a design that works for you. There are standard pages on most websites called: *Home, About Me, How To Contact Me, Links* and so forth. Decide what you want on your site. Write, edit and proof the content. Gather photographs, drawings or graphics you want to use. Be creative and have fun! When you have everything you want to put on your site, you can draw a mock-up of the pages. Review your links, make sure it makes sense and allows the user to get from page to page with relative ease and logic. People like links to work easily and make sense organically.

Step Three: Build It

You do not have to spend a ton of money to build a website, but this is where you may need to hire help, particularly if you are new to creating Web pages. If you can afford a professional, we recommend media artist Jean Hester at *divestudio.org,* whose information is in the appendix. There are some inexpensive "do it yourself" Web design programs on the market. One of them is *e-BIZ in a BOX*, another is *Inet-Toolbox. Nicenet* is a non-profit helping people on the Internet for free or for virtually nothing. Check the Internet Appendix for other resources. Alternatively, many Web designers just starting out can be hired for around $200, depending on the complexity of the site you design It's very important, however, that whoever designs your site follows certain technical rules, such as the placement of "keywords" within the text. Keywords allow search engines to easily locatre you in the massive web of other companies or artists competing for the consumer's attention

Step Four: Update the Insatiable Beast

Websites are mutable beings that transfigure and change or die. As your art grows, so should your website (much like a resume, except it requires more frequent attention). Visit your site often. Update information regularly and check all the links to make sure everything is working properly. Websites need a constant flow of traffic in order to stay dynamic.

So build a website to display your paintings, plays, poetry, whatever you have created. We have thought of a few beginning questions and answers for those of you considering creating a website to help generate income via your art.

What is a domain name?

A domain name is the first thing you need to build a website, and can be used for your "address" on the net. Generally it reads something akin to *yourcompanyname.com*. You will pay a nominal fee to reserve and own your domain name and obtain your URL (Internet address). In its entirety your address will be, ideally, *www.yourcompanyname.com*. If you are using another site as your portal (a gateway to your site), it might make your artwork harder to find. Although it may cost you a little more, it's worth the money to establish your own individual website and to 'brand' your artistic identity.

What is the best way to reserve a domain name?

You will need to get a Web host, which is a service that provides the services and technologies that allow you to post a website on the Internet. As part of their services, many Web hosts will register a client's domain name for a fee, ranging from $25 to $100. To avoid this expense, which is over and above the InterNIC's fee, some companies choose to register directly with InterNIC. (InterNIC is the *Internet Corporation for Assigned Names and Numbers,* a division of the U.S. Dept. of Commerce, *www.internic.net.*) However, this process can be complex to the uninitiated and many find that eliminating the middleman wasn't such a good idea. A hosted website is the easier, more practical way to go. You can get Web hosting service free from places like Yahoo! and GeoCities. However, these sites are free because they are subsidized by banner advertisements, which can be a pain. Also, their services are limited. For example, you cannot have a personalized domain name, nor will the hosting site track the number of visitors who come to view your pages. See appendix for a few hosting companies.

How do I get a fast connection to the Internet?

More and more people are getting DSL and cable because they are the fastest connections and they want their telephones to remain free for incoming or outgoing calls. TI, T3 and fiber optics are other modes of connection to the Internet; however, these are shared methods generally used in office buildings and condominiums. The dial-up connection is the least expensive, but is also slow and extremely cumbersome. Today there are a lot of companies offering fast connections that cost approximately $40 per month; and that $40 saves time and keeps a lot of frustration at bay.

Can I keep track of how many people come to my website?

Many website hosts will have a detailed statistical report on your site's activity which will give you an idea of how many people have visited your website and which specific pages your visitors viewed. This lets you know what is working on your site and what may need to be improved.

Should I update my website?

To keep people interested, update your site regularly. Getting people to visit your site is thrilling; keeping them coming back is gold, or can turn into gold. People will revisit your site more often if you maintain fresh and current content on your site.

Should I use a lot of fancy graphics?

Graphics are fine if they serve your artistic image and are NOT too heavy a download. The Internet is about getting information quickly, and when users have to wait for your site to build itself on their screen, they click on to the next thing. You want imagery, but not at the expense of time and trouble.

What is an interactive site?

The entire Web is interactive. Make sure your site includes ways that people can contact you easily. Most businesses provide an online contact e-mail as well as telephone number and address. You can also include polls, discussion groups, bulletin boards, databases and any other interactive ideas you can think of to make your site livelier.

How do I promote my site?

You can promote your site through free online advertising banners. LinkExchange, one of the world's largest banner ad networks, is a free service that allows members to promote their websites by exchanging advertising space with each other. Make sure to put your website address on your business card. Develop an e-mail list and update your visitors when something new happens on your site. Find other sites similar to your own and contact them to see if you can trade links. The Web is an infinite number of small neighborhoods, and people stroll and shop until they find a neighborhood to their liking. Find yours and join it.

How do people know my site is on the Web?

You can register your site in the major search engines, such as Google, Yahoo, AOL and Alta Vista, to name a few. Although you can go through the process yourself by visiting each search engine and submitting your site one-by-one, you can save time by having someone perform this service for you. One such company is Did-It, which, for a nominal fee, will cover all the major information outlets.

The Internet is what we make of it. If we want to continue doing business as it's always been done, we can buy from the large corporate outlets and businesses, read from the popular magazines and follow the people gossip of the day; or we can make our own way through the ever-shifting maze, surfing where we want, taking only what we want and leaving the rest behind; instilling in our own work and on-line expression only as much or as little anarchy as we would like. It's business-as-usual or a brand new day with all the excitement as well as all the problems inherent in anything new. Remember, "No Rules" is like no guardrail at the Grand Canyon. It makes for a much more powerful view, but you have to pay far more attention to where you're standing.

As for your own "shop," or website, you can model it after a high-end boutique or a tattoo parlor, a serve-yourself deli or an auto wrecking yard. It's your call. Even moreso than when Marshall McCluhan first taught us, the medium *is* the message, and *how* you present what you present makes all the difference as to who sees it, how they see it and, perhaps most important for our purposes, what they do next.

All this, truly, is the beauty of this new expansion of our ability to communicate. Everything is up to each of us, individually; and unlike most other venues, our individual effort has more than just a slim chance of being taken into account.

∞

I self-published my book, Life in Hell. *When I went to the printer, they said, "Well we need a contract, and here, we suggest you use this lawyer," and they introduced me to the attorney I use to this day, Susan Grode. I visited her in her Century City office on the 30th floor. I was completely intimidated. She looked at my stuff and said she would represent me for free. There are attorneys out there who will do that for artists at the beginning. What she said was, "I'm not going to charge you anything and when you make money, I will charge you a lot, and that will pay for the next artist." She stuck to her word and it has been really good.*

Matt Groening, cartoonist/writer

Chapter 6
The Law

The art business is a business like any other, and administering it may require the help of an attorney. Although many legal documents are easy to prepare, you may want to consider hiring a good lawyer for help with the more complex matters, such as contract review and negotiation, commercial leases, incorporation or partnership applications and agreements or establishing your art business as a nonprofit or for-profit company. In the long run, the money you invest to make sure transactions are handled properly and in your best interest is money very well spent. Legal services within your budget are available and certain legal organizations have been established specifically to assist artists.

Volunteer Lawyers for the Arts (VLA) was founded in 1969 in New York City to provide free legal assistance to artists and arts organizations that otherwise could not afford it. Today there are several of these programs across the country, each with its own set of eligibility requirements and rates for services, but all sharing the common goal of providing affordable legal assistance for the artist. In New York, the VLA has created the Artist Legacy Project, an estate planning service, as a response to the AIDS crisis. In California, a mediation program called Arts Resolution Services has been created by the **California Lawyers for the Arts.** And if you do not meet the financial criteria for VLA, they will refer you to an attorney who will help you at a substantially reduced rate.

In our appendix we provide several resources for finding the right legal help. You should also be advised that if you do not meet the necessary criteria, there are also some lawyers willing to work "pro bono," especially for a nonprofit organization. This is where a community of artists can help. Ask around for referrals from friends and colleagues; call people involved in other organizations similar to your own and ask where they obtained legal support.

Copyright

In the simplest terms, copyright means the right to copy. Only the owner of the work, usually the creator of the piece, is allowed to produce or reproduce the work or to permit anyone else to do so. In order for a work to be copyrighted, it must be creative. This means it has to be more than just factual data or public information, though if facts are cleverly arranged, the "arrangement" can be copyrighted. The copyright is immediate upon the expression of the work in a "tangible form of expression," i.e., recorded, written down, photographed, carved or etc. As soon as the work becomes a tangible form of expression, the work cannot be used without your permission. You cannot copyright what you *say* until it has been written down or recorded. The same holds true for choreographed works or performances of any type. They must be written down or recorded. Copyrightable works include the following:

1. Literary works

2. Musical works, including any accompanying words

3. Dramatic works, including any accompanying music

4. Pantomimes and choreographic works

5. Pictorial, graphic and sculptural works

6. Motion pictures and other audiovisual works

7. Sound recordings

8. Architectural works

Titles, names, short phrases and slogans cannot be copyrighted.[1] Ideas, concepts, methods or systems may not be copyrighted. As stated before, facts may not be copyrighted.

Under current law, a copyright will protect your work for your lifetime, plus 70 years.

Copyright Registration and Copyright Notice

Copyright is immediate and requires nothing on your part other than making notes on a napkin or singing into an answering machine. Although the common law automatically protects your work, it is a good idea to take the extra step and register your copyright.

Copyright registration is a legal formality used to create a public record of a particular copyright. Even though it's not necessary to gain copyright protection, there are many good reasons to register your work. Registration:

- Establishes a public record of the copyright claim.
- Is necessary in order to file an infringement suit.
- May be used as evidence in an infringement suit.
- Is necessary in seeking statutory damages and attorneys fees in court. (Without registration, only actual damages and profits may be sought.)

Registration may be done with the Library of Congress. In order to register a work, you must submit, in one envelope or package:

1. A properly completed application form.
2. A non-refundable filing fee (at the time of this writing, $30).
3. A copy of the work being registered.

Submissions are sent to:

> Library of Congress
> Copyright Office
> 101 Independence Avenue, S.E.
> Washington, D.C. 20559-6000

[1] This allows me to write *Just Do It*, and not get sued for it (though if I had included a *swoosh,* I'd probably be in trouble because of trademark infringement, a whole other area of the law); and if it suited us, we could name this book *Planet of the Apes.* (JK)

Application forms are available at *www.copyright.gov/ forms/formtxi.pdf,* or by writing the Copyright Office at the above address. In three to five months after submission you will receive a certificate of proof of registration.

Written works may also be registered through the Writer's Guild of America (WGA) East or West, either online, by mail or in person. Material accepted by the WGA includes scripts, treatments, outlines and written ideas intended for use in film, television, radio or interactive media, as well as novels, short stories, theatrical plays, lyrics and drawings. For registration by mail or in person, the WGA West Registration Office must receive:

1. One unbound loose-leaf copy of material on standard 8 1/2" x 11" paper.
2. Cover sheet with title of material and full legal names of all authors in the order in which credit will be given.
3. Social security number, return address and phone numbers of all authors.
4. Registration fees: WGA members—$10, non-members—$20.

The above should be sent or delivered in one package to the Guild office:

Writers Guild of America, West
Intellectual Property Registry
7000 West Third St.
Los Angeles, CA 90048

Once received, the material is sealed, dated and a numbered certificate is returned to you that will serve as the official proof of registration. Material may also be registered online with the WGAWest at: *www.writersguild.org/webrss/ dataentry.asp.* For questions, call: (323) 951-4000.

For those east of the Mississippi, the WGA East accepts materials to be registered by mail or in person at:

Writers Guild of America, East, Inc.
555 West 57th Street, Suite 1230
New York, New York, 10019
Attn: Registrations.

The WGA asks that a Registration envelope, available upon request[2], be used for all submissions, though if one is not available, a plain envelope, 9"x12", may be used by including the following information on the front of it:

1. Name and address of registrant

2. Title of material

3. Form of material

4. Registration sealed by signature of author (or his/her representative) and social security number.

For recorded instructions, call (212) 757-4360.

Copyright Notices

Before 1978, copyright protection was based upon publication of the work and by the attachment of a copyright notice to the published work. Though this is no longer essential for gaining a copyright, there are still good reasons to attach a copyright notice. A notice identifies the owner, shows the year of first publication, legally substantiates a request for damages and disallows a defendant's claim of innocent infringement. The copyright notice informs the world that the work is protected. It consists of the following elements:

1. The symbol © (the letter C in a circle), or the word "Copyright," or both.

2. The year of first publication of the work.

---

[2] A Registration envelope will be supplied upon request when accompanied by a 9"x12" self-addressed stamped envelope with 78 cents postage, plus 23 cents more for each additional envelope, a maximum of three.

3. The name of the owner of the copyright. And, if you'd like to have your copyright protection extend specifically to Bolivia and Honduras,[3] you should also include:

4. The registration of rights phrase: *All Rights Reserved.*

All together, that would look something like this:

Copyright © 2002, Adele Slaughter

All Rights Reserved

This may be placed on the front or the back cover; on the frame, base or mat of the work; or on a separate label, so long as the label always travels with the work of art. For sound recordings, it's a slightly different form:

Registered ® 2002, Red Crow Records

All Rights Reserved

This must be affixed to the phonorecord[4] or its label, though it is common practice for the notice to appear on both the bottom rear of the jacket and on the album label.

Contracts

A contract is an agreement between two parties that is enforceable by law. Most often there is an exchange of promises: your wares or services in exchange for money, goods, services or rights. Contracts can be expressed in writing or they can be verbal agreements or they can be implied by the actions of the parties involved. Conversations, e-mails and notes can establish a contract even though nothing is ever signed by either party. In short, we're all making contracts all the time, usually without even knowing it. And many of these unrecognized contracts can be legally binding. Of course (and here's the caveat), if

---

[3] I'm not kidding here. Something to do with the Buenos Aires Convention. But just add the All Rights Reserved phrase. It looks cool, and if the Bolivians actually produce your play, you'll get paid. (JK)

[4] Yes, this is an actual word, and is proof that attorneys spend too much time in offices coming up with words that make sense only to other attorneys. (JK)

there is ever any disagreement and you find it necessary to go to court to enforce your "agreement," unless it is in writing and signed by the party to be bound, it will be your word against another's. The best protection is to *GET IT IN WRITING*. Always.

Sample contracts, depending on the deal you are making, are easy enough to find either through the many books listed in the legal appendix or through a lawyer . You can write a contract on a sheet of paper in plain and simple English. No legalese, no "whereof's" or "in that's" or "parties of the first part" are necessary. The contract simply has to state what the two parties agree upon. However, if you have a written contract, make sure it contains *everything* you are agreeing to. Do not leave out those things you are assuming will happen or that the other person has promised you based upon their good will. The law will generally assume that if you signed it, it contains the entirety of the agreement. Be sure to date it and have a witness sign it as well.

If your agreement is complicated and/or if there is any part of it which is unclear to you, you should retain an attorney. If your contract is drafted poorly, it may not be enforceable and may even be interpreted against you, rather than for you.

Aside from the legal aspects, a contract gives all parties a clear point of reference, perhaps most important when working on a project with friends. How many friendships have dissolved over assumptions that were made at the excited beginnings of a project, but which over the course of time shifted and fell away? With any business transaction, be clear and specific regarding the obligations of all parties.

And finally, don't sign anything you don't understand or think you'll want to change a few months down the road. Contracts, like personal relationships, work only as long as all the involved parties are satisfied with what they're giving and getting. Define all the conditions of a contract before your pen hits the paper rather than later in arbitration hearings or contract litigation proceedings.

∞

> *The grants helped but that was twenty years ago. I was nominated for them because of the plays I wrote. I got two Guggenheims and a Rockefeller. It wasn't much money, but it was enough to live on and write and it was quite prestigious.*
> **Murray Mednick, playwright**

Chapter 7

Grants

To save you a lot of time and trouble, we will cut to the chase: there is no such thing as "free" money. As you will see, applying for a grant can take a lot of time and energy. Not even the "genius" grant, the John D. and Catherine T. MacArthur Foundation Fellowship, is free money. The MacArthur gives sizable grants to artists, scientists and others doing valuable work, but you have to have been working and recognized in your discipline long enough for someone to nominate you for a MacArthur; plus you have to have shown extraordinary talent in your field and have a "marked capacity for self-direction." The selection is based on three criteria: exceptional creativity, promise for important future advances based on a track record of significant accomplishment and potential for the fellowship to facilitate subsequent creative work.

Of course if you want to get one of the non-genius grants, you will have to write a grant proposal. The **National Endowment for the Arts (NEA)** gives grants to individual artists, although less frequently now than in the past. Several major foundations remain committed to supporting individuals but, like the Guggenheim and the Fulbright, these grants are generally given to fairly well-established artists. Still, every artist ought to investigate the kinds of grants that are available from the arts council in their home state or geographic region (unless that council has been eliminated).

Today, more and more nonprofits are operating like businesses; and over the past ten years, nonprofits have been relying less and less on grants for funding. Nonprofits can get loans for things like new construction, relocation and other expansion needs. The **Nonprofit Finance Fund (NFF)** can provide money that nonprofits cannot get from other sources. They also provide workshops to help nonprofits become more business savvy. Established in 1980, NFF has granted more than $78 million and serves most of America's major cities. See appendix for contact information.

There are also foundations that will support arts projects such as public murals, staging a play or sponsoring a reading series. Many artists work in school residency programs, such as the Poets-in-the-Schools Program and the nationally run Teachers & Writers Collaborative. (See appendix.) These arts organizations acquire grant money and hire artists to teach in schools, prisons, libraries, senior citizen centers and community settings. These programs, however, are not meant to become a career for an artist and generally cannot sustain the artist indefinitely. They are intended to help you make some additional money while you simultaneously work outside the program to take your career to the next level. Work through these programs offers great opportunities for the beginning artist but can also be time consuming. Many times a "B" job can become more important than the work of making art. It's always a balancing act.

Writing a grant proposal exposes you to the business world and to the world of nonprofit organizations. You will research funding agencies, prepare a budget and think about how you and your art project can effectively interface with society. Grant applications require that you define yourself and what you do, as well as how you plan to spend the money you're requesting. This process can be extremely useful and even cathartic. It can serve to clarify your goals and objectives, open your mind to new and different ideas and introduce you to resources in the community you did not know existed.

When you have won a grant but have not yet received the money, there are Bridge Loans which can offer temporary help with an organization's or an individual's cash flow issues. (See appendix.) Bridge Loans are only available to organizations or artists with a grant they can use as collateral.

Seven Tips For Writing a Grant

1. Make a plan

Brainstorm your arts project. Start a list. Answer the usual questions: Who are the artists involved? Who is the audience? Who are the people who will be impacted? What resources do you need to implement the project? What is the timeline for the project? Where will your work be staged? How will you do what you say you are going to do?

Perhaps the most important question to answer for your proposal is: What societal need(s) are you addressing? Why should this project be funded? How will the community benefit from your creation? Your answers to these questions will evolve as you develop your proposal.

An outline is essential. Using your outlined proposal you can find foundations, corporations, community sponsors or businesses that can support your endeavor. For example, if you want to create art and poetry with underprivileged inner-city children, there are organizations that direct funds to such programs. Other kinds of organizations fund regional theatre, art in the environment and so on. If you seek to arrange a poetry reading series or a performance of new plays, businesses, colleges or universities or museums might offer a space for your performance or buy advance tickets for the event. State and federal agencies often grant funds to support culturally enriching activities.

2. Spend time researching

Agencies and foundations provide general guidelines for proposals. These are available on request. The grant appendix offers a list of organizations that will help you begin your research. You can widen your search by contacting your local arts organizations, libraries, city halls and your state arts councils. Most university libraries will have foundation directories with detailed information on funding levels, demographic requirements, geographic areas of support and descriptions of what they have previously funded.

Do not tailor or alter the content of your project in order to get a grant. If you have a documentary you want to make, a mural you want to paint, a play or a poetry reading series you want to produce, chances are there is a corporation or foundation that will fund the project. Make sure, however, that your project fits into the guidelines of the agency or foundation to which you are applying. Grants are most often rejected because they fail to meet the organization's guidelines.

3. Network and ask questions

Once you have targeted several foundations and begin to make your calls, be gracious. Along with your work, you are selling yourself as someone worth listening to. People give money to *people* as well as to their projects. The NEA and most corporate givers have a staff to help you with the application procedure. The more prepared you are before contacting them, the better off you are. The personal contact is very important as you are making an impression, for better or for worse, with each of the various representatives with whom you speak. Back in the mid-eighties when I[1] was working with New York State Poets in the Schools (NYSPITS), we applied to the New York Community Trust and had an amazing experience. The executive director brought me into the meeting with the funder because I was the poet doing the work as well as the administrator of the program and could best explain the project. The funder we met with suddenly asked me to leave the room. After the meeting, the executive director told me that the funder had asked if she could give NYSPITS an additional $4,000 so she could raise my salary. It happens. Though corporations and other organizations make funding choices based on ideas, making a good impression counts, and your personal presentation can influence the decision.

4. Get support

The grant may require that you show community and peer support. It is a good practice to maintain a media relations file in which you keep letters of support, letters of thanks and articles that have been written about the work you do. Collect support letters from the people

[1] (Adele Slaughter)

you work with, from other artists in your field and if possible from leaders in your community who recognize the value of your work. The input from your peers can also help you focus your proposal before you submit it. Include letters of endorsement from people who will be helping with the project. Additionally, you can offer letters of recommendation from fellow artists or recognized authorities who can comment on your ability to carry out the proposed work. Also, attach any agreement letters you may have obtained from other agencies, organizations or individuals who might be matching or sharing project expenses. An artistic resume may also be required and is useful to show how your career has developed.

5. Prepare a realistic budget

The budget you submit will mirror your credibility. Do not inflate your budget thinking that you will receive less than you request, unless the funding agency recommends that you do so. The days of inflated budgets are over, and as a general principle it is not wise to ask for $30,000 when the project will only cost $20,000. Most people who review grant proposals are savvy enough to know the costs associated with a project.

At the same time, it is important to anticipate and figure in all the costs of your project, and your budget should be consistent with the narrative description in the proposal. Generally, if you follow the grant budget guidelines offered by the organization from which you are requesting funds, you should be on track.

At any rate, you probably will not be requesting all your funding from one source. Most grants include funds from more than one source. And often, successfully obtaining funding from one source can act as leverage to encourage another source to contribute funds. For most projects to succeed they must also have the promise of community financial support, which will indicate that the community supports the project. Meaning, for example, if you are bringing artists into the schools, the schools are putting in some of the necessary funding, or the city will pay for part of the mural project and so on.

6. *Have faith*

Many artists are intimidated by the mystique of writing a grant. True enough, grants aren't easy to get, but they aren't impossible, either. If you have ever prepared a cover letter and an application for admission to a college or university you are capable of writing a grant proposal. Most review panelists and foundation officers work hard to ensure worthwhile projects receive the funds they deserve. Writing grant proposals can be an ongoing process and most likely you will be dealing with the same staff people year after year. Many times they will become your friends with a sincere interest in both your growth and the community you serve.

Follow up once your proposal has been submitted. Call if you said you were going to call. Let the program officer at the funding agency know you are accessible if he needs further information. If you are not notified about the results of the panel review within a few weeks of the posted notification date, write a short note of inquiry. If you are turned down for lack of funds, ask the program officer if he recommends that you re-submit the proposal in the next funding period. If you're turned down because of a deficiency in the proposal, discuss it with the staff so you can make the necessary adjustments before you re-apply. Learn from the experience and maintain your contacts. Have faith.

When you do get the grant, remember that funders are interested in their applicants and want to be kept informed about the anthologies, exhibitions, productions or concerts made possible by their money.

7. *Write a strong proposal*

Every proposal is different in terms of content, substance and style; however every proposal shares certain characteristics. Your proposal must be specific, thorough and clear. A perfect proposal describes a worthwhile project and gives the fundraiser a sense of ownership and pride. Grant proposals are very clear about what they want, why they want it and how they are going to achieve the stated goals. Proposals establish a need for the project and the credibility of the artist or arts organization that can fill that need. The proposals that get the funding ultimately have something unique to recommend the project presented.

Below is an outline of how to write a proposal. Grant writing courses are also available. **The Foundation Center** has a great grant writing program and many state arts councils will guide you to grant writing workshops. Best rule of thumb is when you research foundations to apply to for support, ask them for suggestions on where to get help.

How to Write a Proposal

1. Summary

Although the summary is the last part of the proposal you write, it is the first thing the funder reads. A summary identifies who you are, establishes your credibility and gives an overview of the grant proposal. Some people include the amount of the request and the total cost of the project but, depending on the project, you may decide not to include this figure here. It is a good idea to begin with writing the summary and edit it as you write the rest of your proposal, keeping the big picture in mind.

2. Need

The strongest proposals begin with a description of a broad problem in society that your art project plans to address. Who will your project serve? What is their primary need? How will your project directly address this need? *In the relationship between the societal need and how art can address that need lies the unique essence of your project.* This is the hook that makes the funder read further and eventually convinces the decision makers that your project is worthy. For example, the problem is graffiti in a low-income community. Your solution? A mural project—an artist works with teenagers to create and install relevant murals throughout the city, thereby encouraging creative expression and deterring graffiti.

3. Goals and Objectives

This section clearly outlines the larger purpose of your project. What is your overall goal or goals and what are the actions you will take to meet those goals? This is the verb section of the proposal. Using bullet points, outline the overview of your actions. Will you: Educate inner city youth about art? Establish art workshops? Develop materials? Coordinate replicable programs? Arrange performances?

4. Project Description

This section of the proposal clearly describes the project's activities. Include all aspects of your plan and how you intend to implement them. Describe who will benefit from the program. Be realistic. Can you establish the results of your program in measurable terms? If 100 school children and three teachers will benefit from your writing workshop, say so. If your project has history, describe it here. Be as specific and detailed as you can be so the reviewer will understand exactly how the program will work.

5. Background and Capability

This section applies if you have taken your project to a larger arts organization that is providing basic funding or otherwise sponsoring your project. This information, if applicable, tends to lend credibility to the project and gives the reviewer one more reason to consider it.

6. Evaluation

Not all projects have obvious evaluation measures, but all projects have ways that the success of them can be shown. Describe how you will determine if the program was successful and how these results can be used to help your organization evaluate the success of the project.

7. Funding

In this section you will make a direct request for the funds you need. A concise statement justifying the request can be submitted if necessary.

8. Budget

All projects have direct and indirect costs. Direct costs are those items that can be directly identified with the project. These kinds of costs might include artist salaries, fees or wages, travel expenses, supplies, space rental for the project itself or printing charges. Indirect costs are things that cannot be tied directly to your project— things like administrative overhead, rent, utilities and costs of running the sponsoring arts organization. The amount of indirect costs you include should be cleared with the funding agency before you submit your proposal. You need to be sure that the costs of the program match the outcome.

Sample Proposal

On the following pages is a sample proposal that received many, many grants. It is a solid model on which to base your own proposal.

∞

Teachers and Writers Collaborative Workshop Proposal

Summary

For eighteen years, Teachers and Writers Collaborative (T&W) has been coordinating workshops in writing and other arts for students of all ages and levels of ability. We believe that writers and artists can play a unique role in reaching troubled youth and have therefore developed a new project called Community Artists (CA).

Need

With increases in illiteracy, single parent families, and poverty, predelinquent adolescents are a fast growing segment of our population in New York City. In recent years, adolescents from every economic background have been described as "at risk." Both young men and women are affected by a variety of problems. We are increasingly made aware of pregnant teenagers, teenage drug users and alcoholics, teenage suicides and homeless youth.

The statistics are disturbing and reflect the extent of the difficulties adolescents face today. An estimated 25,000 adolescents are homeless in the New York Metropolitan area. The New York City Youth Bureau alone dealt with 4,000 homeless and runaway adolescents last year and 30% of those youth had no home to which they could return.

In addition, there are terrible personal losses connected to adolescent delinquency. Many adolescents' problems begin with a tenuous relationship with the educational system, a system they find difficult to relate to. A predelinquent adolescent usually gives up first on school and society as well as on himself or herself before turning to delinquent activity. In 1983—1984, 45% of New York City high school students dropped out of school. Many of these youngsters are functionally illiterate, which means they cannot write a check, address an envelope, or read a notice in a store. Often youngsters who are not yet in trouble with the law can be reached and motivated to turn their lives around. The struggle back to a productive role in society must include attention to the adolescent as a potentially creative human being with the self-confidence and self-discipline to change destructive behavior.

T&W believes that when adolescents develop the language needed to communicate more effectively, this process can provide a real alternative to expression feelings in destructive action. In CA, as in T&W's regular school program, we give young people hands-on experience in writing and the arts. These experiences help them develop specific skills, sharpen their critical thinking abilities, and build motivation, concentration, and confidence. Perhaps most important though, for this population, writing and art experience give young people an opportunity to speak out, to create something that is uniquely theirs, to produce something to be proud of, to communicate the often confused feelings that need to get out.

Goals and Objectives

CA's goal is to establish writing workshops for troubled and disadvantaged adolescents in their communities in New York and Long Island. For the coming year our more specific objectives are to:

    • coordinate replicable writing workshops in community settings such as psychiatric hospitals and youth centers,

    • develop writing workshops for specific problem populations such as children of substance abusers and parents of disturbed children,

    • educate artists, educators and mental health professionals in order to expand this unique approach to working with troubled youth and their families,

    • develop materials such as manuals, books and articles that will increase the public awareness of the problems and some solutions to the issues adolescents face.

Plan of Action

In the seminal year of CA, we had three writing workshops at St. Luke's / Roosevelt Medical Center in the Adolescent Psychiatric Clinic; at Veritas, a residential drug rehabilitation facility for adolescents and young adults; and at the Huntington Youth Bureau. At both the hospital and the drug rehabilitation sites, the programs were forty workshop sessions. At the Huntington Youth Bureau, there were two sixteen-week sessions: the first in Commack, the second in South Huntington. We have been invited to continue these workshops next year.

We work in community settings that serve specific problem populations in order to target "high risk" adolescents more effectively. We are already beginning to see the positive results of working with youngsters using this unique and challenging approach. Our program at St. Luke's serves predelinquent youngsters who live in Harlem. Myra Colon, ACSW Program Coordinator, St. Luke's Adolescent After-School Program, says, "Our poet-in-residence has created such wonder helping the adolescents write. For these adolescents, poetry opens up new avenues of expression which enhance their self-esteem."

At Veritas, we are working with drug-free substance abusers. Veritas is a residential facility with the ability to house 66 residents. Generally the residents are ages 16 to 29 and stay at the facility for at least one year. The workshop has been in session since September 1985. After the first three months of a weekly workshop, the participants told the writer leading the group that this was the longest many of them had committed to anything, including school or a job.

A vital part of the process to increase self-esteem and strengthen the skills of the workshop participants is public recognition. Through the publication of an anthology, after the workshop is completed, and at a publication party, CA provides workshop participants with a tangible symbol of their experience. CA intends to publish anthologies of adolescents' writings from each of the workshop sites. The Huntington anthology will be the works written by adolescents from both Commack and South Huntington.

For the coming year, CA has been approached by STEPS, a psychiatric clinic for children of alcoholics and their parents as well as a Therapeutic Nursery for parents who have severely handicapped children.

In discussions with interested community agencies, CA carefully plans workshops to meet the needs of each individual population. In addition, CA believes that for a workshop to be successful, it must be supported by the agency's administration. CA asks agencies to demonstrate their support of our program by cooperating in the scheduling of workshops, by conducting serious outreach to encourage adolescents to participate in the program, and by committing matching funds to the project. We believe that an agency's financial support of the program is an important measure of their commitment and we establish programs only where that commitment is demonstrated.

Background and Capability *(abbreviated version)*

T&W is a nonprofit organization that was formed in 1967 to send writers and other artists into New York schools to conduct writing and arts workshops with young people and teachers. Since 1967, over 300 writers and artists have worked with T&W – teaching workshops or writing the articles and books we publish and distribute. T&W workshops have reached more than 150,000 children, teachers, and adults in the New York City area. *(NOTE: this proposal was written in the 80's. Since then T&W has become an organization offering workshops across the US. If you are working with a larger organization, they will have the necessary language for you.)*

T&W's innovative "Community Artists" builds on T&W's commitment to young people and extends outreach to youth with a variety of problems. T&W has found a lot of public interest in learning methods to help all kinds of teenagers and particularly in finding ways to motivate the "hard to reach" adolescent. Additionally, T&W sees great potential use of the idea that creating art can help troubled youth get in touch with and express their feelings, rather than acting out their destructive impulses. Additionally, through experience, T&W has found that this program not only works aesthetically and therapeutically, but also includes the badly needed work on individuals' reading and writing skills.

Evaluation

CA workshops are evaluated in progress through the anthology publication and the writer who works closely with the on-site staff. Additionally, CA is implementing an evaluational study using the workshops in the Huntington program and with the assistance of the Huntington Youth Development Associations. This study will examine the widely held belief that metaphor or "poetic thinking" can express feelings more precisely than analytical language and thus convey experiences which elude literal and non-metaphorical language. Does metaphor require special processes for comprehension? If so, must these be learned specifically, acquired through growth and cognitive and emotional maturation, or can they be acquired by exposure to metaphorical language?

CA is also planning to edit a future issue of Teachers & Writers, T&W's bi-monthly magazine that reaches about 5,000 educators. This issue will include articles by writers across the nation who have worked with disturbed individuals in a variety of community settings.

There is still much to be understood about how to motivate "hard to reach" youngsters. CA focuses on the special role artists and artistic creation can play in this process.

Funding

Fees from participating sites cover only a part of the costs of the workshops, book publications and developing workshops in new community settings. T&W must raise money to augment the financial support it currently receives. T&W therefore is requesting from *(insert name of foundation or corporation)* a grant of $10,000 to help support Community Artists. Attached please find a budget for the CA project.

Community Artists Project — Projected Budget

Projected Expenses

Writers fees or salaries	$13,220
Fringe benefits	1,980
Project Coordinator	6,600
Professional fees for testing	
& evaluation	1,000
Workshop anthologies	6,000
Project replication	
(special issue of T&W magazine)	3,500
Administration and overhead	9,700
Total Budget	**$42,000**

Projected Income

Earned Revenue	$16,050
Other Foundations	15,950
Request from (name of funding source)	10,000

> *When they are alone, they want to be with others, and when they are with others, they want to be alone. After all, human beings are like that.*
>
> **Gertrude Stein**.

> *I am of the opinion that my life belongs to the community, and as long as I live it is my privilege to do for it whatever I can.*
>
> **George Bernard Shaw**

> *Never doubt that a small group of thoughtful, committed citizens can change the world. Indeed, it is the only thing that ever has.*
>
> **Margaret Mead**

Chapter 8
Finding a Community

Most humans like to congregate, even those who are the solitary types. We like to go to coffee shops, hang out in museums, go to movies together or dance salsa with each other. We like to talk about what we are working on—we enjoy the interaction and we like to share ideas. We like to be in a community of like-minded folks. Artists in particular include interactions with a community of people as part of the creative process and evolution of their work. You'll want someone to listen to your demo, look at the proof sheets for your headshots or tell you where Sennelier paint is on sale. You'll want to be around people who won't think you're weird if you have to weep into your soda on the anniversary of Picasso's death or practice your Irish accent over dinner. Community is where you are reflected, and where you are allowed to reflect. We all need it.

MFA Programs And Other Classes

One way of finding a community is in the academic world, an atmosphere where your art comes first and must constantly be evolving. Take a course, even one outside your immediate area of expertise, and learn about the process of writing, acting, directing, dancing, painting or making music.

Whether full time in an MFA program or a Saturday afternoon life drawing class, the academic life can be a relief, a joy, a great opportunity. You make contacts with other artists in your discipline and others. You meet and study with mentor writers, filmmakers, dancers—groups of artists whose life and work experience can be of enormous benefit to you. Many of these people can become lifelong mentors and friends. By pursuing a Masters in Fine Arts you create an artistic thesis that can help you later to teach or to obtain a coveted job. A degree is a valuable asset. Nonetheless, an MFA is no magic pill. In the end, what will get you the book contract, the movie deal, the show in the gallery, is the work, not your connections or your diploma. Although, in an Inaugural Lecture delivered by W.H. Auden to the University of Oxford on June 11, 1956, Auden talked about primary and secondary creativity. He maintained that someone with primary creativity, which he defined as talent, had to have secondary creativity, which he categorized as marketing skills, in order to succeed. He also implied that one need not have primary creativity in order to be successful, but that secondary creativity, i.e. drive and desire, might garner an artist success, even while they might be short on talent.

Support Groups, Classes, Workshops, Seminars, Continuing Education

There are hundreds of acting workshops, writing workshops, painting classes and music classes that can be very valuable. Check out bulletin boards and look in the free local newspapers in your area—chances are someone is teaching what you want to study. This is a great way to do your art and share it with others, while at the same time keeping your talents honed. There are also self-help groups that can be a great help during stressful or unproductive times. Many *Artist's Way* groups are available and offer group interaction with people who need the same help and support as you.

Artists Retreats

Going to a writer's colony or artist's retreat can be a wonderful gift to the artist within. Founded in 1900 by the financier Spencer Trask and his wife Katrina, herself a poet, *Yaddo* is an artists' community located on a 400-acre estate in Saratoga Springs, New York. Its mission is to nurture the creative process by providing an opportunity for artists to work without interruption in a supportive environment. Another of the oldest art getaways in America, founded in 1907, *The MacDowell Colony* in Peterborough, New Hampshire, is a place where creative artists are given the freedom to concentrate on their work. Writers, composers, visual artists, photographers, printmakers, filmmakers and architects come to the Colony each year from all parts of the United States and abroad. At some artists' colonies, in addition to artists, there are scientists and scholars in residence as well. They all take advantage of the uninterrupted time and seclusion in which to work and they enjoy the experience of living in a community of gifted artists. Colonists say that the opportunity to be in an atmosphere where their work is of paramount importance has changed their lives.

Writers' Groups

Writers' workshops and conferences allow you the opportunity to discuss your work and meet other writers, in addition to agents, editors, and publishers. Generally held in the summer, writers' retreats are a unique opportunity to bask in a community of like minds. Many of America's most well known authors attend these conferences, most ready and willing to share their experiences with their fellows. In the appendix there is a list of some of the colonies and conferences, as well as resources for finding other conferences for aspiring writers.

Writers also form groups in their communities to critique each other's writing on an ongoing (often weekly) basis. Once you get your novel started or have begun compiling your book of poems, it is essential to get feedback. Poets, fiction writers, screenwriters get together to inspire and critique. Some groups form among people who have connected in writing classes and wish to continue the experience after the class is over. You can form a group of your own, go to the local library and find a group or call a writer friend.

Theatre Companies

A theatre company is a collective of actors, writers, and directors—theatre artists who come together based on a common vision and who wish to collaborate. People join a theatre company to keep their art fresh, to be seen by agents, producers, casting directors and directors, to put their art before the public and to gain more practical theatre experience. Performing with a company of actors can be an excellent way to get your start in the business of acting and to have a consistent place to perform. Theatre companies exist in large cities and small towns and are generally always looking for support, especially from volunteers. Membership in a theatre company will expose you to every aspect of theatre, from stagehand to producer, actor to costumer to director. Any and all of these jobs will feed you in your primary art.

> *So I worked on this trilogy of anti-war plays at the Pasadena Playhouse, and then I got on the Pasadena Freeway back to USC and I was the curtain puller on* Imaginary Invalid *by Moliere. I completely fell asleep one time and someone wearing a mask kicked me awake. Scared the hell out of me.*
> **John Ritter, actor**

Companies can form around the work of a certain writer, such as Ionesco or Beckett; around a certain style of work or level of intensity—in LA, The Actor's Gang and Zoo District, in New York, The Wooster Group, as examples; or around a certain teacher or school of acting. Go to Equity Waiver theatre, go to acting classes, audition for shows. By the doing you are already a part of the community. Time will show you your specific place in it.

Dance Companies

The dancers' instrument is the body—perhaps the most vital, but fragile tool of the artist. In order for the dancer to aim for that perfect performance, he must constantly be practicing and physically fit. Dancers learn technique as a way to discipline the physical body in order to manifest the moment of perfection. Most dancers practice a daily workout to keep the body supple and ready. One way is to take classes; another is to join a dance company. There are many dance companies that will help cultivate and nurture young dancers through the rigorous training needed to become a disciplined dancer. The major dance companies include the American Ballet Theatre, the Joffrey Ballet, the National Ballet and the New York City Ballet. For modern dancers, there are the Alvin Ailey, Merce Cunningham, Paul Taylor, Twyla Tharp and Debbie Allen dance companies, as well as hundreds of others throughout the country. See appendix for a list of dance company resources.

Visual Artists

Painters and sculptors are perhaps the most isolated artists. Still, they also have ways to develop a community. Enrolling in an MFA program or securing an apprenticeship with an established artist can be a good way to immerse yourself into the world of fine art. Another way is to visit galleries and frequent art openings. Art shows are listed in weekly local papers—in Los Angeles, the *Times* or the *LA Weekly;* in New York, *The Village Voice* or *Time Out.*

You can also take art classes both to improve your work as well as to meet and network with other fine artists.

Musicians

Music is a strict discipline and generally requires professional instruction and diligent practice. Once again, college. MFA programs. There are, however, always groups to join. Jazz workshops, string quartets, madrigal choruses and local orchestras and symphonies can introduce you to an entirely new and different music community.

If none of these groups suit your fancy, advertise in the local free paper and start your own. Bottom line, find a place to play. John Zorn tells us about learning to play the saxophone so that he could meet other musicians just to be able to have someone to play his compositions. David Speltz talks about his career as a session musician almost as if it were his "B" job. His heart is really with his string quartet (which of course pays nothing). If you are a musician, go to where the music is. Participating regularly in any fashion will pull you to the next level.

Overall, the artist chooses a pursuit that is outside the conventional norm. It is often difficult to stay connected to family or to the community you grew up in, whether for geographic or philosophical reasons. Home may be a thousand miles away from where you are now. In any event, artists need community. Most artists seek out a family of artists, a feeling of belonging somewhere, even if it is only to the group of regulars at your local coffee shop. Creating art is often a solitary and personal experience and can only be enhanced and diversified by a community experience. People to whom we can relate are the single best source for helping us keep our sanity and for giving us opportunities for expression. Community offers opportunities to be of service to others, and often through that process we can begin to find our true selves as artists. We can begin to know what art is really about. Art is not fame or fortune, money or love or security. Art is about using what we have been given in such a way that it adds to the world and to the experience of the people around us.

∞

Chapter 9

Working Overseas

Currency, Politics, Etc.

It is very difficult for artists to find work in foreign countries; and for a variety of reasons, it's likely to become more difficult. Although in years past a few American artists have worked and earned more money in Europe than they have in the United States, even these artists now anticipate a decline in foreign bookings. Dancer/performance artist Tim Miller, successful in obtaining bookings in Great Britain, Austria, Italy, France and Scandinavia, feels the decline in demand for American artists may be a result of the strong impact Americans have had on the work of contemporary European artists. Inspired by their American colleagues, more European artists are producing more work and demanding more government support than they've received in the past.

The extent to which American artists are welcome abroad depends on many factors that have little to do with artistic merit. The current political climate, the currency exchange, the size of a company or production and the level of risk and inconvenience artists are able to tolerate all play a part in determining whether or not they appear at the Edinburgh Fringe Festival or the Schaubuhne Theater.

Politics can play a large role in determining whether or not an artist from your country will be welcomed in another country at a given time, and many governments use the arts for political purposes. Great Britain, which has a very active Visiting Arts program, showed Russian artists a distinctly cold shoulder following the Soviet invasion of Afghanistan. No official government pressure was brought to bear on the Visiting Arts Administration but during that period of time they simply decided to look elsewhere for their cultural imports. In the United States, the United States Information Agency (USIA) is highly selective in the artists and programs they export through their *Arts America* program. For all practical purposes, this agency functions as a propaganda council and generally exports artists most likely to create good will for America. Almost all government-funded cultural exchange programs to one degree or another *are* political. Artists who accept government funding should not be surprised if their performances and exhibitions fit into some agency's illogical (or logical) political strategy.

Should the government pay people to be artists?
"No. God forbid! Keep those rat bastards away."
Hubert Selby, Jr.

The strength of the American dollar can also have adverse impacts on cultural exchange programs. The exchange rate between the dollar and the Euro determines, year to year, how much a European sponsor must pay for any particular act, regardless of whether or not the act has changed its fee. And even if the dollar were in a state of devaluation versus the Euro, European lodging and travel expenses would then in all probability be much higher. If local per diem costs are not included in your contract, watch out. Research all costs before you sign.

The lack of reciprocity between U.S. and foreign governments has also caught up with us. For years European arts councils have not only paid for American artists to perform and exhibit in Europe but have also paid for their artists to come to the United States. Today even our most generous friends in Holland, England and France are beginning to question this inequitable cultural exchange.

Arts International is a nonprofit organization dedicated to facilitating international arts exchanges. Based in New York, their work consists of creating projects and partnerships to help develop cross-cultural work worldwide; developing funding and regranting programs to support artists and arts organizations working internationally; and using new media to connect and educate artists and audiences and cultural organizers around the world.

Through this organization and its partners, funds are available for individual performing artists invited to participate in certain international festivals and for visual artists involved in recurring arts exhibitions. Information, eligibility requirements and applications are available at the program's website: *www.artsinternational.org.*

The size of your company or project is another economic factor that will determine whether or not you are invited to work abroad. Soloists are obviously cheaper and easier to present than a large theatre company with a complicated lighting design and set. You may wish to get yourself established and recognized overseas before you try to find jobs for your friends and colleagues. This in itself can be a huge undertaking and may initially involve paying for your own exploratory tour of the international arts market. Be aware that this is an adventure not everyone sees as worthwhile.

"Right now I'm trying to license three earlier CDs in Europe so that a company there can release them," says David Brown about the work he has produced as the leader of *Brazzaville.* "I can make some money off that; and as people hear them and there's a demand, we can go play in Europe. [But without having an album out] who would come see you? They wouldn't even know who you were. It doesn't make sense."

Tim Miller concurs. "Almost no sponsor will book artists he hasn't actually seen or heard." If necessary, he suggests performing on the street outside important festivals in order to be seen. "Word of mouth," he says, "is very effective in getting your name around. If one sponsor sees you and likes you, he'll tell other sponsors and you'll get more work."

In most European countries, private sponsors and donors receive no tax benefits. As a result, many arts activities are subsidized by government grants. According to Frans van Rossum, formerly the director of the Holland Festival and Dean of the Music School at the California Institute of the Arts, this frees sponsors to present work that might be considered experimental or risk-taking. Without the burden of having to sell tickets to underwrite a performance or exhibition, presenters can nurture experimental work. Avant-garde choreographers, composers, video and performance artists like Robert Wilson, Philip Glass, Bill Viola, and Meredith Monk were supported by European sponsors long before they gained wide recognition and acceptance in the United States.

Composer John Zorn finds his eclectic approach helpful with regard to playing overseas. "Yeah, I go there [Europe] every year, and every year offers an opportunity to try something else. Every year I'd go with a different group, and because I was very kind of.... I had a wild imagination, was very curious and wanted to try a lot of different things, was not afraid of that, so every time I'd go back I'd have a different project, so they'd want me back again to see 'What was he up to this year? *Now* what's he up to? *Now* what's he doing? Now he's into hard core punk, wow, now he's into '50's bebop jazz, now he's into etc. etc.'

"The first gig must have been because someone heard a recording [or] word of mouth—you'd hear about some guy doing some weird thing and then you'd search him out. I played saxophone and duck calls, birdcalls and clarinet, different wind things."

In *For the Working Artist,* Van Rossum suggested that Americans on their way to Europe collect addresses of sponsors, presenters and artists before they leave the country. Once there they can follow up with one-on-one visits. While such informality might not be effective in America, he feels it is appropriate for Europeans accustomed to a much more straightforward, personal approach. In addition to the well-known museums and festivals, he urges artists to contact the many underground organizations that support contemporary work. Rather than slick press packets he specifically advises musicians to prepare a realistic repertoire list which shows consistency, originality and an approach to music which is different from the traditional repertoire sponsors have heard a thousand times. Van Rossum also cautions Americans not to get caught up in "hype." "Sponsors are looking for content and quality," he says. "[In Europe] slick, glamorous press kits are not only worthless, but counter-productive."

Kira Perov, an arts photographer and independent curator with extensive experience in producing video exhibitions and installations around the world, also feels that direct contact is essential for video artists who wish to do international work. "It's better for a video maker to go to one festival in Europe than to write a hundred letters to museums and sponsors," she says. She also suggests that artists may have to subsidize their own initial foray out of the country. "Given talent and seriousness of purpose," she says, "the contacts artists make, the experience they gain and the exposure to fresh ideas they receive will be worth the money they invest in travel."

Short of going to Europe, artists are advised to go to New York or some other city regularly visited by European sponsors and presenters. Many international sponsors and festival directors make annual visits to New York to view work at sites such as La Mama, the Knitting Factory, P.S. 122, the Brooklyn Academy of Music, Dance Theatre Workshop, The Kitchen and Danspace. European sponsors rely heavily on recommendations from trusted colleagues and will make a point of going to a particular gallery or performance space if referred by the executive directors of Dance Theatre Workshop or BAM.

Contracts

Negotiating contracts can be a dicey business in any country and the subject is covered at length in our Legal Chapter. Many presenters have a standard contract which, if necessary, you should have translated before you sign. The method of payment can be very tricky and you should clearly understand whether you would receive your fee in the currency of your foreign sponsor or in American dollars. As a general rule you should not accept more foreign currency than you expect to spend during your visit in the country (or in the EU). Is there a fixed exchange rate or not? To whose advantage is it set up? You should also request an advance payment of at least 25% of your total fee one month prior to the time you leave the U.S. Technical riders attached to your contract should be translated before you send them so that you and your sponsors have a clear and accurate understanding of your technical requirements. If at all possible, consult an attorney (see Chapter 6 about getting legal help) before you sign a contract with an overseas sponsor. If legal advice is unavailable, ask artists, curators, managers or arts administrators who have worked abroad to review your contract before you sign anything.

Three organizations that will provide you with information about working overseas are the *International Theatre Institute/US*; the *United States Information Agency (USIA) "Arts America" Program;* and the *Canada Council Touring Program*. Contact information can be found in our appendix. Some embassy and consular staff will also provide good information about their cultural and international touring programs.

There are a limited number of fellowships and scholarships made available here for artists who wish to perform and study abroad. These stipends can make up for certain expenses for travel and housing, and in lucky instances may pay the way for the entire venture.

Fulbright grants for creative and performing artists offer funding for a year of study and training throughout the world. A more regional organization, *Partners of the Americas,* develops exchange opportunities for artists to trade places with fellow artists in Latin America and the Caribbean basin for stays of one month and longer. The *National Endowment for the Arts* has fellowship applications for those artists who may wish to visit Japan and France.

The prospects for touring for individual artists and troupes are difficult, as we've already mentioned. The issue of artistic merit often tends to take a backseat to considerations like the political climate, level of risk (both monetary and physical), exchange rates and inconvenience you will encounter on your sojourn abroad.

You're very unlikely to receive bookings from foreign producers who've never encountered your work, so a good deal depends on your prior visibility in the States, especially these days when the Internet has made the world community so small. To be seen anywhere can translate into being seen somewhere else, with or without your knowledge (or your permission, for that matter), as David Brown has learned. "We supposedly have a big following in Russia," says David, "Because some guy, a critic, got hold of our CD and played it on the radio there and someone else bootlegged them and they're available in the stores. So we have a cult fan base in Russia, of all places."[1]

∞

---

[1] In November of 2003, Brown and his band, *Brazzaville,* spent two weeks on tour in Russia, playing to sold-out houses—young women screaming, young men envious and admiring—one of (perhaps the only) positive aspects of piracy.

HAMLET
> *Good my lord, will you see the players well
> bestowed? Do you hear, let them be well used; for
> they are the abstract and brief chronicles of the
> time…*

LORD POLONIUS
> *My lord, I will use them according to their desert.*

HAMLET
> *God's bodykins, man, much better: use every man
> after his desert, and who should 'scape whipping?*

From *The Tragedy of Hamlet*
by William Shakespeare

Chapter 10

Acting

There are perhaps few professions more thankless, or less thankful, than that of acting. To be an actor requires the dedication of extraordinary amounts of time, energy, sweat and tears on work for which you are paid nothing or next to nothing, or even for which you must pay. Most acting, after all, is done in acting classes (for which you pay) or in small theatres (which pay next to nothing) or in auditions (for which you are never paid, and which may cost you a considerable amount for coaching, wardrobe, transportation and time off from your "regular" job). Of course it's a bit Vegas in that respect. You put up your money and you take your chances, betting that you're going to score—if not this time, then eventually. Nor is acting a profession that engenders much respect. We've all seen the Shakespeare-era signage that states, "No dogs or actors allowed," but the sentiment is not that far removed from today's view. Successful actors are treated as royalty and revered in our culture, yet if the next Tom Cruise is waiting on your table at a restaurant in between auditions and classes, he is afforded little credibility. It's a tough and competitive business. The point is, you really have to want to do this if you're going to do it. It's too much work and too much grief and there is too little chance to make it for anyone who does it for any reason other than for the love of acting.

> *An actor's life is not to be envied. It consists mostly of losing out, of being turned down. Unendurable, such a life, for most of us. I will never know how actors manage to persist.*
> **Michael Shurtleff in *Audition***
>
> *Actors endure long periods of unemployment, intense competition for roles, and frequent rejections in auditions...the work, when it is available, is hard, the hours are long, and the pay is low.*
> **—*Occupational Outlook Handbook***
> ***2002—03 Edition,***
> **Bureau of Labor Statistics,**
> **U.S. Department of Labor**

According to the U.S. Department of Labor Bureau of Labor Statistics, median earnings for those dues paying members of Equity who were able to find work in 2000 were less than $10,000; and the average income that SAG members earn from acting is less than $5,000 a year.

The truth is, if you are an actor at heart, no amount of wisdom about the impossibility of an acting career is going to dull your spirit one bit. You'll look at the statistics, but they won't alter your drive or ambition to act—you'll do it anyway.

What separates the SAG and Equity members who are working from the ones who aren't? Talent, of course, must have at least *something* to do with it. Timing. Luck. Training. Looks. Persistence. The ability to take an interview, do a cold reading. All these things matter to one degree or another, but here's the big one: commitment.

> *When I was younger I would have walked barefoot across the Sahara Desert at high noon to get a part in a play. Money was not an issue. To a great extent, this is still true, although now I would probably wait until sundown and steal a camel.*
> **Fionulla Flanagan, actress**

That's what you're up against every time you go out for a role, whether it's to sell soap or to play Stanley Kowalski in the new Broadway revival of *Streetcar*. If you don't want it as badly as that, it's a guarantee that someone else will.

Actor Peter Coyote weighs in with his views on the difficulty of the profession: "I made no money as an actor until I was thirty-eight," he says, "and I think that's okay. It's a great gig and it should be difficult. One of the ways to keep people who are not serious about acting out of the profession is to make it hard." Coyote, whose vision and energy contributed to the shape and substance of the California Arts Council, a state agency that until this year provided grant support to theatres and theatre people throughout California, has had considerable experience reviewing requests for support from talented actors willing to work in schools, prisons and community centers. " Young actors who want instant fame and success are too greedy," he says. "They're concerned about the wrong things. I don't suggest that the cream necessarily rises to the top, but if they're good and stick to it, they'll make it."

Training and Preparation

One of the oddest things about the acting profession is that, unlike law or medicine, auto repair or plumbing, many people look at it and say, "I can do that." And perhaps some of those people could "do that." Being an actor is about being human, after all. And of course we all know what it is to be human; but how many of us can be emotionally and openly vulnerable to the process of living in what are generally extraordinary situations, saying someone else's words as if they were your own, amid the silent cacophony of the boom man in your eye line, the camera creeping in for an extreme close-up and you staring at a taped "X" because the actress had to go change her hair for the next scene and you're about to lose the light? How many of us can do it fifteen times in a row, keeping it new and fresh and alive each time, until all the elements fit and you get a take everyone is happy with? And the stage has a whole other set of difficulties and challenges that are not met by the standard criteria of being a human being. You may have innate talent, but these are learned skills.

> *If you go to an acting class and they're working from a television script, walk out. You may never do Shaw or Ibsen or Shakespeare, but working from these kinds of scripts will prepare you for anything you do.*
>
> **Barbara Bain**

How do you find an acting teacher? Where should you study? What technique is appropriate for you? You can ask a hundred actors and get a hundred different answers. Each will have his or her own history and experience to draw from, and each will have his or her own preferred method of training.

First and foremost, if you are serious about being an actor, you need a technique. You need some set of principles and guidelines, some set of questions to ask yourself for each character you approach which will allow you to fulfill the obligations of that role, allow you to come alive on stage or on camera as this character. You must be able to analyze the script, place yourself in the world of the play, know what your motivation is and know what is at stake. You must be able to access your own inner world, your emotions, your own thoughts and feelings and needs. You must be able, as Sanford Meisner said, to "live truthfully under imaginary circumstances."

Most of the acting techniques available today can in some way be traced to The Group Theatre of the 30's and their embrace of the work of the Russian master, Constantin Stanislavsky of The Moscow Art Theatre. From this group of young actors came Sanford Meisner, Robert Lewis, Stella Adler and Lee Strasberg, each of whom developed his or her own approach to the work and each with students, and students of students, still teaching today. Which approach is right for you? First, ask yourself which professional actors you are drawn to, and why. Find out who they studied with, what technique they use, what they studied after they got their main technique. How long did they study? Do they respect the craft of acting or not? This research may help guide you toward an approach that works for you. There are many books written by these teachers and by their protégés. Read, study and see what you're drawn to.

Evaluating an Acting Class

Many schools or teachers will allow you to audit a class. Take advantage of this. Sit in on as many different types of classes as you can and answer the following question:

- How large is the class? Will you be able to work in each class session and get sufficient individual attention?
- Do you feel as if you can trust the teacher with your vulnerability?
- Is there a definite goal to the work of the class and can the teacher articulate that goal?
- Is the technique being taught the way it was originally taught, or is it an offshoot or further evolution of the original? If it is other than the original, is this a positive or a negative?
- Is the focus of the work on the emotional truth of the character or on the emotional truth of the actor inhabiting the character? Is the work about hiding who you are or expressing who you are?
- Does the work you see exhilarate you or scare you, or both? Do you feel challenged?
- How much does the class cost? Does it fit in with your schedule? What is the time commitment?

Photographs and Resumes

When you are ready to audition for roles, you will need a picture and a resume. These two items, usually presented together, will be your most important tools in getting through the door to audition for stage, film and television roles, and are necessary even for finding an agent or manager.

Art That Pays

Photos

Ask other actors whose pictures you like for information about their photographers and shop around until you find one whose prices you can afford. Trade publications such as *Backstage* and *Backstage West* will have ads and listings of photographers who specialize in headshots, but personal referrals are always best. Getting a photo that really works, that really represents what you are selling, is of paramount importance. It can represent your first, last and only chance even to get in to see a particular agent or casting director. You are a sales person with one very specific product in your inventory. Be sure it is presented in its best possible light.

When you find a photographer who you think may be right for you, interview him/her and ask to see his/her book. When you look at the photographer's work, try to put yourself in the role of a casting director. Do the eyes "pop?" Are you drawn to the person in the image? Has the photographer captured the essence of the actors in the book or do they all look the same? How is the hair, the make-up? Do the clothes serve to enhance the face or to draw attention away from the face? A good photographer will be able to work with you to present yourself as well as is possible.

Next: Are you comfortable with the photographer? Do you feel you can really be present and trust that you are in good hands? Ideally you can be present no matter who is behind the camera, but any actor will tell you that still photos are more difficult than just about any other work they have to do. It is no fluke that people like Annie Liebowitz make the kind of money they do for being able to show celebrities in ways that thrill us.

And then: how does the photographer work? Does he shoot one or two rolls and give you an 8" x 10" of whatever photo happens to be the best? Or does he shoot until he thinks he's got what you need? Is he willing to talk to you about how you see yourself being presented? Does he have his own ideas? Does he seem like someone who sees his work as a collaboration with his client or are you just another hour's worth of income? And then, of course, how much does he charge? Can you afford him? If you can't, are you willing to work a little harder to be able to afford him? Remember, this picture will be your representative out in the big bad world of those-who-can-hire-you. It's worth paying a premium if it's going to get you in a door.

If you absolutely cannot afford a photographer, you may be able to trade some modeling for a headshot. There are photographers who are just starting out who need help putting together a book of their work. Check the bulletin boards of local art or photography schools for this sort of exchange.

All you really need is one or two good headshots from about the shoulders up. The final product should be an 8" x 10" glossy, black and white, which looks like you. Many beginning actors have expensive composites made before even getting an agent. This is an unnecessary expense. (A composite is a group of photographs arranged on one sheet showing different poses, clothing and background.) Most agents, if they want you to have a composite, will want to advise you on what they need. Many people choose to have a make-up and hair person at the job to help them pull it together. Some photographers offer this service along with their work. Don't overdo the clothes. Simple is always better. Plain as opposed to patterned. Don't have the photographer do glamour shots if you don't normally look glamorous. If you are clean-shaven and have a two-inch scar on your forehead, don't have the scar airbrushed out and grow a beard. All the photographs you use should be up-to-date and reflect something true and basic about your personality. Casting directors dislike being misled, and your two inch scar will not hurt your chances nearly as much as deception.

Go over your proofs carefully and get as much feedback as you can from others. If they need improvement, meet with your photographer again. Keep on till you get it right. Photographers depend on word-of-mouth. They want you to be satisfied.

These days most quantities of headshots are printed as lithographs rather than as glossy reprints. Lithographs are much cheaper than, and do not look all that different from, the glossies. There are numerous businesses that specialize in reproduction and most advertise in the actor's trade magazines. When you order your copies, have your name printed at the bottom. If you do not yet have an agent, be prudent in how many you order; for while the price per copy drops considerably as the size of the order rises, you do not want to be stuck with a pile of eight by tens if your new agent wants you to re-shoot, or suggests you put their name at the bottom alongside your own. When your order is ready, be sure to check the quality of the copies as compared to the original before you leave the shop. If you are not pleased, ask the lab to redo your order. Any reputable lab will comply.

Update your photos occasionally in order that they reflect the reality of your life. You may have looked great as a perky nineteen year-old, but if that was ten years ago, it's probably time to update. Remember: there are roles for all ages and for all types.

Resume

Your resume should reflect integrity and good sense, as well as your experience. Don't list all your high school credits, unless that's all you have, nor pretend you were featured in a Spielberg film if you were an extra. Don't lie about being in movies or television shows. There are many stories about actors making up huge lies about being on jobs they'd never done only to find that they were actually lying to the producer of that project. Needless to say, none of these stories end in, "and they all lived happily ever after." If you have few acting credits, design your resume to include as many related experiences as you can. You can always emphasize your background in workshops and classes. Everyone has to start somewhere.

Your resume should be no longer than one page. Name at the top, credits for film, television and stage separate from each other, and then training and special skills, e.g. dialects, fencing or martial arts skills, juggling, dance, ability to ride a horse. It should be printed to the same size as your picture and stapled to the back.

Your resume can be modeled after any one of several different formats, but whatever format you choose, you should observe a few basic rules:

- *Spell check.* Spelling errors make a much bigger impact than you might think. Your spelling and grammar should be flawless.
- *Phone Number.* Leave a number where you can be reached or a message can be left day or night. An answering machine or service is preferable until you get an agent (as opposed to, say, your cell phone). When you do get an agent, their name and number should be listed prominently at the top of your resume either directly above or directly below your own.
- *Updating.* If you're fortunate enough to have a computer or access to one, keep your resume on disk so that you can easily add to the credits as you begin to work more. Always add your new credits as soon as you have done the job. Nothing pleases those who hire more than knowing you were just hired by someone else.
- *Appearance.* Remember, along with your picture, your resume is the only reference they have to identify you and your work. Everything you submit should look good, neat, clean. Print it on light-colored, quality paper. Always make the process as painless as possible for your target audience.

A standard format for a theatrical resume will include the following:

- *Name.* Your name should be prominently placed at the top of the page. Use bold typeset and larger lettering, though don't over-do it or make it too fancy.
- *Agency Name.* Include the name, full address and telephone number (with area code) of your agent.
- *Height, Weight, Hair Color, Eye Color*
- *Union Affiliations.* Use abbreviations.

- *Credits.* In Los Angeles, television and film credits are listed first. In New York, list theatrical credits first. Use discretion and select work that best represents what you want the reader to know about you. It is a good rule of thumb to list most recent credits first. Credits should include:
  - *Film*: Name of film, studio or production company, name of director;
  - *Television*: Name of show, billing (regular, recurring, guest star, featured), network;
  - *Stage*: Name of play, name of role, theatre where performed;
  - *Commercials*: State "available on request" (unless commercials make up the bulk of your experience).
- *Special Skills.* Anything you do really well (or reasonably well) and/or have training in;
- *Training.* List teachers or studios that are recognizable and/or highly regarded;
- *Education.* List schools attended and degrees/certifications achieved.

Finding an Agent

The easiest way to get an agent to see you is to have a fellow actor, a producer or a casting director put in a good word for you. Some agents who take on new clients also have a relationship with an acting coach or teacher from whom they will take referrals for new clients.

If the above options are not available, you must use the method that most actors employ when first starting out:

1. Get together a list of agencies that you think you would be right for and who actually consider new talent. Be realistic. (There are several good sources for information on agencies in our appendix. You can also purchase packages, which include mailing addresses.)

2. Send out your picture, resume and brief cover letter to each agency on your list.
3. Record each agency's name, address and phone number, the name of your contact at the agency and the date of your mailing on a file card.
4. Follow up with a phone call within a week to see if anyone is interested in meeting with you.
5. Make a note of their remarks and whether or not there may be a chance with them at some time in the future.

Once you have an agent interested in seeing you, set up a general meeting. Dress casually and use the interview as an opportunity to find out something about the agent as well as an opportunity to let him know you. Prepare to do cold readings. The agent may ask you to bring in a scene you have prepared with a scene partner. (This is where all that scene study you've been doing in class will come in handy.) Rarely will film and television agents want to see monologues (though for theatre you should have in hand two three-minute contrasting monologues). Be sure that the scene you choose to do showcases you in a role for which you are eminently castable, and be sure that it is not a scene which belongs entirely to the other actor. In your meeting, try to let the agent see something of the real you. There is no need to be devastatingly funny, dynamic or wonderful throughout the interview. Actor Ed Harris warns about trying too hard. "Five minutes of wonderfulness is about three minutes too much for most agents," he says.

In New York, it is permissible to have more than one agent representing you in each field without a signed contract. In Los Angeles, an exclusivity rule stipulates that you may have only one agent working for you in each field.

Sometimes an agent, usually at a larger agency, will offer to carry you as a "pocket client," meaning he will submit you for jobs and will act as your agent but the two of you will not have a signed contract. This can be a win/win for both parties in that the agent, without really risking anything, may end up with a client who can make money and you may, at least temporarily, get the representation you need. The disadvantage, of course, is that if you do not produce quickly the agent can simply stop taking your calls. Obviously it is preferable to have an agent who says he is with you for the long haul, that he believes in you whether or not you book something in the first year; but at the beginning of your career, the most important thing is to be seen by people who will hire you, and for that you need an agent.

The amount of personal attention you get from agents will vary. Basically, you can expect a reliable agent to:

- Be aware of what is casting and submit you to the appropriate casting directors.
- Negotiate billing, fees and business arrangements.
- Read and check contracts for you.
- Return your phone calls within a reasonable time frame and take an active interest in your work.
- Represent your interests in good faith.

You must view your relationship with an agent as a two-way affair and be conscious of your responsibilities to him. It is important to establish a relationship which is businesslike and professional, but it never hurts to also take a personal interest in people with whom you have a lot of contact. In addition to offering personal interest and courtesy, you should:

- Keep your agent supplied with pictures and resumes.
- Provide a composite if he requests one.
- Be available on short notice. Casting can happen very quickly and your agent should be able to find you at all times.
- Be a real professional. Prepare for a good audition, be on time and be informed about the business.
- Keep your listing in the Academy Players Directory current.
- Pay his commission promptly.
- Investigate new projects on your own and let your agent know about any new developments in your career. If you are appearing in an Equity Waiver production or studying with a new teacher, let your agent know.

Try not to be a pest. You must have a certain amount of faith that he's working for you and will not have time for daily phone calls inquiring, "So what's new?"

The various kinds of agents available are:

- Theatrical – Agents who handle talent for television and motion pictures.
- Commercial – Agents who handle on-camera talent for television commercials.
- Legitimate – Agents who handle radio and off-camera television work, voice-over, announcing, cartoons, etc.
- There are also agents for modeling (printwork, trade shows, advertising) and variety agents for nightclub work.

Most actors will want to be represented by both a theatrical and a commercial agent, and if you plan to work on the East Coast you should have a legitimate agent as well. You can find out which agents are franchised from the local union offices. Lists are free to union members and are available to non-members for a small charge.

You can research different agents and what kind of service they render through SAG's "agents' talent lists." These lists may not be copied, but as a union member you are free to view them to your heart's content. Look for total number of clients (are there too many, will you be lost in the shuffle?), recognizable names of people whose work you respect, conflicts with you in your "type" (are there three other actors who could be cast in your stead, and where would you fall in the pecking order? Can you trust an agent who would sign you at the expense of another of their clients?).

Talent Agencies Fact Sheet
What is the difference between a legitimate talent agency and one whose purpose is to separate you from your money?

The legitimate talent agency does not charge a fee payable in advance for registering you, for resumes, for public relations services, for screen tests, for photographs or for acting lessons. If you are signed as a client by a legitimate talent agency, you will pay such agency nothing until you work. From then on you will pay them ten percent of your earnings as a performer. Few, if any, legitimate talent agencies advertise for clients in trade papers, newspaper classifieds or through mail solicitation.

Are legitimate talent agencies licensed by the State of California?

Yes. Talent agencies are licensed by the California Labor Board as Artists' Managers. The Screen Actors Guild also franchises most established agencies in the motion picture and television field. You should be extremely careful of any talent agency not so licensed.

What about personal managers and business managers?

There are many personal managers—some long established, some very new. Some will take on new and unknown talent, some will not. Unlike agents, personal managers are not SAG-franchised, nor are they licensed by the state, so you are very much on your own with regard to sussing them out. Most will charge ten or fifteen percent of your gross income for their services. A good manager can be beneficial in helping you to get signed with a good agent and will work in tandem with that agent to find you job opportunities. Managers can also have contacts the agents don't have and can use those contacts to your advantage.

What about photographers?

If a purported talent agent seeks to send you to a particular photographer for pictures, what should you do? Chances are he's a phony and he makes his money by splitting the photographer's fee. If you need photographs, choose your own photographer and try another agent. Under no circumstances should you pay anything in advance.

Unions

Performing artists just getting into the business are advised *not* to join unions until they're certain they're finished with community theatre, tours, nightclubs and dinner houses which prefer to hire non-union artists. It's very difficult to work in Hollywood without a SAG card but it's also difficult to turn down non-union work when you haven't had a job in six months. Once you join any union, you may not do outside work unless you have been granted an exception or are working in an Equity Waiver theatre. Unions provide their members many wonderful benefits but guaranteed employment is not one of them. Unless you are ready to compete with experienced professionals for professional jobs, don't go without food and shelter just to become a union member.

Once you decide you are ready you should learn about the many paths that lead to that elusive union card. You should also have plenty of background information on all the unions in order to intelligently decide which ones you need to join.

There are six performing arts unions grouped under one national organization called the *Associated Actors and Artists of America (4A's)*. These are: *Actors Equity Association (AEA), Screen Actors Guild (SAG)*, the *American Federation of Television and Radio Artists (AFTRA), American Guild of Musical Artists (AGMA), American Guild of Variety Artists (AGVA)*, and the *Screen Extras Guild (SEG)*. You will find contact information in our appendix.

The notion that you can't get into a union without a union job and that you can't get a union job without your union card is somewhat true, but while it is difficult and expensive to get a SAG or Equity card, it is not impossible

Equity

There are actually several ways to obtain your membership card in Equity:

- *Equity Contract.* You may join the Association by virtue of employment under an Equity contract. This can be accomplished by apprenticing with a summerstock theatre or working as a nonunion performer in an *Equity League of Resident Theatres (LORT)* production. If the producer or director decides to hire you under a union contract, this contract and your initiation fee will establish your eligibility to join Equity.
- *Four A's Affiliation.* If you have been a member in good standing of one of the sister unions (such as SAG or AFTRA) and have worked as a performer under that union's

jurisdiction, you are eligible to join Equity by paying your initiation fee.

- *Equity Membership Candidate Program (EMC).* If you secure a position at one of the participating Equity theatres around the country, you may then register as an EMC candidate. The registration fee is credited against your future initiation fee. When you have worked for a total of fifty weeks under this program (not necessarily consecutively) you are eligible to buy into the union. The disadvantage here is that you may be working in these theatres at a pay rate substantially less than the other Equity actors working beside you. The advantage is you're able to act and get paid for it.

- *Crewing.* If you have technical skills, you may want to try signing on with the crew of an Equity Production. If you can eventually work yourself into an Assistant Stage Manager's job, you'll be covered by Equity and will automatically be eligible to join the union.

AFTRA

The easiest union to join is AFTRA. Basically, anyone with $1,000 can walk into an AFTRA office, fill out an application form and become a member. You can then use your AFTRA membership as an entrée to other unions as well as to jobs in television (taped, as opposed to filmed) and radio. As of this writing, AFTRA is once again holding talks with SAG about the possibility of a merger. What effect that would have on all of this is still unknown.

SAG

Although it is difficult to get into SAG, it is not impossible. Here are a few possible paths:

- *Taft-Hartley.* If a producer decides to hire you as a nonunion member in a union film, she can file a Taft-Hartley [1]report justifying her reasons for hiring you rather than a guild member. You will then be eligible to join

---

[1] The Taft-Hartley Act of 1947, while being seen as a friend indeed to many a nonunion actor trying to get his union card, started life as something else entirely. As an amendment to the National Labor Relations Act of 1932, it was presented as a way to restore balance

SAG by paying the initiation fee of $1,310 and one-half of your first year dues.[2]

- *Four A's Affiliation.* Like Equity, if you have been a member in good standing for at least one year in a sister union and have worked under that union's contract, you may buy into SAG. See above for amount.
- *Extra Work.* Finally, you may join if you have been cast as an extra by a SAG signatory producer at full SAG rates and conditions for a minimum of three days and by paying the initiation fee and one-half of your first year dues.

The performing unions provide artists many benefits and guarantee you and the future you's decent working conditions. Their pension plan, welfare funds and health and dental insurance are excellent and vitally important to struggling performing artists and help the lifetime professional to know she will be taken care of in the last years of her career (for most performers never truly retire). More important to those of you just beginning your careers, union membership symbolizes to others and to yourself that you are serious about your work, you consider it your profession and that you expect all the protection and respect your union demands and you deserve.

∞

to the Management/Labor relationship (which some thought had tipped too far in the direction of Labor). In fact, according to some union people, it went much further than that by, among other things, re-instituting court injunctions against labor strikes, allowing the government a way to break strikes by ordering an 80 day "cooling off" period, banning certain types of picketing, giving employers the right to hire scabs as permanent replacements for striking workers, banning sympathy strikes by one union with another where a contract was in effect and requiring union officials to sign affidavits disclaiming any affiliation with the Communist Party before the union they ran was allowed to seek the help of the National Labor Relations Board. (This last section was eventually overturned.) Just a little labor history for all you future union brothers and sisters.

[2] SAG dues are based on all earnings under SAG contracts in the prior calendar year. Each SAG member pays basic annual dues of $100.00. In addition, there are percentage dues of 1.85% of all earnings up through $200,000, and .5% on all earnings from $200,001 through $500,000.

photo courtesy of Tom Ormeny

Tom Ormeny

The Actor's Life

In our research for this chapter we were able to conduct some wonderful interviews with people who have made acting their life. Here is one of those interviews.

Interview with Tom Ormeny

Tom Ormeny is an actor and an acting teacher. With his wife, Maria Gobetti, herself an acting teacher of some renown, he runs the Victory Theatre in Burbank. The theatre has been in continuous operation since 1980 and hundreds of actors have passed through its doors and are the better for it. Tom is someone who has scrapped his way up and through it all and is still standing to talk about it.

When did you get started as an actor?

My mother was a big star in Hungary. She starred in forty feature films. And my father was the chief engineer of the National Theatre System and we lived across from the National Theatre, so I was hanging out in the theatre from the time I can remember. My earliest memories are of being on the boom coming down, watching my mother act. So I'm Hungarian. I'm a refugee. We came here in 1956 and I started acting when I was twelve in New York in radio drama for Radio Free Europe in Hungarian. My mother was working for Radio Free Europe/Voice of America, and whenever they needed a kid, they would just bring me in and I would do it. It was great fun. So I actually got my Social Security card as an actor when I was twelve years old.

My parents really didn't want me to be an actor, so I got into sciences. I went to Santa Clara as a pre-med student and really hated it. I walked by an audition one day and thought I could do better than that and walked in and got a part and that was that. By the end of my sophomore year I was flunking out and had to tell my parents "I'm going to be in the theatre," which drove my father crazy. I told my mother, "If anyone can understand why I'm doing this, it should be you," and that sort of clinched it. 'Cause she really, to this day, has a passion for the theatre.

Was getting an MFA useful?

Yeah, it was useful. It was pretty dramatic. When I went into [the UCLA] program, they really had a professional program. They had three or four teachers who were professional. They had a fabulous movement teacher and a mime teacher and a vocal teacher and a Shakespeare teacher and an acting teacher, and at the end of my first year there all those people were gone because they were out of money. So I organized a strike and wrote a letter to the dean and said you should just cancel the Master of Fine Arts program at UCLA because there is no reason for it to exist, and it just blew the lid off of everything.

And I wasn't going to come back, [but] I heard that they had hired an acting teacher, Ed Kaye-Martin. I didn't know anything about him, so I went and sat in and after three classes I did a late registration because I knew that this guy was brilliant. So I studied with him there for a year, got my MFA and sort of left, then came back a year later and saw a production there and decided this guy…Ed was a maniac, really crazy. He was a functioning sociopath. That's really who he was. Why are you laughing? But he was brilliant. He was really an incredible teacher and he gave me a technique that I treasure and use and teach to this day. It's a Meisner-based technique. That's [also] where I met my wife.

When did you start teaching?

I started to do little things here and there and they were really unsatisfying to me. An enormous amount of energy would go into trying to get a day-player gig. I really loved the training with Ed and I really loved the theatre, so Maria and I started teaching. Ed was in and out of town. He kept referring people to us. Every time he would leave he would sort of throw ten, fifteen, twenty students our way. And it was fabulous because I was learning so much by teaching.

What was I learning? Well, you know they say "Those who can't do, teach"? Well, I've got a different saying: "Those who can't teach it don't know it." And if you can't communicate to a human being what you do and how you do it, then fuck you. Give it up. Or go get some therapy. I mean, if you really want to be human, what you have is there so that you can give it away. That's what it's about.

What is it you love about acting?

This is to me really the king of the arts. There isn't another art like acting. The raw material of it is the human spirit, and that has to be treasured and it has to be nurtured and it has to be valued, and anyone who even has an inkling of it is a gift to humanity.

I've got a class now at a college with thirty kids and I put them through a meditation at the beginning of each class; and I'm meditating with them yesterday, and I'm looking around at all these kids lying on the floor…they've been with me for maybe a month, and the transition from the first time I got them into a meditation to last night when I got them into a meditation was so clear to me. The air in that room had a tone to it that was so clear and so calm and so…it had that spiritual kind of vibration that was exciting, that made your hair stand up on end with joy. And all I could do was just give thanks. I mean, my God, what a privilege to be allowed to really talk to people about real meaning, of what I know about real meaning, whatever that is; and a lot of the time, when I do that, I know I'm channeling, because I don't know where some of this stuff comes from. Yes, it's like real acting. If you can really leave it alone, if you can really get out of the way, you can really be in the moment. It's spiritually orgasmic. It's just wonderful. You're really creating in the moment—here, now—which is as close as you're going to get to infinity. There is an essential being of the experience that is so distilled that it's humanity at it's best.

How did the theatre come into being?

I got real tired of the whole thing. I was teaching and working as a waiter, and I got fed up. I said, 'Screw this,' and we had like $7,000 in the bank. We found the building in Burbank and then spent ten weeks to build one theatre and about five months to build the second, because by that time I was exhausted. Beth [Henley] was in Maria's class [and] we opened the theatre with *The Miss Firecracker Contest* right about the time that she won the Louisville

Actor's Theatre playwriting contest with *Crimes of the Heart.* It won the Pulitzer and suddenly all of the people who were saying no to us for the last three years said, "Wait a minute, maybe these people know something." And that's how we started to produce and establish the theatre.

So, we opened with her play, which we scraped together with friends, did a little limited partnership deal and were very successful with it, and had to close it to get married. That was the next production. We closed a hit show so we could get married. And then I went back to waitering to support the theatre. What most people don't realize is, you go to the theatre, you pay twenty bucks and the theatre or someone else is paying another twenty dollars so you can sit in that seat.

It was hard to make a living?

I wasn't getting any acting work, [just] enough to get insurance, [not] enough to earn a living. And I had some skills: I knew about wine, I knew about food. I was raised in a family that prided itself on its style, so I got jobs at very expensive, very high-paying restaurants. And when I wasn't in a restaurant, I did direct sales. I was a Fuller Brush salesman. I literally sold Fuller Brushes door to door in Hollywood when every other door was a massage parlor. I was selling to all the prostitutes in Hollywood. And I was making three, four times the money that most of the people I was selling to were making because I wasn't going door to door in a neighborhood where people weren't home. I was going door to door in a neighborhood where people were there and appreciated being attended to and being delivered to, and the product was good. I did that for two or three years. And it was always stuff that I could work around. So, yeah, it was really tough. Maria was teaching, and whenever we could put the money together, we would produce, and whenever we could rent the theatre, we would rent the theatre. And if the theatre could cover itself it would give me a little breathing room to develop something for the next thing. But that's the only way we kept the theatre up. I usually don't tell this story quite this honestly because I sort of want to show an image that everything's together…but, you know, it's really tough.

Bottom line advice to the young actor:

I just had that conversation last night with a student who's really talented and has some real skills and is a lifeguard. An expert athlete in a lot of things. All of his buddies are becoming professional lifeguards or firemen or paramedics, which is a very clear thing. You go to school, you take these classes, you get a certification, you do your thing and then you can make a decent living and you're respected and you're part of the community. And this kid says, "What'll I do? I'd like to have a plan like my buddies have a plan." I said, "You should have a plan, but it's not going to be the same kind of plan your buddies have." And I said, "Look, you're never going to be an actor, a professional actor, unless you start to reach out and do something. Get *Backstage West* and start auditioning for whatever you can audition for, and then if you get something, you'll have to arrange your life to be able to do it and whatever that takes is what you'll have to do." [I asked him, "What else can you do?"] He said, "I've done everything. I've been a carpenter, waited on tables." And I said, "Well then you're perfect acting material."

You really have to become part of the underground. And I say that specifically. You can't be a civilian and be an actor. You really have to become sort of like a bandit. You have to have a mentality of how do I fit into the society on a legal basis where they will allow me to survive and for me to continue to be an artist? To be legal and be an artist.

So there's a real challenge of how to be outside the mainstream, but enough a part of the mainstream to survive. Because if you take a straight job, you can't be an actor.

Is it all worth it?

It's been a great life. It's been an amazing life. When you look at the fact I'm sitting here and I'm 56 years old and I'm in this same theatre twenty-some years and we produce stuff every year that is recognized as being a substantial artistic accomplishment, I couldn't be happier. I grew roots and that is part of my baggage. I had to escape from a country [where] we were under siege. My parents were very vocal during the revolution. [My mother] was one of the leaders. So I don't move easily. It was extraordinarily difficult for me to be uprooted at the age of ten. I was out on the street, I learned how to shoot a machine gun. I came home with a piece of shrapnel in my leg and I didn't tell my parents because I didn't want them to know I was where I shouldn't have been. I was in a war when I was eleven years old. That's not something you eliminate. It is something you learn from.

It has been very rich. I've done thirty years of Jungian therapy and I bought a house. I convinced my wife that we should stay there. I felt that it was the only way I could feel safe and continue to express myself. In some ways it is kind of conservative, but I think that you have to limit yourself if you want to go and take flight because you cannot do it if you don't. That has been my entire life; I have wanted to have the freedom to fly. And to have the freedom to fly in that very rare area.

I had a Jungian therapist who I was complaining to about how hard it is and he said, 'What do you expect? You think the collective is going to reward you because you stretch it? All they are going to want to do is knock your fucking head off.' And when you look at it that way, it is really true, when you take the collective and you push it to another level of realization, whether you're an artist or a scientist. You talk to the people who do the major scientific discoveries and the torture that they go through before they make a discovery is the same thing that we go through, except we do it more often. We do it with every role. I die every time I do a substantial role. It's like going mining. You go into a mine and when you find that vein you've got to follow it wherever it goes and it's painful. And you know what you're mining for; you know what you're going for. And once you get to my age you trust and believe in your craft and you know where you're going and that's what it is.

∞

Chapter 11

Dance

E ach of the performance arts—theatre, music, dance—is ephemeral: each live piece of theatre is like an apparition performed on stage; or like an epiphany, a sudden illumination, a manifestation of the divine. And like every manifestation of something greater than the self, it is a fleeting moment. Once performed, the dance lives on only in memory. And, like music, dance speaks a universal language. It speaks eloquently across cultural barriers using the language of the body. Dancers illustrate life's vigor and joy, the creative spirit and our common humanity. Dancers communicate despite one's social standing, religion or political beliefs.

Practically speaking, dance is a body moving through space in time. The dancer's instrument is the body—perhaps the most vital, but fragile tool of the artist. In order for the dancer to aim for that perfect performance, that moment of self-actualization—be she practicing jazz, tap, modern, ballet, or ballroom dance—she must be ready and physically up to the challenge. Most dancers begin when they are very young and end when they are still quite young— dancers retire at an age when most painters, writers, and musicians are just beginning to become successful making art. This paradigm is changing a bit. Today, Broadway shows are hiring mature, experienced dancers for shows like *Chicago* and *Fosse*. New union rules have made it possible for a dancer to continue after having a child. Dance careers have lengthened and many dancers can perform into their 30's and 40's. In order to keep performing, though, dancers must work against fatigue, pain, injuries and time. Forty-year-old dancers gain insight, wisdom and discipline as well as a body that requires more rest, care and motivation. Nevertheless, most dancers claim it to be a satisfying and rewarding profession. Since dancers begin their career early and finish early, they work hard to perfect their craft and value every physically healthy moment.

Training

Dancers need formal training. This much is a given. How they get this training varies from dancer to dancer. Some people go to school and get a dance degree, others join a company right away. Some people audition for a Broadway show; but rest assured, if they land the audition, they have been studying, they are trained and they know how to move.

Fred Strickler is a dancer/choreographer who has received fellowships from the National Endowment for the Arts and the California Arts Council. As a modern dancer he was a founder of Eyes Wide Open Dance Theatre and was a featured soloist with the Bella Lewitzky Dance Company. He was also a founding member of the Jazz Tap Ensemble. Since 1967 he has been a Professor of Dance at the University of California Riverside.

"Having a dance degree makes a big difference. I don't know that it's necessary, but you get a broader education. You get some contact with dance history. Versatility. You need to be proficient in a lot of things to make your living through dance. Of course, if you know you're not going to be a choreographer and you're not interested in how dance works, than perhaps college isn't absolutely necessary. It will always be helpful, though, and if you have the ability and the means to get a college education, you should."

Strickler also notes that dance is passed on from person to person. There are no books that can tell you how to become a splendid dancer, capable of flight. It is important, then, to find a mentor, a guru.

"You must be willing to listen, work hard, have patience and determination and be willing to grow. The first week I came out to California I met Bella Lewitzky. She had already developed and matured in whole areas that were just beginning to appear to me as directions in which I might want to move. She was involved in the evolution of CalArts. I was fortunate to be in on that process as one of her company members."

Rebecca Wright, who was a dancer with the Joffrey Ballet and a soloist with the American Ballet Theatre (ABT), offers diametrically opposed advice. "By the time I was out of high school, I was in a company. As a ballet dancer, that's what you have to do. You can't go to college for four years and then join a ballet company. By 21 you're too old. Ballet companies want dancers who are between 16 and 19. A ballet dancer knows by the time she's eight that she wants to be a professional dancer."

However, that does not preclude training, says Ms. Wright, currently the Artistic Director of American Ballet Theater Summer Intensive programs around the country. "Training gives you the freedom to express yourself and if you want, create something new. If you don't have a solid background, you don't have enough information about the classical part of it to go on. If dance students don't want to go to an art institute or college and they plan to go to New York to study, I suggest that they try to get into a company school. Young dancers need to be aware that there is not only one place and one way to dance. You have to go to the place that nurtures *you*."

In 1972, Donna Wood joined the Alvin Ailey American Dance Theater, eventually becoming a leading dancer with the company. Wood has guest-starred with the Hamburg Ballet, the Vienna State Opera, and the Royal Danish Ballet. In 1985 she left the Ailey Company and took a two-year faculty appointment at CalArts. In 1991 she and her husband, Peter Michael Sanders, created the Donna Wood Foundation, "to assist young dancers as they are embarking on careers, giving advice on additional education and skill development" necessary to survival in the dance world.

"You need to work with teachers and mentors who are as enthusiastic about dance as you are," says Wood. "It's very important to instill the joy of movement and the joy of dance. Training with respected teachers tells everybody else how serious you are. There are very few teachers who really give you a well-rounded perspective of movement and I suggest that you study with a series of teachers. You need different perspectives and techniques to become an integrated dancer. When you study with three different teachers at one time, the information you get from teacher A feeds into teacher B and C so that you connect in a different way.

"At CalArts you have to choreograph, you dance in other people's choreography and you learn every aspect of production. You learn to costume, sew, produce, and dance. You take responsibility for your own education. This makes you strong and shows you how to take care of yourself and be independent."

Auditions

Rebecca Wright suggests that you come to an audition dressed for the part, be it a Broadway, modern dance or ballet audition. "You have to be neat. You have to be trim. You have to be clean. You have to know how to present yourself in auditions. How are you going to look? How are you going to wear your hair? What is your face going to look like? You don't have to look like a pale, gaunt little girl who wants to get into a company. A little bit of glamour can help a lot. You have to be sure your physical body form [weight] is in its proper place. That's your maintenance. You have to make sure that the shoes you wear are clean and neat. Keep them the same color as your tights—one long line.

"If you've made up your mind that you want to join the company, the only way to go into the audition is center front. You let them know you want them. If you stand in the second line off to the left, they're going to know that's exactly where you want yourself to be placed. Put yourself out front.

"You have to know a wide range of styles and movements: classical, neo-classical, modern en pointe, modern in jazz shoes, modern in tennis shoes. You have to know how to count your music because they might not count it for you. Being able to develop a rapport with your teacher or auditioner is very important. Send out vibrations of being able to absorb. Don't be afraid of criticism; take it constructively, not negatively. Don't be afraid to ask questions. Always be prepared. Have the shoes that you need and the right tights. Always take a needle and thread, Band Aids and safety pins. Always think of the most disastrous thing that could happen to you. The ribbon on your shoe breaks, your pointe shoe breaks. You always need two pairs of shoes in case one breaks down. Your bra strap could break. You don't want to think negatively, but you want to be prepared for anything that might happen."

Fred Strickler believes that networking helps you get work in the relatively small dance community. "You talk to people about what you're doing and they'll say they've got something coming up in six months and they need someone to do a tap dance thing and ask if you're interested. Getting work is not always done through formal auditions. I think developing a really healthy social persona is important for a dancer. If you know somebody you're interested in working with, let him or her know. Most choreographers choose people they've already met. Use the *Dance Magazine Directory* [e-mail them at *directory@dancemagazine.com*] to locate someone whose work you admire and call and introduce yourself. Say, 'I'm doing a dance program and I'm very interested in working with your dance company at some future date. I would like very much for you to come and see my work.' Nobody ever gets offended by having you say you want to work with them."

Strickler admits that you might get turned down, but reminds the dancer he will get rejected just as most artists will. Young inexperienced dancers have to work for those plum jobs.

"It's really about paying your dues. You work your way up— dance small parts, dance in workshops for free to get exposure, work with different choreographers. Learn to be psychologically flexible as well as physically. Rehearse for free and get minimal wages for performances. Sometimes you'll even have to pay money to get a certain experience. [But] get lots of experience. That's what paying your dues is."

Contracts

Sometimes dancers might be able to work with people with whom a letter of agreement or a simple standard artist contract agreement will suffice. It doesn't have to be spelled out in minute detail. But the larger and more established ensembles will have their own fairly complicated contracts. Strickler says that with the Jazz Tap Ensemble, which tours frequently, they have a fairly difficult and detailed technical rider that is about eight pages long.

"I would recommend that you consult a lawyer if you are trying to work out a standard contract you plan to use over and over again," says Strickler. "A lawyer can check it out to see that it covers all the territory it needs to and that it's legal, that you're not asking for something that is illegal, such as a quick change room by a fire exit. A lot of arts presenters are not aware of your specific needs. No matter how basic and obvious you think your needs are, it's quite likely that at least once those will be utterly missed by a sponsor. They will not know that you need time on the stage before the performance. Sometimes they do not tell you that you will be working around a set. You need clear, open space of minimum dimension. You need to specify those dimensions. You need to know what lighting facilities will be available to you. Figure out what all your needs are, how you want your art to be presented. Spell it out."

Agents

Many beginning dancers and dance companies serve as their own booking agents. Not only can this prove to be frustrating and arduous, it is also time-consuming. A good agent is talented, patient, persuasive and worth the expense. You will rarely come across a dancer whose skills as an agent are on a par with his artistic skills, and unless you find it absolutely necessary, don't be both dancer and agent. Some options to consider include:

1. Forming a non-profit arts management organization with other dancers or dance companies. Sometimes groups of artists get together and form an agency to handle bookings and to implement grants writing, marketing and management services for artists in the collective. Sharing the costs, services, and office enables dancers and choreographers to save money and reach a wider audience.

2. Hiring a commercial booking agent. If you can afford one, you will benefit from the rapport and clout the agency has already established with sponsors you don't know. In addition to finding bookings, commercial agents will often make travel arrangements, including hotel reservations. They will also provide the press with press releases, up-to-date reviews and a press packet.

3. If you are a dance company, an arts administration intern, a volunteer from the Board of Directors or your company manager can serve as an agent (generally for a limited period of time. This is not a job that everyone can do well.).

If you know a dancer who is happy with his booking agent and you like the gigs she's getting, ask the dancer to introduce you so you can find out if the agent might be willing to consider taking you on. The best agents are the busiest agents. An agent who can give you part of his time may be worth a lot more to you than an intern with lots of time and no contacts.

Unions

American Guild of Music Artists, referred to as *AMGA,* is the union for ballet and concert dancers (as well as for choreographers, opera singers, choristers, stage managers and stage directors). Many dancers also belong to *SAG (Screen Actors Guild)* and *AFTRA (The American Federation of Television and Radio Artists).* The *American Dance Guild*

(ADG) is another helpful union. It is a national non-profit membership organization concerned with promoting the art of dance. Since 1956, the *ADG* has been serving the needs of performers, choreographers, teachers and students through all stages of their development and careers.

In the Company of Dance

Deborah Oliver, who got her MFA from CalArts in 1981, currently has her own dance-booking agency in Los Angeles and represents various performing arts venues.

"After graduation, dancing became secondary to survival," notes Oliver. "I never lost my strong desire to be a choreographer. I luckily worked with organizations that taught me the business of being an artist, and I learned to be a producer. Learning to work with video, to be a stage manager and to design has all helped make my work stronger. No experience is ever wasted on the artist."

Donna Wood, who began dancing with the Dayton Ballet Company where the competition was not as fierce as it was when she came to New York to dance with Alvin Ailey, has a clear philosophy: Be filled with the essence of dance and don't do anything halfway.

"You have to be open," says Wood. "You cannot go into a class and say, 'I don't like this. I'm not going to do it.' You have to be completely submissive in order to expand your knowledge of dance. Do whatever they tell you to do. Learn everything— every aspect, every technique of dance—in order to discover your true strengths and challenges.

"There is a company someplace for everybody. New York City is not for everyone. Investigate other places. A lot of New York companies are fed from other places. Many people need a secure foundation before they can deal with the major companies. Of course you need training, but you need life too. You have to have a balance. Dance is about people dancing, not just technicians. It doesn't matter if you can do ten pirouettes if you are a bore."

Wood was skilled and fortunate. She was able to leave one of New York's finest dance troupes to make guest appearances. She felt that guest appearances tested her mettle and demanded from her that she take command and move beyond her comfort zone as a dancer.

"My ultimate goal in a performance is a total sculpting of an entire ballet. You have to be able to play with the choreography without changing it. Although you strive to make every step perfect, the artistry comes in when you fall out of a pirouette. You must cope with it as gracefully as possible, as if it were choreographed, and keep on going. You can't spend the rest of the ballet knocking yourself for missing that pirouette because the entire rest of the ballet will suffer. In performance, you must command your space and magnetize the audience with your energy. You can't do anything halfway."

Serendipity stepped in for Fred Strickler, who helped form the Jazz Tap Ensemble. "After our first concert in January, 1979, we started getting about a booking a month, regional stuff. By the end of the year we were in New York at the Dance Theatre Workshop, a very, very good place to be because it is certainly one of the most established places for new dance companies to perform. Recognition and success came quickly for us, perhaps because we combined art with entertainment. We brought a modern dance choreographic sensibility into an art from that was associated with entertainment.

"It was intensely creative. It was popular. It came just at the right time, when there was a big upsurge and interest in tap dancing, and we were doing it at a pretty high level of artistry. We were a good package that was organized and could be toured. We also got good reviews, which is very important.

"It's tough doing collaborative work, because ultimately a decision is made by mutual agreement or through struggling until one person's idea wins out. In our first two years we did more than thirty productions on practically no money. Public relations is essential and that's a lesson I learned with Jazz Tap Ensemble. It doesn't matter how good your work is, if nobody knows you're performing, it's not going to pay off. You have to do continuous PR in order to compete in the marketplace.

"We found a manager and a booking agent. We wrote our own press releases. In the beginning, we did it among ourselves. We would call and send letters. We began to get photographs of ourselves and started sending out press packets, piecing it together, Xeroxing reviews. A lot of the funding came out of our own pockets. We weren't smart enough in those days to know that we needed a non-profit corporation. If you want to dance, you make it work. You fight, you're willing to go through the artistic battles to get what you want."

Career Transition for Dancers

Dancers face uncertain employment, poor working conditions and often the lowest income from their art form. Dance companies are considered successful if they can give their members 20 weeks of employment in order to qualify them for unemployment insurance the rest of the year. Most dancers' careers end when they are young enough to begin a whole new occupation. There is at least one organization interested in helping dancers translate their skills to other jobs. The Caroline and Theodore Newhouse Center for Dancers offers career counseling and grants to dancers to help empower them and develop a "life after" performance.

"Keep in mind that more than probably 90% of people who have dance careers are finished with their performing careers between ages 35 to 40, sometimes earlier," says Strickler. "You have to think, even at 18, about what else you can do to support yourself. Develop something else. Perhaps a business skill. Find something else that you can do to make money, something with flexible hours. Dancing is not an economically viable occupation for 95% of the dancers.

"There are other dance-related fields: dance management, teaching dance history, research assistant, dance notation, dance therapy. Broaden yourself in all of the arts. Know art history, contemporary art, the various arts media like video and film. Learn to read music, a great advantage to a choreographer. Get involved. Go to the theatre. Go see films, go see all kinds of art. Dance does not exist in a vacuum. We are influenced by other artists. Get involved in your community so that you're in touch with what is going on around you. Don't isolate yourself by being an artist in a hothouse studio. There are distinct advantages to concentrating on your own vision, but if your vision is not bigger than yourself, it's not a very big vision. You have to know who else is out there in your field and who is influencing them."

For some people a teaching job offers the kind of security they require while others are able to make the leap into professional dancing, join a company and make a name as a dancer. 'Life is what happens when you're busy making other plans,' says John Lennon. For some, teaching offers rehearsal space, health and dental insurance and the occasional opportunity to perform.

Staying Power

Deborah Slater is a choreographer and founder of the Deborah Slater Dance Theater (DSDT), a professional dance-theater company dedicated to the creation and production of evening-length works that explore timely social issues using original movement, text and music. She has worked outside the box for most of her dance career.

"I didn't really appreciate what it would mean to be a dancer in this country. I chose what I loved to do without being aware of the economic repercussions. In any other profession after twelve years of hard work, I'd have a steady income, a health plan, a decent car and be able to think about putting a down payment on a house. As an artist doing non-traditional work, that's simply not possible. San Francisco prides itself on its individuality, but it doesn't support its artists and galleries.

"I have never regretted being an artist. When I'm doing my work and it supports me, I'm ecstatic. I can do public relations and arts management, but it's not really satisfying. The event is much more compelling than the work that makes an event happen."

Today, twelve years after she gave the above statement, Slater says that "The DSDT extravaganzas are bigger and so is the workload. But obviously I still love it 'cause I'm still doing it. The rehearsal process is a wonderful thing; it is where art really lives— as we excavate and discover. I don't want the word *work* to mislead people in terms of the creative process, which is the heart and core of continuing. The word *work* in this case refers to all that is not the creative process, which at this point, I now enjoy that too."

Professor and Creative Arts Program Coordinator Yen Lu Wong, who was Artistic Director and principal choreographer of TNR/Moebius, has this to say about making a living as a dancer. "Survival depends on where you live. If you live in New York where there are good support systems, it's easier to survive than it is in Los Angeles. We don't have an organization like Dance Theatre Workshop in LA. There's no cluster space, no organization to impact critics, to address problems with marketing, insurance and developing rosters of good affordable designers and technicians. Survival is always difficult for artists, but in some cities it's almost impossible."

∞

Interview with Lula Washington

Dancer and co-founder of the Lula Washington Dance Theatre, *Washington has been dancing since she was 22 and educating young dancers for the past 23 years. She has performed at the* Academy Awards, *with* Cher *and choreographed the* Little Mermaid *movie. Her choreography reflects her political views and her personal interests/experiences with pieces such as* Let Their Voices Be Heard, Check This Out *and* What About Watts, *all explorations of the search for freedom. Her dance troupe has performed all over the United States and Europe.. This fall they will appear at the Kennedy Center in Washington, DC.*

Breaking the myths

I didn't discover dance until the 12th grade. It wasn't dancing—we were exercising to music. I started really dancing when I was 22 and I had to work really hard. Once I decided that that is what I wanted to do, I just kept working really hard.

I was always honest with myself and my assessment of where I was. One thing that set me apart was I was never comfortable with the level of training that I got from the university. On the weekends I would take other classes outside the university. I took training from other prominent teachers and they would move me to the next level of my dancing. When I was a student, they [UCLA] didn't really have any jazz classes, so I took them elsewhere. Because of this I was able to get movie auditions as a student, whereas my friends could not because they couldn't do the double pirouettes since they only took modern dance.

I never let anybody tell me what I could or couldn't do. I believe you can do anything that you want to do. The only person who stops me today is myself. You have to be willing to go the distance. If you don't get the job don't be mad at someone else.

People are dancing beyond [the age of] forty and they can because they maintain the body. It depends on who you are and what you do and how well do you keep your instrument. If you let yourself get out of shape, you won't be able to keep dancing. It depends on how much time you are willing to invest in yourself. Twenty years ago you would have been pushed off the stage.

Auditions and advice

When I was at UCLA and I went out on auditions, I was really naïve. This is why I advocate studying every different style of dance. When I went on the auditions, I saw the real world. It isn't just doing a simple pirouette; you have to put more heart into it. You have to put passion and technique and all of yourself into it. Those are the kind of things you learn when you go into different classes with different teachers who teach different ways of moving than what you're used to. Dancers have to be prepared. It's like the old saying, 'You have to be a triple threat.' You have to be able to dance, sing and act. The downfall for a lot of dancers is that they don't take any acting classes. If you don't have anywhere to go into inside yourself, you don't have anything to bring out and can't give the choreographer something close to what he is looking for. If you can only do a step, you have no range. And they aren't looking for people who can only do a step.

Find the classes that exist throughout the city. Take all the classes from African classes to ballet. Right now the hip-hop dancers are at the top of the chain. To me dancers have to be competitive. They are competitive if they have knowledge and confidence.

∞

And, Finally...

We give the last word to Fred Strickler. "You're probably never going to be rich. Any dancer who has the ambition to be a professional performer/choreographer has to absolutely work hard. Don't ever expect it to be easy. Follow your own advice more than anyone else's. Don't mess around in performance with self-indulgent stuff. When you ask an audience to sit in front of you and watch what you do for an evening, or even for ten minutes, it behooves you to do your absolute best. There's just too little opportunity to perform. When you do your best, you'll be satisfied. I've done self-indulgent work and it doesn't work. What happens is that the references are so internalized that nobody can connect with them. Dancing is a language of communication. Don't expect your audience to work so hard in order to understand your art. Just give. The best dancers are always givers."

∞

photo courtesy George Lange

David Brown, leader of *Brazzaville*.

Chapter 12

Music

Preparation

When preparation meets opportunity, people call it luck. That's misleading because opportunities are always out there. You can't control that. The only part of the equation you can control is the preparation." So says Warren Christensen, the artistic director of the Los Angeles Garden Theatre Festival, an event that grew in three years from a $60 backyard party to a $1.5 million month-long arts festival. "So long as you put yourself out there, continually study and prepare, believe in yourself, and even when you feel terrible get yourself out to be seen and heard, an opportunity will eventually come along."

What constitutes preparation in the field of music? Talent, of course, would seem to be an essential (though there are, today, many examples which would seem to belie this truth, but that's another subject).

In addition to talent? Practice, practice, practice. In cities like Los Angeles, New York and Chicago, your chance for success is completely dependent on your ability to perform. Henry Mancini said that in Los Angeles, "You have to be an excellent musician if you plan to do studio work. There is simply no time to practice at home. Studio instrumentalists must be first-rate readers and extremely flexible. A sax man might have to play a musical comedy score in the morning and switch to a big band sound in the afternoon."

In order to gain experience, many young musicians take their instruments and haunt nightclubs, waiting for a chance to sit in. They work dances, bars, organization dinners and church picnics.

Blues pianist Bob Riedy advises young musicians to "study and play along with recordings of favorite artists to learn their techniques." (He also suggests that musicians "be prepared to give up *everything* for music.")

David Brown, songwriter, composer, leader of *Brazzaville* and saxophonist for Beck, has spent his life collecting music and musical ideas from the streets of Hollywood as a young runaway to India, Venezuela, Thailand and Nepal. He knows a few things about preparation. "When we first had label interest I was extremely inexperienced as a singer. Basically I was terrified. From the moment I got onstage 'til the moment I got offstage it was just one huge terrifying tidal wave. You know, it got a little easier, but particularly at shows where there would be label executives in the audience, it was as if you had a shotgun in my mouth and were just pressing on the trigger ever so lightly. So this guy who was acting as our manager brought a bunch of executives out to see us and we did this one show that was atrociously bad. They went back to their offices and said 'It was nice to meet you.' And in all honesty, I was not ready to be signed. I was so full of a combination of fear and self-importance I would just have been one of those idiots you read about leading a pathetic existence after a while."

Preparation, Part II:

"I needed experience," adds Brown. "I needed three more years of playing a lot of gigs and recording a lot of music before I felt I belonged onstage and I had a right to be there. For a long time I wondered what the hell I was doing and how I slipped by the guards. I was waiting to be discovered for the fraud I really am. You can't perform from that perspective and have it be anything too great. So you've got to put in some time, I think. Maybe some people don't, but I did."

Bob Monaco and James Riordan, in their book *The Platinum Rainbow: How to Succeed in the Music Business Without Selling Your Soul,* put all of this into their concept of goal setting to good effect: "Before you do anything, you must formulate [a] plan for success. Use the one I've given you in this book [*The Platinum Rainbow*] or make up your own, but have one. And follow it.

"Once you have your primary goal set, you need to break it down into four or five secondary goals. Then you're ready for your working goals, which in some ways are the most important of all. Let's say that you decide the best way to work on your live show is by playing clubs, so your first working goal is learning twenty songs by other artists. Your second working goal might be to write or discover ten original songs. Before you can pursue other secondary goals, you must master these two working goals.

"You've got to discipline yourself, and one of the best ways to do it is by having a schedule based upon achieving a working goal. After you achieve one working goal, immediately set another. If your time limit runs out, immediately figure a new one. Goal setting is one of the only ways to keep an artist working effectively toward his dream. Take it one rung at a time. Make sure you do it right before you move on, and you won't have to go backwards. Remember that the more things you do well in the beginning, the easier it will be in the home stretch. TAKE YOUR TIME."

When you're certain your performance skills are as good or better than other musicians you know who are recording, performing and bringing in a regular paycheck, and after you've set realistic goals for at least one year, you need to consider the following issues:

Promotion

Document everything. Record your dates. Make a list of all the clubs you've played and the concerts and tours you've done. Save any press you may have received. Get someone from your family or a friend, if necessary, to take black and white pictures you can use in a promotional package. Have the best writer in your band compose a promotional letter you can use when you contact A&R people, club owners and booking agents.

Once again, David Brown. "A lot of press nowadays uses digital. People will have electronic press kits. People will have all their press quotes, their bio, their pictures—everything can be e-mailed. But, people still send packages, physical packages. We mostly send out actual CDs. So a good package will include a CD, photo, bio and press release. Make sure your mailing and e-mail lists are up to date and include everyone you want to inform about your performances. And remember that, as opposed to the post, e-mail is free and nearly everyone you want to inform uses it. Send your press materials well in advance of your performance and flood the community in which you're performing with fliers, window displays and newspaper announcements."

All this has to be done weeks before your performance in order to accommodate newspaper deadlines. Involve local record stores and university music departments as much as possible in promoting your concerts.

If you're in school, before you graduate, ask some of your more distinguished professors and teachers to write general letters of recommendation. Don't wait ten years or let another two hundred students pass through their doors before you make your request. Larry Stein, the National Program Director of Young Audiences and a producer of the Olympic Arts Festival, emphasizes the wisdom of this strategy. "You always need to build up your portfolio. It's a lot of little things that say to other people you have it all together."

Demos

A demo represents your talent and demonstrates the kind of work you do. It can be made for you to evaluate your own performance or to send to a record company. Larry Harris, the co-founder of the now-defunct Casablanca Records and Filmworks, says, "You should do three songs on a demo, ten-fifteen minutes long, just enough to let someone know you have the capability of cutting a hit record. You have to make the tape sound as professional as you can. If it sounds muddy or scratchy, the record company is not going to get past the first song. If you don't have good original material, take old songs and revamp them. Bring them up to date. The tape should show what the group can do, especially their vocal ability. Be creative when you send in the tape. Do some creative packaging and grab somebody's eye. Don't just send it in a little brown wrapper because it will go in the pile with the hundreds of other brown wrappers. Try sending it in a gift box."

Larry Stein suggests sending CDs to booking agents and producers whether they ask for them or not. "I'm really big on excerpts," he says. "I send short CDs, no more than seven minutes long, thirty seconds to a minute of different kinds of things. I also include a page that says what it is, what instruments they're hearing and when it was recorded."

And here's yet another point of view. "You can send out unsolicited packages," says David Brown, "but chances are they're just going to end up in a gigantic pile somewhere. Sorry to say, but that's just the way it is. If it's a major label, they get thousands of unsolicited [demos], and a lot of them won't even open them—some kind of legal reason like people will claim they stole their song. So it's kind of a waste of time and money to do that. There are lawyers and managers who have relationships, music lawyers who have relationships with heads of companies or A&R people or whoever, but they'll get it to someone who will listen to it. So that's a better way to go: to find a lawyer that believes in what you're doing."

Management

Larry Harris says, "It's managers who have relationships with record companies. They've dealt with them in the past so they can get their tapes to the A&R people. Booking agents can also do it and music lawyers can do it. They get people signed because they've dealt with the record companies for a long period of time. Record companies do not want to deal with artists directly. There are too many times when the record company has been accused of ripping off unrepresented artists. It's also very awkward to listen to an artist's tape with the artist sitting in front of you. Record company people don't like to put themselves in that position. A manager will take care of all the business with the record company and will make sure that the record company is behind the group. A good manager will also make sure the group has an agent, the correct lawyers and accountants, and will monitor the airplay a record gets. When a record company has hundreds of artists, a group can get lost in the shuffle if a manager doesn't stay on top of his group's progress."

Musicians and performing artists pay their managers as little as ten percent and as much as fifty percent of their earnings. If your manager is someone who has been in the business for a long time and has the knowledge and access you need to get your career off the ground, it may be smarter (and more profitable) to give away a large percentage than to hold onto ninety percent of nothing. If you've already tried to manage and promote your own career for a few years, you'll have a sense of what you're buying with your twenty or thirty percent.

"In California, your manager is not supposed to book shows for you. It's a conflict of interest," says David Brown. "So you have a booking agent, they book all your shows. You have a manager, they take care of all your business. They make a budget for your tours, they talk to the record label, if there is a record label; they are the buffer between you and the world. They can find a record label, but also lawyers do that. I've had a couple and at this moment I don't. They're not hard to get, though.

"A lot of times managers don't even require a contract—I don't have one with mine—because it's the type of relationship that if it's not working for one or the other, you can't do it. It just doesn't make sense.

"They have to believe that what you do is valuable and important. They also have the benefit of not being the artist; so they can talk to whoever it is—booking agents, clubs, record labels, commercial people, whoever it is—and you can say anything to them. They're not the artist. And they won't take offense. You need to have that objectivity in somebody, and it's not going be anyone in the band. And also they can be objective with you about your work—they can say, hey, this song is much stronger than this song for a single—to a degree. And also, they're there to help you strategize as far as, okay, what do you need to do to take something to the next level. What do you have to do: Do you have to tour? Where are you going to tour? How many times do you have to tour that place to build up a good following? How are we going to get records in the stores there? What about the press? You know, all that comes from the manager. It's not easy. It took me four or five years to find somebody I really liked, and I went through several.

"You can either try to get a big time manager, they'll have a lot of connections, but they'll also have a lot of acts who take up about ninety-nine percent of their time and energy; or, if you get a smaller manager, someone who hasn't hit the big time but you feel is competent, they're going to work for you. They're really going to work for you, because you're their priority. That's how a lot of bands did it. Bruce Springsteen, the Beatles—they had their one guy and they were his band, and they took them all the way and stayed with them forever.

"It could be anybody. It could be someone at a show who is intelligent and educated and is trying to become a manager, or maybe it never even occurred to them until they saw you. It's a very strange position. You know, there's no manager school. And it's not rocket science. Somebody could read a few books and kind of get the gist of what's needed."

Most managers and agencies aren't going to take on musicians at the beginning of their careers. Until you're ready to sign with a record company or book a national tour, you really don't need high-powered management. This is just one more chore that you and your long-suffering friends will have to learn to handle. And five years down the road, you'll be glad you did because you'll know whether or not that big-time manager deserves thirty percent of your earnings for the next five-year period.

Unions

When you make more money as a union member than as a non-union member, you might want to go to the nearest American Federation of Musicians (AFM) office and apply for membership. Application must be made in person and each chapter has its own fee structure. California is Local 47 and as of this date, annual dues are $162, semi-annual dues are $84 with a one time Local 47 initiation fee of $25 and a one time Federation initiation fee of $65. Check with each chapter for the minimum down payment. Attendance at one orientation meeting and an audition are also required.

Union membership not only guarantees wage scales but provides numerous benefits and services. Many branches offer low-cost rehearsal space, free published help-wanted and audition notices, contract preparation and consulting services, job referrals and listings on agents, managers, record companies and nightclubs. The AFM insurance program includes coverage for health, retirement, disability and death benefit group insurance. Low-cost instrument insurance, credit union membership and notary public service are also part of the generous benefit package provided through the AFM. Please see our appendix for contact information.

The union may, however, not be right for everyone. In some ways it seems mainly for the benefit of session players. "Union? I've paid many dues to the union," responds David Brown, "but I'm not a member. It's a very strange thing. They never made me join, but they just took money from anything I made. Whenever I'd be on TV, whenever I'd have something in a movie, they would take their cut, but….why bother [joining]? It's not like it's SAG where you get some amazing health insurance or anything. It's a very weak union. Basically they get you your, you know, $271 per session, or whatever, but it's a pretty weak union, from what I can tell, at least in California."

Composers

Within the field of music, no one has a more difficult time than the composer. Young composers fortunate enough to sign with a publisher soon realize that it represents only the beginning of a long struggle to let the world know about them and their music. Carl Stone, now famous for his live computer music, is currently on the faculty of the Media Department of the School of Computer and Cognitive Sciences at Chuyko University, Japan and hosts a weekly program on KPFA in San Francisco's Bay area, has this to say about getting started. "When I graduated, I figured I would just sit and wait for the commissions and performances to come rolling in. After about a year, it hit me in a blinding flash that nothing happens on its own. In this day and age the marketplace is such that if you want to have your music performed and you want to have it performed reasonably well, you have to be intimately involved in the production. A lot of people don't want to be bothered with that. They think their job is to compose the music and someone else's to produce. That's perfectly fine, but if you feel that way, you're going to sit around waiting for the performances, the commissions and [for] the record company to call. It might happen, but you have just as much chance of winning the Irish sweepstakes. That is why I worked with a group of colleagues, all composers, to start ICA, the Independent Composers Association, which was dedicated to producing performances of our own music.

"I don't think there is always a direct relationship between talent and success. If you want to succeed as a composer, and if it's as important to you as actually making music, you have to put energy into all aspects of getting the music out. That ranges from entering competitions, joining ASCAP or BMI, calling up radio stations and bugging them to get on their shows and joining up with friends to put on concerts of your own music. You have to do everything you can possibly think of to get your music out there. If it happens without you [being involved], it's right up there with the burning bush and walking on water."

While no one will look out for a composer as well as a composer will look out for herself, support organizations have sprung up around the country which offer many important services as well as information on funding and performance opportunities. See the appendix for information. The *American Music Center* also maintains libraries and resource files designed to help composers stay abreast of the most current information on publishing, recording and commissions.

∞

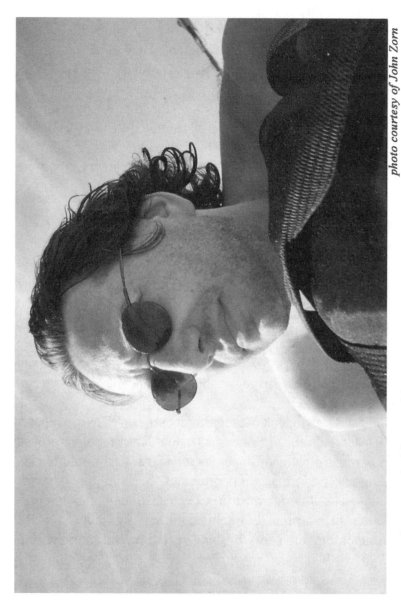

John Zorn (self portrait)

John Zorn Interview

We had a truly pleasurable conversation with composer/performer John Zorn. Based in New York, he has recorded or composed the music for over sixty albums and is the founder of Tzadik Records, which is dedicated to recording and keeping in print music that otherwise might not exist for us.

"B" Jobs:

I did shit jobs in my life. I mopped up floors after midnight, I bike messengered, I worked at a record store. After I dropped out of college. You just have to survive….survive somehow.

Make it last:

I was very frugal. Back in those days, I found a place to live for twenty dollars a month. I just went to this building, I went to the super and I said, "Do you mind if I live in the basement next to the boiler?" And I just swept this little space out and I gave this guy 20 bucks a month cash. And eating—I ate potatoes. Potatoes were five cents a pound and I'd buy a 20-pound bag of potatoes for a dollar, and that would last me almost a month, a 20-pound bag of potatoes. That's a big fuckin' bag. I'd buy some oil to fry it up in, or bake it or boil it. Mayonnaise, fried potatoes. That's what I ate. But I was happy as a lark, man.

Community:

I played with people because a composer, man, that is really isolating, to sit and write music. Then who do you get to play it? Unless it's played, it doesn't really mean anything. So I learned to perform on the saxophone and I improvised with a lot of people as a means of meeting them and getting together. As we would get more comfortable with each other, I would bring the right pieces of music for that group of people. And year by year I would meet more musicians. It took a long time. In the beginning, there were just one or two people I could play with, who understood, [who] were going in the same direction. Each year I'd meet one or two more, and as the years went on the pool of players, the community, got bigger and bigger and bigger. So, it's a slow process, but a great process.

Ambitions:

I don't have big ambitions. I'm not one of these people that are, you know, goal oriented people. One of the great things about my life is that I've never really had like a goal, like, 'I want to be on the stage at BAM,' or, 'I want to write an opera for the Metropolitan Opera.' You know, fuck that. So whoever I was involved with, I wrote for the people who were right there at hand. Very practical in that way.

Self-Taught:

Back then it was an exciting search of going to different neighborhoods, looking in record stores. If you wanted an Indian record, you'd have to go to the Indian neighborhood, you know? Go into Nagma House, which sold appliances, you'd go in the back there'd be a few records. It was a very different world. An exciting world. You'd hear about a record, you'd look for it for *years*. And then you'd be on tour in maybe Ohio and walk into some record store and look around and the guy next to you would pull it out of a stack and you'd start sweating and shaking. You'd think, "I hope he puts it down, oh my god, I been looking for it for eight years!" Now you go on the Internet, you press a button, Google search and there it is. So you know, you go to the library, whatever you can, you look at scores. This was all on no money. I'd take hundreds of records from the library, I'd check 'em out, tape 'em and listen to 'em. It was fun. It was a lot of fun.

My first gig [in Europe]? Must have been because someone heard a recording, also word of mouth—you'd hear about some guy doing some weird thing and then you'd search him out. I played saxophone and duck calls, birdcalls and clarinet, different wind things.

Follow your muse:

The same thing over and over again—I couldn't do that. That's not who I am. The thing that kept me interested and kept me going all through the years is that I did what I wanted to do, and that was it. And I didn't give a *fuck* who thought what about it. I did what I wanted to do. Whatever that was. And I followed my particular muse, where, you know, sometimes I went into different dark corners. If it goes into dark corners, so be it. I just did what I had to do, what I felt like doing, what I was *compelled* to do, without any regard whatsoever to what people *wanted* me to do, I did what I had to do. You try to second guess people, what they want you to do, you're going to get *all* fucked up. And I've seen it happen to people, you know, who think they should be doing such and such; or that if they do such and such, then they're going to get the gigs. And they end up, usually, dropping out and not even continuing. Because they lost touch with why they got started with music in the first place, that kind of youthful curiosity that I tried never to lose, that keeps you young. I'm not going to use the word "happy" because that's really irrelevant to the whole thing. It's not about making yourself happy. That's for fuckin' yuppies, you know? The American dream is just some distraction so the government can keep you under control. The search for happiness is a crock. Sometimes I'm happy, sometimes I'm not. Sometimes I'm cold, and sometimes I'm hot. Sometimes I'm sick, you know what I mean, and sometimes I'm well. It comes and goes. It's got nothing to do with that. There's a deeper thing going on. You're connected with a tradition.

Be Unique:

The best music I find is written…it writes itself. It's like I'm not even there. It's writing itself and I try not getting in the way. You gotta connect yourself up and just, you know, I'm here to get some *work* done. I'm not here to make myself happy. How shallow is that? So you do what you gotta do. And you get a deep satisfaction in not just accomplishing something for the culture, for the tradition, but involving other people, taking responsibility for your actions and responsibility for taking care of the musicians you work with, responsibility for your community. You know, those are words that have become a little bit outmoded in a certain way. Too many people are concerned about career, success and happiness. And that's not something that I *ever* thought about. I was more concerned with keeping my integrity. Being responsible to the people around me. Being dedicated and loyal. Those are the things that kinda fueled me.

You have to struggle [to keep your integrity] because the world doesn't *want* you to succeed. They *despise* you for your integrity. They are afraid of people that create new things, or that create things. It's a threat, and they want you to go away. And it is a struggle every day. And I'm not Howard Rourke [the protagonist of Ayn Rand's *The Fountainhead*], I'm not a god, I'm constantly tortured and hounded by doubts. What if I'm wrong? What if *this* is just a crock of shit? I mean, you listen to a piece by Stravinsky, or a solo by Charlie Parker, and you just want to blow your brains out. But you keep pushing, you keep working. And it's sometimes very painful and unless you have what it takes to stick with it, you go under. And not everybody has what it takes. It's difficult. I'm not sure that you're wrong when you say maybe you're born with it and that's it. Maybe that's what it is.

Believe in Yourself

You've got to have a certain messianic belief in yourself, a certain trust, to go out on a limb and take a chance and say, "I'm not certain where I'm going here, but I'm going to check it out because that's why I'm on the planet. I'm not here just to celebrate somebody else's discovery, I'm here to check out something that hasn't been done, so let me try it. I'm not afraid to fall flat on my face and have people say that I'm a joke. I'm going to do this." And there's a reason.

Stay Interested

But it's a trick to stay interested in what you're doing over the course of a lifetime, and I'm not going to use the word *career* because career is a crock of shit. You're here to do work and that's what you do. I've seen bands that make one good record and never another. I've seen directors who make one or two good films and never another. I've seen composers who have five or ten good years, or maybe one or two good pieces and then they never get it again. I used to be excited, when I was young, by these outrageous works of art that may be the only good thing that guy did and it's fantastic and *wow*! Now I'm more interested in composers, bands, performers, who developed a body of work over the course of thirty, forty years, and remained interesting and curious and interested and continued to question and challenge themselves. As I get into my third decade of making music, I find it is a challenge to continue making good work, year after year after year after ten years, twenty years, thirty years; and there's all kinds of ways to keep yourself interested, and I think that goes back to trying to stay young, trying to stay curious, trying to stay open; consistently researching new and unknown areas, finding inspiration in new artwork and what have you.

∞

David Speltz Interview

For twenty-five years, cellist David Speltz has made a living, a good living, as a session player in Los Angeles. By his count, he has played on the soundtracks of some 700 movies, including Chinatown, Jaws, Schindler's List *and* The Matrix, *to name a few, and on innumerable albums. He was able to give us a unique perspective on what he sees as perhaps a dying branch of the music business. What he has to say will be of interest to anyone who is seeking a career in classical music or in session work. Like everyone else we spoke to, his way into a career was uniquely his own.*

I started cello late. I was eleven. I know it doesn't sound late, but these days it is. I got distracted in high school, played bass in a rock and roll band. Came back at eighteen, and even then I was pursuing a degree in math. But after a couple nice circumstances I was inspired to come back and then after a couple of years being heard by the right people, I decided to give up the math and pursue the cello.

I got heard on KFAC [a Los Angeles classical music station]. They had a chamber music series every Sunday and I got together little groups to play on it every week. Through that I was given an opportunity to expand, like with the Pasadena symphony. From there, I had the opportunity of meeting people and was recommended to contractors in the commercial business.

From there it grew. One thing led to another. It's being in the right place at the right time, being heard. Being recommended is far better than sending out resumes without backing by an already established musician. You can send out hundreds of records and reviews to prospective employers—if you can't back that up with somebody saying something, it's usually of no use; because the big contractors, in LA for example, are overwhelmed by people sending them things. But when someone they respect calls them and recommends you, that's your ticket.

Unfortunately, these days there are very few slots for soloists, so with all that preparation [college, MFA program, master classes] you end up either teaching or becoming a chamber music player, like in a string quartet or a trio; or you play in an orchestra as a section player in the rank and file; or if you're really good, you might get a principal cello job in a major orchestra, like the Los Angeles Philharmonic. The other option is do what I did and do commercial work.

Thank God, I've been very lucky and made a wonderful living for twenty-five years. I probably earn twice as much or two-and-a-half times as much as a section player in the Los Angeles Philharmonic. And do a lot better financially than a member of a string quartet, even a well-established string quartet. But if I had my druthers, I would have liked to play in an ensemble like a string quartet or a trio for a living. But it's a very hard life and I wouldn't have been afforded the life style I have now.

Agents

No, I don't have an agent. Again, if you're in an ensemble like a quartet or a trio, if that's how you make your living, you have an agent, called a manager. As a freelancer in the commercial business, it's just a matter of being established. I belong to the Musician's Union, Local Number 47. They furnish nothing. They don't find you work; they only regulate the work in terms of establishing minimum scale for, say, a recording session. They provide health and welfare. Healthcare and pension. Though I have supplementary health care through the motion picture industry. For those musicians who don't do MP [motion picture] work, the union covers them. Someone who just does orchestra playing or club playing is covered by the Musicians Union.

Community

I guess we do have somewhat of a community because the same people generally are on the calls. There's a contractor in Los Angeles who is the main contractor in LA, and she generally calls the same people. Her "A" list, I guess it would be.Once in a while you'll see someone you haven't seen in awhile because the composer requests those people. And we lunch together and very often we'll see each other outside of work at parties or gatherings.

Advice for Young Musicians

Best advice? Today it's difficult to say because I'm not sure I'd encourage young musicians to aspire to what I do. I've been very lucky. I was able to experience a lot of good work and plentiful work. But it's changing, and luckily I'm at that age where I can start winding down and saying goodbye.

But young people, I'm not sure what their future is in this business, because so much of the work has disappeared. Either they're doing it on synthesizer, which has been around since 1980. (On most of the TV shows, if there's any music, it's synthesizer. We do about three or four shows, like *Voyager* or *JAG*. Some of the few shows that are still using live music.) Or it's scored somewhere else. That's the other problem. They're finding it cheaper to do it in Canada or Hungary or Australia. I'm probably doing thirty-five percent of the amount of movies I was doing ten years ago.

But in terms of encouraging young people to go into this business, I would suggest they gear up to pursuing a career in orchestra. They're suffering, too, but I think there'll always be orchestras. Or chamber music. But again, that's a hard way to make a living. Even if you play in a well-established quartet, you have to find a way to supplement it.

∞

Connie Kupka Interview

Connie Kupka is a violinist for the Los Angeles Chamber Orchestra. She also happens to be married to David Speltz, so we were afforded the opportunity to interview her as well.

[Getting started], a lot of it, things just kind of fall your way or not your way and you just kind of arrive at it. You come out of school and you have to support yourself and you play every little job there is that's around. [You] come out of school and start auditioning for just about any orchestra across the country, and then you sort of work your way up into better orchestras as you get experienced.

I wasn't really interested in playing full time in a symphony, so I never did audition for the Philharmonic. I used to sub with them and go on tour and I really enjoyed that a lot, but I wasn't interested in that large of a job. I kind of liked the freedom of playing here and playing there. Playing in the Burbank Symphony and the Pasadena Symphony and church jobs, doing anything that comes along to make ends meet. And then you hope for better things, hope for opera, for ballet when it comes to town.

You just know about a job. You get to know the people. If you're new in town, it's actually a little bit easier because you contact the personnel manager of every organization and you say 'I'm here and I'd like to play for you or send you a tape,' and you put your best foot forward.

We don't go through an agent. You just have to know the contractors for the various organizations and the orchestras and you get yourself in that way; or you play with other people and hopefully they will recommend you for jobs that they are doing."

Advice to Young People:

Advice? Nowadays, the competition is so incredible, there are just so many young people coming out of school and they're top notch and I pity anybody who has to compete in that environment. Of course they do [compete]. I see young people in all of the jobs I do. You just get out there and you try.

The chamber orchestra [was] something I really wanted to play in. It's a small orchestra and terrific caliber and great literature and it's not a full-time orchestra. It's a smaller season. It's kind of just the right size. You can do other things and not be tied down every week like you would be in a major symphony. [And] I think that's probably my greatest love. Chamber music.

We had our own string quartet for about ten years and we learned a lot from that struggle. [We] traveled and played and endured and it's the hardest way in the world to make a living, but it's really great. That kind of playing, you get paid for it, but it's not something you can make a living doing unless you happen to find a great group and you have some success. But we consider ourselves working so that we can play chamber music. 'Cause you can't make a living playing chamber music.

Just going to a good school and just getting started on that auditioning process is the best thing you can do. If you spend some time sitting in an orchestra somewhere, that's going to be very beneficial.

Art That Pays

I think young people should not start out trying to work in studios. I think it's bad for them. And right now it's so tenuous, who knows just what's going to be available for people in the future.

But I would think, really, [just] going through the ropes. Putting in your time in a professional group is what will serve you later on when you're hunting for another, better position somewhere.

∞

Chapter 13

Visual Arts

> *If I ran an art school and if I were king, I would not allow anybody to graduate with an MFA or PhD or any of those other wonderful letters without having a secondary skill with which they can earn money.*
> **Josine Starrels,**
> **former Senior Curator,**
> **Long Beach Museum of Art**

When artists get together to discuss the frustrations and hazards of their work, it's difficult for eavesdropping non-artists to understand why they don't give it all up and enroll in the nearest computer-training program. The ongoing struggle to pay rent, maintain a car in operating condition, buy supplies, eat regularly and survive with any kind of dignity is so common among visual artists that family and friends frequently question their judgment and more often their sanity. Outsiders too often see only the artist's isolation, the lack of public understanding and appreciation for complex and difficult work and the almost chronic inconvenience and poverty most artists endure in order to continue creating new work. They do not see the joy and delight an artist experiences when he and his work go in a new and exciting direction. That joy and delight doesn't do much to salve the inconvenience or humiliation of an eviction notice; it may, however, explain why there are not hordes of artists pounding on the doors of institutions that offer re-entry job training programs.

How much easier artists' lives might be if Josine Starrels *were* king and all artists graduating from art schools were given secondary skills that would allow them to pay the rent while getting established as artists. In an arts survival workshop she gave for CalArts students, Ms. Starrels said, "If you ask me about survival, I recommend you try to earn the maximum amount of money for the minimum amount of time so that this secondary endeavor you do to pay the rent takes as little time from your art as possible."

She went on to say, "Art schools which send young people out into the cold world without a secondary skill and with the cockamamie idea that they'll support themselves off their art eventually forces them into some sort of compromise. The commercial world is the commercial world and gallery owners who also have to pay rent and bills will look at the work young artists bring in and question whether or not that work will sell. So young artists, in order to be successful and receive approval, may end up producing work that helps everybody pay their bills. If you want your poetry to remain pure, you may have to make a living repairing TV sets or fixing other people's sinks and garbage disposals."

> *If you cannot sell your work, of course you have to work somewhere else; but never work too hard on that other job. You have to find a job where you can earn as much as possible and work as little as possible, because that's an awful spiral that can drag you down. It doesn't get you anywhere if it pulls you out of your own career.*
>
> **Hubert Schmalix, painter/**
> **professor/gallery proprietor**

In a book entitled *Starting and Succeeding In Your Own Photography Business,* photographer/author Jeanne Thwaites tells about a family whose members, no matter how lofty their ambitions, learned a trade. Although they attained varying degrees of success in the corporate world, they always knew they could work as carpenters, mechanics and housepainters. The knowledge that you can always support your vocation and your family with a back-up trade can do a lot to reduce the stress of contemporary life, regardless of your profession.

In addition to developing a marketable secondary skill, young artists embarking on a professional career can minimize their hardships by learning a few basic techniques of presentation. Grantswriting skills are, of course, de rigueur for visual artists. See our grants appendix for a list of publications and websites that provide resource information. If you don't learn how to write a grant proposal before you graduate from art school, you should refuse to leave. It's as basic as learning to put your portfolio together or learning to write your resume. Since preparation of slides, cover letters and resumes will all be part of a complete grant proposal, preparing a sample proposal is a good exercise for artists about to step out into the harsh world of galleries, museums, dealers and art critics. If you don't believe a secondary skill is as important as we seem to thing it is, at least read about grantsmanship in Chapter 7, learn to write a simple, straightforward cover letter and resume, prepare your slides and portfolio and practice a few introductory telephone calls on a patient friend before you dash out to take the art world by storm. It can't hurt.

Training

Should a painter, a sculptor, a photographer go to school? Does university have anything to offer? Well, yes and no, according to our sources.

"We have a different system in Europe," says Hubert. Schmalix, a painter born and raised in Austria. "We don't have the bachelors or the masters degree. You go to an art school, which is equivalent to a university, and you get a diploma that says you finished school. It's equivalent to the bachelor's degree, maybe. In Europe, ninety-nine point nine percent of artists go to school.

"The biggest advantage? Meeting people who were doing the same thing as I was. The interaction, the discussions…[discovering] we were all the same. And I think that's the most [valuable] and maybe only reason for going to the university."

Shane Guffogg, another artist we interviewed, had a rather varied experience of university. The first run at it was not that positive. "College? I was painting and my teacher was angry with me [because] I was teaching *myself* how to paint. We got to be very competitive. He would pull me aside and say 'You could be a star, your girlfriend is holding you back.' We had a push/pull."

But another school, and a whole other experience: "The next thing I did was go to Cal Arts. At the time, they accepted only thirty students a year and it is the best of the best. The first thing they did was to pull the rug out from under me. I had no idea what it was [they were teaching me]. It was a whole new language. Words I had never heard of. So after class I would ask the teachers what words like *appropriation* meant. I didn't understand how it applied to art, but I learned. Cal Arts is great for not teaching what you should do, but teaching what you should not do."

Shane tells us, though, aside from college, there are many ways of learning. "I grew up on a farm in the San Joaquin Valley where the only culture is agriculture. I knew nothing about the art world. I didn't even know if the way I was painting was an acceptable way. I had read about painting and started experimenting with it because I had a lot of images in my mind and I wanted to get them down. I was reading about the Renaissance Masters and how they all did apprenticeships with Masters before they became their own painters and I thought, well that would be the way to do it.

"Cal Arts came about through this artist, Joe Goode. He had a ranch up in the Sierra's, which was about forty-five minutes from where I lived. I'd heard about him and called him to see if I could meet him and do a studio visit. I was nineteen years old. I took some slides of my work and he said 'The first thing you need to do is get out of this area, and be with other artists.' He suggested Cal Arts because it was such an open forum.

"After I got out of Cal Arts I worked with the artist Doug Huebler. He was my mentor at Cal Arts and working for him was a great way to keep my hand in the art world and meet people and see how other artists handle their careers and how they make their art.

"[Then] I sat down one day and thought about who are the artists that work in LA that are successful enough to hire and need a full-time assistant. I thought Ed Ruscha, Sam Francis and David Hockney. I picked Ed because I really admired his work and his work ethic. I found out what gallery he showed at and took my resume by there, but I never heard back. Then about a year and a half later I called Joe Goode up again just to see how he was doing. We got together and I told him I was looking for a job as a studio assistant. He hired me on the spot. The first day on the job, he took me over to Ed Ruscha's studio. That's how I met him. It was one of those things that I set it in motion, but it took a year and a half to come around, which is what I usually find happens in my life. It's never when I think it should be."

Preparing Your Resume

The purpose of a resume is to let someone else know who you are and what you've accomplished. Place yourself in the employer/gallery director/curator's chair and ask yourself if your resume:

1. Shows you are qualified for a particular job or show.
2. Provides a curator with a good representation of your exhibition experience.
3. Documents your qualifications for a residency or grant.

Your resume should *not* describe your artwork or philosophy. If you feel the need to provide a lengthy statement, enclose it on a separate sheet of paper. Remember that most readers will give your resume less than a one-minute glance, and therefore the physical appearance of a resume is extremely important. If you don't feel secure in putting it together in a professional manner, hire some help. If you have it on your computer you can easily shift things around, add and subtract, in order to stress the entries you think would be most attractive to a particular position. Your resume should include the following information:

- Name
- Residence/home address
- Studio address or mailing address
- Phone number/s
- Fax number
- E-mail address
- Date of birth/age (optional)
- Education and degrees
- Honors
- Awards/Grants
- Bibliography
- Group exhibitions
- Less than 3 person shows
- More than 3 person shows
- One-person shows
- Collections your work is in
        (public & private—not relatives)
- Professional appointments
        (jobs in the art field/lectures)
- Professional memberships
- Employment objectives (optional)
- Employment history (job-related only)
- List of previous clients
- References

In summary, remember that a good resume will contain only relevant information, with items arranged in relative order of importance.

As was noted above, resumes can and should be rewritten as needed to reflect your qualifications for various positions, and should be accompanied by a cover letter that is as clear and straightforward as your resume.

Portfolios

A portfolio is the most important job search tool a visual artist can develop. It is therefore necessary to present your best work in your portfolio and to consciously delete any items that emphasize your limitations.

The following recommendations for preparing an effective portfolio are reprinted with the permission of the California Institute of the Arts, publishers of the *National Directory of Arts Internships:*

1. If your work is 3-D, make photographs or slides of it from more than one angle.
2. Whatever format you choose, be consistent. If possible, cut mats of the same size. Avoid having a hodge-podge look to your portfolio. Your work should be easy to view.
3. If you cannot shoot decent slides of your work, it is worth your while to find someone to shoot them for you. Remember to keep a set of original slides for yourself, in case the others are lost or damaged. Duplicating slides is very expensive and they will not have the same quality as the originals.
4. *Do not* have smudges, tears or uncovered work, especially of pencil drawings or pastels that rub off onto other pieces.
5. *Do not* include several examples of the same problem.
6. *Do not* include too much work in your portfolio. This can be as bad as too few pieces.
7. Should your portfolio have to be mailed out, be sure it is self-explanatory.
8. Generally, your portfolio will be mailed out only after a prospective employer has seen your resume and

talked with you. If possible, show your portfolio at the interview.

9. Prepare carefully for a short interview of about fifteen minutes, but be prepared with "back-up" material should the interviewer be interested in seeing more.

10. Include only your own work.

11. Include: working drawings, design work, graphics and related artwork (painting, ceramics, etc.).

12. The following adjectives should describe your portfolio: conveyable, durable, revisable, neat, professional and self-explanatory.

13. It is not necessary to have all color photographs.

14. It is not necessary to have all 8" x 10" photographs.

15. *Do not* reduce working drawings to less than 11" x 14".

16. *Do not* use tracings. Instead, make sepia, black line, Photostats or blueprints.

17. It is usually advisable to show some original artwork as reproductions.

Tips On What to Include in Your Portfolio

A. The Commercial Portfolio

- Show work that demonstrates the diversity of your technical skills, especially those pieces that show what you can do for the company.

- Quality is more important than quantity. Limit your portfolio to no more than fifteen or twenty examples that represent your best work.

- Your fine art work is of interest only if it shows some skills that the company can use (e.g., your drawing ability).

- Get professional advice and criticism on your portfolio from people in the field whom you respect. Always ask the interviewer for criticism of your portfolio if you do not get the job.

- Always include a resume.

- Research the company before your interview. Know their clients and campaigns. Know the technical language as well as possible. Select examples of your work that you think best illustrate your problem solving ability and creativity. Try to show what commercial illustration accomplishes that photography does not.

A good book to read in helping you prepare your advertising portfolio is *How to Get Your Book Together and Get a Job in Advertising: 21st Century Edition* by Maxine Paetro. Among other things, you will learn from it the necessity of being familiar with storyboards and campaigns.

B. The Gallery Portfolio

- Galleries look for maturity and direction. Apart from quality, your portfolio should demonstrate consistency and professionalism in a body of recent work. Do not include earlier work unless you think it necessary to show your development.
- Research the gallery to learn what kind of image it tries to project and take this into account in selecting pieces for your portfolio.
- One or two pages of slides (ten or twenty) are probably sufficient. Be sure to include some good detail slides. Slides are usually the accepted format, but some artists prefer to show color photographs.
- Since galleries have different policies about looking at artist's work, check out the policies of the various galleries you'll be visiting. (Some will reserve certain hours for looking at work; others want artists to leave slides with stamped, self-addressed envelopes.)

Some artists will benefit from portfolio variations:

Illustrators sometimes use 8" x 10" or 5" x 7" transparencies rather than slides. Transparencies are easier to view than slides when simply held up to the light; cumbersome equipment is not necessary.

Photographers should include both color samples and black and white samples. The recommended size for all samples is 8" x 10" or 11" x 14".

Graphic designers must often ignore the uniform size rule, since finished products will vary greatly in size and shape. If you prefer a presentation of uniform size, you can use a slide or transparency portfolio rather than originals.

Studio artists most often use the slide format due to the cumbersome shapes of their work. In addition, they will probably need to mail a portfolio more regularly than commercial artists, and slides provide the simplest form for mailing. Studio artists dealing in three-dimensional forms should have at least two slides for each work, showing it from different angles.

Filmmakers' portfolios consist of film samples—at least three very different, brief pieces that quickly and clearly deliver a focused message.

All items in any portfolio should carry clear labels summarizing the work in two or three words. For certain types of portfolios, especially slides or transparencies, it is vital to identify the top and bottom as well as the front and back.

Whenever possible, an artist should present the portfolio in person. If asked to mail it (as is common for museum/gallery exhibitions), you can use slides but should keep duplicates. A stamped, self-addressed envelope will help ensure that slides are returned. For portfolio presentations that take place in person, the quality of the presentation holds just as much importance as the quality of the portfolio itself. The applicant must be able to discuss the artistic choices made for each entry. This requires that you articulate the development of your ideas as you were producing each piece. After his comments, the employer needs ample time to review each item in silence. You should not speak again until the employer poses questions or moves on to the next portfolio item. While it is inappropriate for artists to apologize for their work, it is also inappropriate for them to become overly defensive. You must strive for the delicate balance between pride in your work and a humility and openness to creative suggestion. Repeated practice with faculty members or knowledgeable friends who can critique your efforts is a huge help in coming to the place of being able to successfully present your work.

After the portfolio presentation, a resume is left for the organization's files. Students might also consider preparing a small package of reproduced samples to leave with the employer. The resume serves as a reminder of only experience and education, whereas actual samples allow easy reference to finished work as well.

Once you have your portfolio together and you have exhausted your friends and relatives by making them participate in mock interviews, you should be ready to take on the gallery/museum world. Bear in mind that curators and gallery owners are in the business they're in because they love what they do. For the most part, they like artists and enjoy being part of the process that presents artwork to interested viewers and collectors. Although you should treat these people with the same courtesy and respect you show your mother, your doctor and your mechanic, there is no need to work yourself into a frenzy prior to a viewing.

If you do have the misfortune to run into a rude, insensitive dealer or curator, make a hasty exit and remember that you will have dozens, even hundreds, of future viewings that will be more successful. As Toby Judith Klayman points out in her *Artist's Survival Manual,* "We, too, can accept or reject. After all, galleries and museums need *us.* Without artists, there would be no dealers, no curators, no museums, no arts administrators or National Endowment for the Arts. It's important to remember that *we make* the goods *they're* interested in handling."

Tips for Approaching Galleries and Museums

1. Be prepared. Research the gallery or museum you're approaching. Find out about their viewing policies, the kind of work they handle, the special interests of the curatorial staff.

2. Be aware of the importance of personal appearance but also dress in a way that is comfortable for you. A viewing with a

gallery owner is no time to try out a pair of four-inch heels. You'll have enough to worry about without worrying about when you're going to topple into the gallery owner's favorite potted plant.

3. Reconfirm your appointment the day before and arrive five to ten minutes early so you can relax.

4. Establish a track record before you try the gallery/museum circuit. A museum is not a jumping-off place for artists without an exhibition history. Enter local juried exhibitions in your area, at schools, banks or through art associations. Those exhibitions are frequently juried by museum staff and provide a good opportunity for you to be noticed.

5. Participate actively in the interview process. Make a checklist of the items you want defined if the gallery agrees to accept your work. If you are dealing with a museum, you should have some sort of formal written agreement outlining exhibition dates and other commitments you and they have made verbally. Discuss such issues as the size of the catalogue, the identification of the gallery space, insurance, sale of works and your responsibility to provide photographs, research materials, etc. Formalizing all these items in writing can be tedious but the process will clarify what all participating parties are expected to do. At the same time, written agreements and contracts will protect both you and the museum. Although the emphasis of your relationship with a gallery will differ from that with a museum, the same kind of paperwork is necessary. Be prepared to question the gallery owner or staff about your mutual responsibilities, whether or not you will be participating in group shows or one-person exhibitions, where and how your work will be stored, promoted and priced. Define the duration of your relationship with a gallery, whether or not your relationship with them restricts you from exhibitions in another gallery in the same geographic areas and how soon and how much you'll be paid after each sale. After you and the dealer have covered all the issues to your mutual satisfaction, put everything in

writing. The agreement can be a simple letter that both parties will sign, date and have witnessed, or you can use one of the many sample Artist-Dealer contracts available through the sources recommended in our Law appendix. Remember that both you and the gallery owner are business professionals, and clarity between you will represent a greater potential for profit as well as ensure a more satisfying business relationship.

6. Establish prices for your work before you sign a contract with a gallery. Any agreement you sign should stipulate the price of your work and, although the gallery owner can and should advise you, the final decision on pricing is yours. It's foolish to overprice your work because this will make you inaccessible and difficult for a gallery to handle. On the other hand, if a piece means a great deal to you and if you want to be perceived as a serious professional, you won't want to begin with bargain basement prices. It's always possible to raise your prices but it's very chancy to lower them. If a collector has paid $400 for a watercolor, he's not going to want to see a similar piece on the market a year later for $250. You must also consider your overhead and costs when you establish your prices. While it doesn't make much sense to charge by the hour or the square foot for your work, you should consider the cost of framing a piece, materials such as handmade paper and the commission you will be paying to the gallery. You should also guard against art patrons looking for a quick "deal" who try to buy work directly from your studio in order to avoid a gallery commission. You have a responsibility to protect the dealer or gallery by keeping your prices consistent. A gallery owner who discovers an artist underselling him has every right to drop that artist. It's very complicated and you will need to discuss pricing with your fellow artists, with your gallery, and with curators who understand your particular market. After you factor in all the advice, your attachment to the work and, finally, your own financial need, you alone must fix realistic prices and *STICK TO THEM.*

7. Unless the curator or dealer has been extraordinarily rude to you, send a follow-up thank you letter expressing your appreciation for their time, advice and their interest. There are far more artists than there are curators and it can't hurt to identify yourself as an artist who is courteous, considerate *and* professional.

Publicity

Almost everyone in the art world resents the type of artist who indulges in "hype," but no one I know in the media or in arts management positions resents artists who provide them with clear, timely information. Communicating with journalists, critics and television staff who run free public service announcements is just another task artists have to take on if they want people outside their immediate circle of friends to know about their work.

Press releases, personal letters of invitation to critics, public service announcements, flyers, posters, post cards and targeted mailing lists will all play a part in developing a market for your art. If you want to create a demand for your work, you must let people know about it. If you're lucky, you'll have a support network of family and friends who will help you; and as you get to know collectors, curators, arts managers, dealers and other artists, your support system will grow. In the beginning, however, you may have a support system of one and it may fall on *you* to write the press releases and public service announcements, design the post cards and develop a mailing list. It's time-consuming work and it takes talent as well as time to do it well. It's also necessary. No one will come to your studio and drop offers in your lap, and on the day you decide to become a professional artist, you should also begin the process of self-promotion. You can begin simply by attending art events and openings where you'll meet other artists, art patrons and the arts press. By exchanging cards over the cheap white wine, you can begin assembling a mailing list. Eventually you'll build up a reliable list of people who have a genuine interest in the arts; and when you add your relatives, your dentist, the neighbors and your mom's best friends to your new collection of art patrons, you'll find you have a pretty decent support system.

From day one, begin assembling materials for a promotional package. Reviews, your resume, slides, photographs, press releases and any articles written about you or your work should all be part of this package. When you have enough material to make a favorable impression, you can start sending it around to curators, gallery owners, presenters and collectors. Whether you're seeking an exhibition, sales or grants, you'll need to provide good, clear information. There are too many good, accessible artists around to compete for the limited time and resources curators and presenters have at their disposal. Don't make it hard for them to find you, because unless you were born lucky, they're not going to make the effort when Xenia Hausner or Shane Guffogg's press packets are just an arm's length away.

Henry Geldzahler, author and former Commissioner of Cultural Affairs for the City of New York, reminded us in his article, *Career and the Artist,* that no amount of self-promotion and technical business skills will help an artist make better art. "Success is a reward," he says. "Making honest art is the goal." Publicists and promoters must always bear this in mind. It's very easy to get caught up in the style and splash of self-presentation. Self-promotion *is* necessary, but if the work you're promoting is not solid, honest and original, you're going to be found out and discarded so quickly your head will spin. Keep it all in perspective. Be a professional and learn to present yourself professionally but always stay in touch with the reason for the press releases and promotional kits. If you find yourself spending more time working as a publicist than as an artist and that your press packet outshines your art, it is time to assess who you are and what you're doing and whether or not you're confusing your goals with your rewards. Of course this is our opinion, but we value the process far more than the result. Results are nice, but the process is the gold.

∞

Photos courtesy Shane Guffogg

The Us of Me, oil painting by Shane Guffogg, and (inset) the artist.

Shane Guffogg Interview

Shane Guffogg received his B.F.A. from Cal Arts, where he interned with Gary Stephan. From there he worked as Studio Assistant to Ed Ruscha from 1989 until 1995. He works in many media: oil on canvas and paper, watercolor, gouache and pastel on paper and traditional zinc plate etchings. His work expresses his own painterly language of patterning, light and visual depth, the results of which are reminiscent of everything from the expression of the human spirit to the "unseen worlds of Quantum Physics and Super String Theory." The artist makes his home in Hollywood with his wife and son.

Advice to young artists?

Make yourself part of the landscape wherever you are. Go to every opening. Get a feel of which galleries are doing what; get a feel of where they are going, because it is a waste of their time and yours to approach a gallery that isn't working in the direction you are. Invite everyone you can over for a studio visit. It doesn't matter if they collect art or are involved in the art world or not. The more people that see your work, the more well known your work becomes. How many people know of Picasso's work and how many of those people actually collect it?

Get to know as many other artists as you possibly can, because artists recommend each other to dealers. I do that. People always think of the artist in solitude, making their work. That is true but art is also a language and the more you speak it the more fluent it becomes. There is never one artist in history that creates an *ism* (*Popism* or *Abstract Expressionism* for example); it is a *group* of artists that create the *ism*. They may or may not even know each other, but chances are they do and chances are they talk about their process and their work with each other. I do that with my artist friends and in the end we inspire each other. All that said, the most important thing for the artist to do is just do your work. So many artists are so concentrated on trying to strategize and make sure they are talking to the right person at the right party to further their career. So often they spend more time doing that than making their work, and it shows. Rarely do you see work that has been fleshed out and resonates with the artist's truth and I think that is one of the main reasons why.

Painters Paint

Everyday I go into my studio. I've had people say that I have had the luxury of doing that, but when I was working a forty hour week for somebody else, I would get up at 6:30 in the morning and paint and then when I came home I'd paint and I got at least five to six hours a day painting. Art is not something you do; it is a way of life. You cannot live without it. It's like *Letters to A Young Poet* by Rilke. I have been a construction worker and come home so tired and wondered how I could go home and make my work, and maybe I would go four or five days without doing my work and I'd just get cranky. My life didn't seem to make sense if I wasn't doing my work.

Something About Success

Success to me is not about fame and fortune. Success to me is about giving myself or creating an opportunity that allows me to live up to my fullest potential. That, to me, is success. That is what I always aim to do; I don't care if I'm working out of a shoebox or a huge warehouse. And you cannot allow money or fame to be barriers. When I am finished with a painting, I step back and am happy and satisfied with it…I know it has a life of its own and it will be telling its story outside of me. Then I am successful.

∞

Hubert Schmalix Interview

The Austrian-born Hubert Schmalix is often associated with that country's so-called 'Wild Painters,' a group of youthful artists who, in the late seventies and early eighties, developed an expressionistic painting style antithetical to the de rigueur minimalism of the day. He is known for his nude portraits (a series begun in the Philippines in the early eighties), images of Christ and, of late, the bird's eye view geometric shapes of tract housing in Los Angeles, his home since 1987. He has exhibited widely, from Vienna to New York and London, he operates the Black Dragon Society Gallery *in LA's Chinatown (the gallery name inherited from the former occupants) and he teaches painting at UCLA.*

Advice to young painters:

"There's not really any advice you can give to a young painter other than to work a lot. You can't tell them *what* to do. That's something they have to figure out. They have to surprise you with what they are doing. And they are the ones who show you what *will* be done. As the older person, and maybe established, you do what *you* know how to do and you are more or less a finished person.

But these young people, they are doing something new. They show you what has to be done in the future. So you cannot teach somebody or tell somebody what he has to do."

Would you ever discourage a student you thought wasn't talented enough?

"I wouldn't dare to discourage someone. My teacher discouraged me from doing art. Hopefully I proved him wrong. Teachers used to be that way. They thought they had the authority to tell you what was good and what was wrong. Maybe at that point he was right, because I didn't do a lot and I was a really bad student. I changed after school. I worked much harder after school than during school. And the hard work, that's what makes you an artist. There's no 'talent.'"

How often should a painter paint?

"I paint every day."

photo courtesy of Jeff Kober

Painter Hubert Schmalix in his Mt. Washington studio.

∞

Art That Pays

Chapter 14

Writing

> *How I kept myself from getting completely depressed was I considered that every form of writing, even typing up a classified, was a piece of writing and I tried to make it as good as I could.*
>
> **Matt Groening, cartoonist/writer**

While writing is often portrayed as the loneliest of professions, writers are a generally social bunch, for the most part, and have well-established support systems that provide advice, legal aid, health insurance and even emergency funds for sick, disabled or downtrodden, about-to-be-evicted writers. There are also organizations, guilds and publications which provide contact with other writers and offer valuable insight into how to turn your writing into a paying, thriving business. On the Internet there has been an explosion of sites that help writers find freelance work.

This chapter will help you come to terms with how to get an agent, a small press publisher, a distributor, as well as how to find funding and places to apply for awards. Also, we can point you toward some writers organizations that help and support writers.

Every poet, playwright, fiction writer, screenwriter or journalist has her own way to approach the business of a writing career. The artists we interviewed for this book spoke to practical matters as well as digressing into the process of creating. We interviewed writers in each of the disciplines to get some practical tips on how to cope with being a particular kind of writer; but similar threads from everyone's stories began to weave together, showing us the commonality of all writers. Everyone had to fight to find a way to make money to pay the bills, and then sneak off to write something of their own. The *how* of that for each of them is fascinating. But first, some practicalities.

Agents

It is not necessary to have an agent to be a successful writer, but there are some reasons to consider getting one. And if you find yourself at William Morris, sitting across the table from a smiling Young Turk, your manuscript on his desk, there are a few things to know. Besides reassuring you that the last editor was insensitive and wouldn't recognize good writing if it bit him, a good literary agent will also:

1. Place the writer (you) with an appropriate publisher.
2. Negotiate the writer's contract with the publisher.
3. Collect all payments due the writer from the publisher.
4. Follow-up and confirm that the publisher is living up to the contractual agreement.
5. Create bidding wars or auctions on the writer's manuscript. (Manuscripts are submitted to publishers and other possible buyers with a deadline and often with each potential bidder knowing that he has to fight for the property. This helps the writer receive the maximum advance.)
6. Develop other markets such as film, television and foreign sales for the writer's work.

The written agreement you sign with the agent should reflect these duties as well as what percentage he will receive, if he will be reimbursed for expenses and when this contract will be renewed. Generally, contracts are drawn up for a one year period. If you cannot get friends to refer you to an agent they like, which is the best of all possible options, you will have to write a "cold" letter of inquiry. Get a list of agents (see appendix) and start sending out letters. In the fifth edition of *Literary Agents, A Writer's Guide*, Debby Mayer found that many agents actually will respond to cold queries, though very few will read unsolicited manuscripts, so save yourself the trouble and write an interesting letter of inquiry first.

Query and Cover Letters

All query or cover letters should be brief.

Letters to Agents

Your query should include a short sample or description of your work, your education, training and publication history. Be clear, to the point, and print a clean crisp letter. Agents who do respond will probably ask for sample work. Include a self-addressed, stamped envelope to improve your chances for a reply. Do your homework and direct your letters to a specific agent and don't be discouraged by the rejection letters.

Once an agent expresses an interest in reading your manuscript, submit a polished, clean version of your work. Ask that he or she respond within two weeks. When and if the work is returned, thank the agent and repeat this procedure until you have found an agent to represent your work. If you set yourself a goal of sending out "X" number of manuscripts per week, you will eventually find an agent to represent you.

Letters to an Editor

Before even submitting poetry, fiction or non-fiction to a magazine, there are at least three things you can do to increase your chances of success.

1. Write well and clearly, develop a unique voice.
2. Know the market, read the publication before submitting your work.
3. Persist. Rejection is inevitable.

If you are writing a query to a magazine editor, your goal is to grab his attention and impress him with the content of your piece so he will buy your story for his publication. If you are making a book query, you want to interest the editor in seeing more—either a book proposal or the entire manuscript. If you are a poet, you are simply writing a cover letter and including the poems you wish to be considered in your submission. Although there is no formula that will guarantee your acceptance, there are some standards for letters of inquiry:

- Keep your letter to one page.
- Find the name of the editor to whom you are writing and use the formal address, i.e. Mr. or Ms.
- Write a strong opening. For pitch letters, your opening is often meant to be the lead for the article. Use a professional tone; do not write to the editor in an overly familiar voice.
- Give the editor a clear idea how you will develop the article or book, which requires that you do your research. Editors are impressed with depth of information.
- Make a direct offer to the editor to publish your article; include your suggested word count and the time frame in which you can get it completed.
- Show yourself in the best light. If you have clips, send some. Develop a brief biographical paragraph, or outline your education.
- If you wish to get a response, include a self-addressed stamped envelope.

Often writers just starting out are hesitant to send a query, thinking the editor will get a better idea by seeing the whole manuscript, but in today's busy world editors prefer to be queried. The yearly updated *Writer's Market* is a comprehensive book on submitting work to publishers and agents. There is also the web site: *www.writersmarket.com* which is an amazing resource for writers. Subscribe to it. Also, we liked Moira Allen's comprehensive tome, *The Writer's Guide to Queries, Pitches & Proposals.* She delves comprehensively into the art of writing a pitch, and her book is a tool every independent writer must have.

The following are two query letters: one that worked and one, as of this writing, that has yet to work. We have taken out the names and the addresses of the editors. These letters are placed here as samples in order to give you the flavor of a possible pitch. They are not templates within which you can just plug-in your own ideas.

Friday, January 31, 2003

Magazine
Address
City/state/zip

Dear Editor,

There's a killer on the loose. He committed the perfect crime right in front of millions of Americans. Not only did he get away with murder, he profited handsomely. He even got an award. David Milch killed Bobby Simone on NYPD Blue and took his time, carefully planning his death

I'd like to offer you the first opportunity to publish "Confessions of a Dangerous Pen," a feature article, around 3,000-words, about how writers write about death. You know the old saying, "If it bleeds, it leads?" Dying is Heaven for network television. But it has to be real—so writers have to create an accurate portrait of death. But how do some of Hollywood's best TV writers deal with death and dying?

The piece will feature Milch who won a writing Emmy for an episode of NYPD Blue that portrayed Bobby Simone's death. In support, I'm including an interview with Milch's brother, Robert who is a physician and a palliative care expert. Dr. Milch helped David accurately portray Bobby's death.

Additionally, I'd talk to Jack Orman, executive producer of the ER episodes that witnessed Dr. Mark Greene's final days. Orman will discuss the TV 'formula' for death. Favorite characters die slowly — ER needed two years before finally letting Anthony Edwards' character pass away. Not surprisingly, the death formula worked. Ratings peaked for Dr. Greene's final goodbye.

I will also be interviewing Matt Tarses, who wrote a recent episode of Scrubs that explored how some patients want the option to die on their own terms and how this deeply personal choice clashes dramatically with medical hubris. Many doctors feel that death is a "failure of medicine" rather than the inevitable culmination of our human experience.

Writing about death may resurrect high ratings but the topic requires skilled handling. Death is difficult for the living — in life and in drama. As Flannery O'Connor is reported to have said, "I always hate it when one of my character dies."

I can complete this feature article within 48 days of your approval. Thank you for your time and consideration. I look forward to hearing from you soon.

Sincerely,

Adele Slaughter

Art That Pays

Wednesday, August 27, 2003

Dear Editor,

James Cameron, who brought the Titanic back from its watery grave, is directing our attention to another ship, this one on a mission to stop the death of the world's coral reefs. Coral reefs reflect the health of our planet and they are dying. With 10% of these "rainforests of sea" gone and an estimated 58% of all reefs endangered, not only are the fish and natural habitats vanishing, but this destruction is also threatening the air we breathe. Phytoplankton in the ocean creates the majority of the world's oxygen as well as absorbs the greenhouse gases.

"Our destiny is interlocked with the destiny of the sea," says Cameron. "If the seas die, we die."

"Coral reefs are dying at an alarming rate worldwide," says Cynthia Lazaroff, Vice-President of the Planetary Coral Reef Foundation (PCRF). "The RV (Research Vessel) Heraclitus chartered by the PCRF is working to turn the tide."

I'd like to offer you the first opportunity to publish "2003: An Ocean Odyssey" a feature article, around 4,500-words about the coral reef crisis and the new information gathered by the crew of the Heraclitus on their mythic voyage. The Heraclitus is returning to California this October after setting sail from Oakland in 1975. The ship is due in Los Angeles on November 18, 2003.

Where has the Heraclitus been? For the past 28 years the RV Heraclitus has circumnavigated the globe, from the headwaters of the Amazon, to the Antarctic Peninsula and most recently Papua New Guinea and The Solomon Islands. For the first time in history, scientists are pioneering the technology to create the first comprehensive baseline map of living coral reefs. Thanks to this unlikely giant, an 84-foot motor and wind-powered boat made out of ferro-cement and her crew, we have the first vitality studies and maps of the planet's coral reefs. The Heraclitus brings back real solutions to an environmental problem, equal in scope to the destruction of the rainforests.

I propose to compile a timeline that will include selected adventures culled from the 28-year history of the Heraclitus alongside the global shifts, which have contributed to the decline of the reef ecosystem.

The piece will feature James Cameron, who is hosting the ship at a Captain's dinner while it is in Los Angeles this November to raise awareness and money to preserve the reefs. Additionally, I will include an in-depth interview with Abigail Alling, a marine biologist who has been an Expedition Chief on the Heraclitus and is currently President of the PCRF. The piece will also include some of the current crew, who will give personal accounts about their recent dramatic voyage across the Pacific.

I can complete this feature article within 30 days of an assignment. Thank you for your time and consideration. I look forward to hearing from you soon.

Sincerely,

Adele Slaughter

Resumes

As a writer, your resume not only lists your credits but also reflects your skills. The writer's resume will tell the reader at first glance a lot about the person behind it. A resume is something that sells you. Your resume should reflect what makes your writing unique. A busy reader wants to know what you are offering in the first few moments of glancing at your resume.

Writer's resumes, like most general resumes, detail your education and your *relevant* work experience. (Leave out the interesting, non-essential jobs.) A writer's resume should also include a section headlined *Publications* in which is a list including the title, publisher or periodical and date of each article, story or book you have published. If you have no works that have been published, emphasize your education and writing experience at any of your past or current jobs, or your experience with writing workshops. You can even include odd jobs such as writing ad copy, drafting biographies or any other writing work you have done for businesses.

Small Press Publishers

The major publishing houses are generally interested in bestsellers, because this is where their profit lies. Small presses are the best bet for unpublished novelists, and perhaps the only real option for poets and playwrights. You should investigate each of the different small presses to see where your work fits. Early on, *Ecco Press* was one of the most established small literary presses publishing well-known literati such as John Ashbury, Paul Bowles and Joyce Carol Oates. In 1999 they were acquired by *Harper Collins* and although they still publish poets, they cannot be considered "small" anymore. *Hanging Loose Press* (they first published Sherman Alexie) is usually interested in new writers. They have a stable of writers they publish and, as with most houses, they will develop writers they believe in.

Consult the 20th edition of the *CLMP Directory of Literary Magazines and Presses* for the most current and complete information on how to get your work published. There are hundreds of small magazines that publish poetry and fiction as well as the more established magazines like *The New Yorker* and *Harper's*, all of which will publish good work. Getting published is a business, like any other, and the only way to get published is to keep writing, keep researching, keep putting together submissions and keep mailing them out. Have your next packet ready to send out so that when you get a rejection, you have another batch ready to mail out. Do anything to not take the rejection personally. Once you have some publication credits, put together a book manuscript and send it out to the various writing contests or small presses for consideration.

> *Wherever you are in life, you need to finish the work you're doing and it needs to reach an audience; if it's a poem, you have to give it away; if it's a comic book, it has to be Xeroxed and you give it away. It has to be seen by someone at whatever level you can show it. With luck, you can actually get paid for it.*
> **Matt Groening, cartoonist/writer**

Writers Service Organizations & Sources of Funding

There are many local and national service organizations for writers that provide information, professional assistance, teaching and other job opportunities and financial aid. These organizations have helped writers advance their careers with grants, awards, internships, readings and writers-in-residence programs. They have also helped writers establish relationships with agents, editors and publishers. Most important, however, they have urged writers to develop the skills and expertise they need not only to survive but also to be successful professional writers. The appendix contains a list of these writer's organizations. Many of these writers service organizations offer awards, fellowships, prizes and grants; and as you look deeper into *The Academy of American Poets* or the *Playwrights Award* websites, you'll find contests to which you can submit you work.

∞

Writer Interviews

We interviewed Hubert Selby Jr., Richard Jefferies, Murray Mednick, Dana Gioia and Jim McManus. Each of these writers has achieved success in a particular field of writing, as well as the respect of their peers.

Hubert Selby, Jr. Interview

*You realize how vital the man is when you remember he's been working on one-half of one lung since about 1946. Hubert Selby, Jr. (*Requiem for a Dream, Last Exit to Brooklyn*) has suffered in this life from tuberculosis, placental strangulation and the odd ill-advised cigarette; yet when we walk into his apartment there's no oxygen tank, no breathing tubes, not a hint of illness anywhere. It's just a nondescript, cozy, one-bedroom apartment in West Hollywood, one of so many others like it.*

Cubby (Selby's nickname) is one of those rare individuals who has lived on both sides of the dragon's mouth, learning his own version of the nature of life and reality, and has taught himself how to write it down. Not in some 1990's memoir, tell-all spew of experience, but as genuine literature, shaped so that others can maybe catch a glimpse of what he has learned about the weight of being, about the pain of breathing in and out.

He seems to be sipping air as he exhales, so little there to breathe out it must be conserved to give his body the illusion it is getting enough oxygen. Since he tires easily, we quickly set up the recorder. There's a brief moment of guilt for putting him through this, but then he gets going and we are in the experience of his life force and there is nothing but the moment and the sound of his voice and the certain knowledge that each moment you are here with him is a gift. He seems to sink into the cushions, a small man but never insignificant. Up close it is easy to see how, and even why, Cubby has written such brave, more-real-than-reality fiction.

photo courtesy Jeff Kober

Hubert Selby, Jr....more than just a pretty face.

Selby on Writing

> *It's not owning that you're a writer, it's accepting it. I think it's Leonard Cohen who said, "Being an artist is a sentence." So you accept the fact, yeah, this is not a choice. I can't do anything else.*
>
> **Hubert Selby, Jr., writer**

I've kept showing up to write. I've written, what is it, six books and a collection of short stories and a couple of films. *Requiem for a Dream* and one that's being edited now, *Fear X,* and I did some rewriting on a couple of things. *Fear X* is an original thing I did with this young Danish director. He contacted me, wanted to make a movie with me. And no, there's no training for a writer, not other than reading and writing.

I realized what I have to do, as an artist, is understand the story that's been given to me. That's why, for instance, when I pick up a book and they talk about the color of the clothes—'Fuck you. Get outta here! Let me know where life is, fer God's sake!' Nothing to do with anything. 'He ran his stubby fingers through his red hair…' (Laughs).

How did you write and work at the same time?

I worked as a clerk, as a secretary, any old thing. It took me about six years [to finish my first book]. I came home every night from work and just wrote. There's a part of *Last Exit* called *Tralala,* it's about twenty pages long. It took me two and a half years to write those twenty pages. And I'm writing every night after work—couple of hours every night. And I eventually realize, what I'm doing is thinking out loud. I don't know how to just sit and think. And then I realized, one day—one night—that this story was given me to write so that I could reflect the psychodynamics of an individual through the rhythms and tension of a prose line. Then the story just wrote [itself] as fast as I could type.

I wonder: if I didn't have to spend so much physical energy on jobs, if I'd have had another six books. I don't know. Maybe not. It just takes a lot out of you. I don't have much, physically. I guess I have a lot, but I tire rapidly.

How have you survived?

Precariously. I just had all kinds of jobs. Besides being a clerk, I computed group insurance and administered pension plans for a while.

Anyway, I don't have to work now because I got Social Security, and I finally got my disability benefits from the Second World War. So I've finally got enough coming in.

Do you think that the government should pay people to be artists?

No. God forbid! Keep those rat bastards away.

How did you get an agent?

At the end of six years, I had this book, and Seymour Krim, a guy I hung around with, said he knew some people and he arranged for me to have lunch with some editors at one of the big publishing houses, I don't remember which. And so I had lunch with them, had some Old Granddad Manhattans, probably had some food, too. And they said, "Look, we'll give you a contract to write a regular novel, and after we publish that, we'll publish *Last Exit*, because, as you know, these kind of books don't sell."

I went down to the bar, after work—the Cedar Street Bar—and Roy was there—Amiri Baraka—and I was telling him what happened. And he said, "Well, why don't you get an agent?" And I said, "What do I know from agents?" And he said, "Go up and see Sterling Law, that's Jack's agent." Jack Kerouac. And I don't know how it happened, but I called him. The guy said, "Yeah, come up." A few days later he calls me. And this is one of the few people who said, "I read your manuscript and I think we can make money together." I mean, usually, producers and agents are, "I know it's an art and bupbuppaboopitah…" And this guy said, "You did your job and I know my job. Now let's see what we can work out." And so he gave it to Barney [Rossett] at *Grove* [Press] and that's how it got published. And we all lived happily ever after.

How do you handle letters to the editor?

Once, I had a bunch of short stories, and I thought, "Well, maybe I should try getting them published." So I sent a letter to like *Harper's* and *Esquire* and people like that. *Esquire* wouldn't even reply. They wouldn't even say "No." I am not regarded very highly in literary circles. And *The New Yorker* turned down everything I've ever written. A woman there once many years ago asked if she could see my stories. So we sent them over there and she had some very negative things to say about them. This was eight years ago. I get turned down for grants—well, not anymore, I don't apply, but…NEA's, I tried twice, Guggenheimers…nobody'd give me a penny. Not one penny. According to them, there's only two thousand writers a year who are better than me. This could be true. I doubt it, but I'd like to read them, I'll tell you. 'Cause I've finally accepted, at least to some degree, that I'm pretty good. That I've done things—I've read enough now to see that I've done things that hadn't been done before. I've accepted what people like [novelist/screenwriter] Richie Price have said to me—"You made it possible for us to write." But, that doesn't impress magazines.

Have you done any book tours?

I've never been asked to. I've done a couple of signings.

Do you have an agent and a manager?

Yeah, I have an agent. Manager? There's a manager in the [apartment] building. What's to manage?

Do you have health coverage through the WGA?

If you make money, they get you hospitalization. Medical coverage. No, I haven't made enough money.

Do you teach?

I've been teaching down at USC in the graduate school for about fifteen years. I don't call it teaching. I have a fiction workshop in the graduate school. They have a program called Masters of Professional Writing. Really nice program. The guy who's the head of it, Jim Reagan—wonderful guy, wonderful poet—I've been there all these years.

What about MFA programs?

Well, I'll tell you, I suppose MFA programs are great because at least you don't have to go out and work for a living. If you have an MFA, you can get some kind of sinecure somewhere. You can get grants and things. And from what I hear, if you really know how to work it, you can grant yourself for the rest of your life, if you do those things. But as far as MFA for me or for someone like myself, why bother? When it comes to something like the visual arts, like a painter, an MFA might be helpful.

How about a community for artists?

Community? Absolutely. And I think that's the biggest advantage of this thing I'm involved with at USC, and I tell the students that each semester. That's where the real learning happens—with your peers. You hang out with each other, you lie, you bullshit, whatever you do…you drink, you get drunk. That's where it really happens.

∞

Richard Jefferies Interview

> *Give screenwriting up early. Because it's so hard, and if you think there's the slightest chance you might give it up when I give you that advice, then you should. Because only those who are absolutely dedicated and will settle for nothing less in life, then maybe you've got a shot. It takes that much perseverance. That's how hard it is to make it, to make a living at it.*
>
> **Richard Jefferies, screenwriter**

Richard Jefferies works in the pool house on his property. He writes every day. He works very, very diligently. He bought his house in this posh neighborhood, south of the boulevard (Ventura), before it got so pricey. He remodeled it himself. He has been working in

Richard Jefferies at the *Cold Creek Manor* film premiere, September 13, 2003

Photo courtesy Mark Kirkland

Hollywood for twenty-five plus years and, through sheer perseverance, Jefferies has climbed to the top of the pile and is in the coveted "A" list of writers. Most recently his script, Cold Creek Manor, *was produced by Touchstone Pictures, directed by Mike Figgis and starring Sharon Stone, Dennis Quaid and Stephen Dorff.*

We asked Jefferies about how he became a member of the Writers Guild.

That's a Catch 22. Everybody who joins the Writers Guild has an impossible story like this. It's like joining any union. How do you get in? What happened to me was I got signed at William Morris through a friend of a friend. She read a couple scripts of mine—which were the same couple of scripts that had been floating around for years. Finally somebody who knew someone meaningful read them. She said, "Oh, by the way, do you have an agent?" I didn't at the time. I really had nothing going. I had no agent, no lawyer, no job and my wife was pregnant. I was actually talking to two different agents. I hadn't made a decision yet, and Dodi Gold from William Morris called and said, "I know you haven't made a decision yet, but I've already found a job for you if you want it." Well, given the fact that my wife was pregnant and I had nothing going and money was running out, I said, "Sure, you're my agent. What's the job?" And the job was script doctoring on a Michael Jackson project. You know, for years it wasn't significant to say that, but now he's in the news again so it's sort of creepy and cool that yes, I shook the man's hand and yes, I worked with The King of Pop—and that was an expanded music video to a song called *Smooth Criminal.*

Advice to young screenwriters:

What it took for me? I did carpentry work, special effects work—anything I could get. It's those years after film school, you have a few friends in the business and when you have work, you give them what you can from it and when they have work they bring you in. I wrote in my spare time not making a dime. How did I persevere? I had to pay the mortgage. Seriously. For a few years I thought, psychologically, if I can't take this anymore, I'm just going to get into real estate, remodel houses and flip them, but then one day I realized I couldn't even make nearly as much money doing that, and would I be as happy, really? Could I be? All the same sort of issues come up there. Sure, you design a house, but then a person doesn't want it to look like that. They want it to look stupid. So then, do you make it look stupid just to get the check? It's all the same issues as screenwriting.

It's taken twenty-five years since film school. It took nine years to get an agent who could move me into the mainstream. I had three waves of "you're hot, you're not, you're hot, you're not." I know in the long run it's a steadier course if you stick to what really excites you creatively, and when you find people as allies, stay in touch with them. Most of them, many of them, quit the business; but if you meet them, stick with them. When you meet people you get along with, maintain those relationships.

∞

Murray Mednick Interview

> *Being a playwright is exactly like being a poet: it's not a vocation that will sustain you financially. You don't do this kind of thing as a career choice. I don't have a career. I am a playwright.*
> **Murray Mednick, playwright**

Murray Mednick, who founded the Padua Playwright Productions (which you can find online at www.paduaplaywrights.net/publications*), insists that there is no such thing as a career for a playwright. He says that being a playwright is much like selling snake oil. Mednick has kept himself alive by teaching the craft of playwriting at many universities, and privately as well.*

Can you earn a living as a playwright?

I hardly ever get paid when a play is produced. If it's regional theatre, they might pay a thousand or five hundred dollars. And if it's a commercial run, you get money when the investors get their money back, but very few people get to that point. What kept me going was that I enjoy writing plays. I had a calling to do it.

Advice to young playwrights

The first thing I tell young playwrights is that they [must] have another economic foundation. For example: get a "B" job, hope to receive an inheritance or find a rich boyfriend.

The second thing I tell them is, if you really want to do it, you have to do it from the inside out. Get involved with theater. You aren't going to learn by taking a class in a college. Because by calling it a career they are already starting on a bullshit basis, so there is a lie there which is to promote the teaching but has nothing to do with the art of writing plays. You don't learn much in playwriting classes. They don't teach it like an art. If you work with a playwright as an artist you learn more. Get a mentor. That is the best way to learn. You have to do things on your own.

Still, don't rely on the theater world. You get co-opted and become a playwright, not an artist, and it is an act to satisfy these theatre people. Your plays are what they expect you to write and they have a certain sound like all the other plays. They all sound the same and have the same conceits.

Another thing: many people think writing plays is like writing television or movies, but it's not. The characters are alive on stage and it's in the present. It is a different kind of writing altogether, a different kind of mind. I wrote screenplays, and it's an interes   Ing form, but very different. When most people think of playwriting, they think in terms of television storytelling, which is very shallow and not the medium for which theater is intended. In plays, characters talk more and it's more about ideas. Characters are live on the stage and there's something that happens in theatre which is akin to catharsis. [It's a form] based on our old masters, the Greeks and Shakespeare, and if you study them, you find you can do things in playwriting that cannot be done in any other medium. There is nothing like it. It is a very high art.

How do you get an agent?

It's a commercial thing. If they think they can make money on you, they'll call you. You'll attract them with your work.

Work habits?

I work every morning. For maybe two hours. There is no such thing as retiring. It's like being a painter. It's not like a business. Unfortunately, it's run like a business, but it's more like an art. And no, I don't have a retirement fund. I have to keep working.

Is it worth it?

It's a wonderful art, but it's not a career. I cannot emphasize that enough. The best way to learn is to be involved in a good theatre company. You need to be prepared for all the ego and vanity that goes down. It has to be a calling. Ask yourself this question: "Are you obliged to write plays?"

∞

Dana Gioia Interview

> *Being a poet is very impractical.*
>
> **Dana Gioia, poet**

Dana Gioia, poet, is the current head of the National Endowment for the Arts. He has three books of poetry published with Graywolf Press. *His third book won the* American Book Award. *Gioia has written countless essays, including the controversial* Can Poetry Matter? *(originally published in* The Atlantic Monthly, *then later in book form). He's written an opera libretto, compiled many anthologies and was a businessman at General Foods from 1977 until 1992. We spoke with him in between meetings in Washington, DC, to get his perspective on being a poet.*

What do poets do?

Very few poets in history only write poetry. Poetry is a calling, rather than a business. If you do it well enough, you can make a living from it—not, probably, from writing poetry itself, but from writing poetry, reading your poems, talking about poetry, reviewing poetry, anthologizing poetry, doing programs about poetry, teaching and writing poetry and teaching literature. And a poet should not over-specialize. Being a poet should allow you to do other things, from book reviewing to staging works to teaching to performing. And one of the advantages of poetry is that you could have another job, as I did or many other poets did, and write on your off hours.

Woody Allen said, "Ninety percent of success is showing up." And there is wisdom in that remark. I mean if you are a good writer or musician or whatever you should welcome opportunities to travel and perform, even if they are exhausting. And you should welcome opportunities to introduce your work to new audiences. These gigs will be magnificent. Some of them will be unsatisfying. But the cumulative impact of doing this will be to develop and sustain a reputation. The bigger one's reputation, the greater one's freedom. There was a famous opera singer who once said that success is the freedom to say no. And what she meant by this was that success is the freedom to say no to those things you really don't want to do, and not have to do them because you're desperate for money.

Agents, Unions and PR

I've never had an agent. No, I've never belonged to a writers' union. I suppose I could use an agent for my prose works, my anthologies and my theatrical works, but I prefer to work directly with my partners—publishers and things like this. The thing is that no poet needs an agent to succeed. If you are sufficiently successful, an agent might save you some work. But it's ridiculous for poets to think that if they have an agent it's all going to be done for them. Even then, prose writers start by writing and sending out their own work. An agent should come to you because they see how good you are.

I've made a very good living being a writer for twelve years without an agent, without a manager, without a publicist. But I also work seven days a week. Most people don't want to hear this. They want to hear, "So what's this little formula I need to succeed?"

Advice

The artist's first and foremost task is excellence. Whether an artist is concerned with commercial or aesthetic success, the focus of his efforts should be on being the best artist possible. I do believe that a bad painter or a dull writer can adopt the most disciplined and reasonable marketing strategy and still fail because the works themselves are not engaging or memorable or powerful.

I got a letter yesterday from a poet [asking] how can he find an agent and get his work out there, and I think that that question is in itself the wrong question to ask. One should ask, "How could you write better to attract people to your work?" Now, I think it's important if you are a writer to understand the possible markets for your work and try to understand where your talents overlap with places in the market. But having said that, I think it is almost always a mistake to write in some narrow sense for the marketplace. Ironically, what makes a writer saleable are those very things that make him different from the other things that are being sold. A writer needs individuality and the unique quality that cannot be found elsewhere. For example, those journalists who are most successful are the ones that have an identifiable personal voice.

My advice would be: to be commercially successful, be artistically successful. In order to be commercially visible, be artistically identifiable. Create the voice, the style, the vision that differentiates your work from the other work around it. That task can only be accomplished by looking inside yourself and developing what you honestly possess. There's no formula for it.

∞

James McManus Interview

> *Luck is huge, perseverance is bigger.*
> **James McManus, writer, professor**

We spoke to James McManus over the telephone and found him to be full of life experience with tools of excellence useful for readers of this book. McManus has written four novels, a collection of short stories, a couple of books of poetry and a non-fiction work, Positively Fifth Street, *which began as an article about the World Series of Poker for* Harper's Magazine *and ended up as a book published by* Farrar Strauss. *He also teaches at the School of Art Institute of Chicago.*

He told us how he survived and got representation at the beginning of his career. He's had a literary agent for twenty-two years. His first agent responded to something published in a literary magazine, and his next agent was the agent of one of his teachers. He won an NEA fellowship for poetry in 1979 and published his novel, Out of the Blue *in 1984. He supported his family with a part-time teaching job until his writing started to pay off. Here are the principles that McManus followed to become a writer of note.*

Drop the post-modernist bullshit

I think that so many young artists feel that they have to make something that middle-class parents hate. They despise the mainstream. They wear their alienation on their sleeves. They think, "Well, because I'm alienated, I should be an artist." I don't think there's any real connection between alienation and artistic talent. So many people who are just angry, depressed and politically estranged go into the arts. I think that is the absolute wrong approach. Anyway, if you want to get paid for your work, you probably shouldn't have that attitude.

Put your obsessions to work

Probably the best place to start is to write what you are obsessed about, what you can't shut up about. Given the same level of writing talent, work done with passion, enthusiasm and expertise will carry the day.

Make it maximally good

Whatever entry-level writing you're doing, whether for the school paper or the local *Gazette*, try to make it maximally good; because generally you move up in stages based on how good your previous piece was. So you're not going to write for *Harper's* or *The New Yorker* right off the bat, but you need to do a killer piece at every stage. Don't toss stuff off. Go for the best possible version of whatever it is you're writing, no matter how humble the forum.

Write longer pieces

The actual writing process tends not to be thrilling. There are moments of "thrillingness," but by and large you need to grind it out. Writing longer narrative prose is the best way to earn a living as a writer—maybe not the best, but you're more likely to earn a living writing narrative prose.

Socialize, but remember your roots

I'm not a community-type guy. I think that community, in the sense that you get fellow readers in the classroom workshop, is helpful. You can also form useful advisory and editorial relationships with older writers in MFA programs. People can get the illusion that they are being a writer by going to literary parties and the like; but I think it's important to remember the main action is the writer alone in a room.

Persevere

I think you have to have your ass in the chair many hours a week. A lot of young artists seem to have the impression that art is a game, the opposite of a job. But it is a job. A work ethic is underrated in the literary arts community. Without talent a work ethic is not going to get you very far, but I think that is the *sine qua non*, what's the Latin translation of that? "Without which nothing will happen." The talent is the easy part. The work ethic is the hard part.

∞

Art That Pays

Appendix A: Job Resources

Links

Academy of America Poets, 588 Broadway, Suite 604, New York, NY 10012-3210; Tel: 212 274-0343; www.poets.org/academy/

Administrative Service Announcements American Symphony Orchestra League, 3 West 60th Street, 5th Floor, New York, NY 10023; Tel: 202 776-0217; E-mail: league@symphony.org, www.symphony.org

AECT Career Information Center Association for Educational Communities and Technology, 1800 North Stonelake Drive, Suite 2, Bloomington, IN 47404; Tel: 812 335 7675; Fax: 812 335-7678; E-mail: aect@aect.org www.aect.org

Affirmative Action Register, Joyce R. Green, Editor, Affirmative Action Register, Inc. 8365 Olive Boulevard, St. Louis, MO 63132; Tel: 314-991-1335, 800-537-0655; E-mail: aareeo@concecntric.net www.aar-eeo.com

Americans for the Arts
Washington Office, 1000 Vermont Avenue, NW, 6th Floor, Washington, DC 20005; Tel: 202 371-2830; Fax: 202 371-0424; *New York Office,* One East 53rd Street, New York, NY 10022; Tel: 212 223-2787; Fax: 212 980-4857; www.artsusa.org/

Art & Design Career Employment Sponsored by Northern Michigan University Dept of Art and Design. Contact lists in all fields of the visual arts, listing of art and design employment agencies and links for international employment opportunities. Department of Art & Design, Northern Michigan University, 1401 Presque Isle Avenue, Marquette, MI 49855-5339; Tel: 906 227-2194; art.nmu.edu/department/home.html

Art in America Art in America, Inc., 575 Broadway, New York, NY 10012; Tel: 212 941-2808; www.artinamericamagazine.com/

Artjobonline Lists job and internship opportunities. 1743 Wazee Street, Suite 300, Denver, CO 80202; Tel: 888 562-7232, 303 °629-1166; www.artjob.org

ArtCareer Network Membership web site devoted to employment opportunities in the arts. www.artcareer.net/

Artist Resource Lists jobs and internships in the fields of art and design and jobs for writers. www.artistresource.org/jobs.htm

ArtSearch, Theatre Communications Group, 355 Lexington Ave., New York, NY 10017; 212 697-5230; E-mail: tcg@tcg.org   www.tcg.org

Artsjobs Employment information in arts administration, graphics, photography, music, theater, arts education and other areas of the arts, both in the US and abroad. groups.yahoo.com/subscribe.cgi/ARTSJOBS

Artslynx International Arts jobs information. www.artslynx.org/jobs.htm

Associated Writers Programs, George Mason University Mailstop 1E3, Fairfax, VA 22030-4444; Tel: 703 993-4301; E-mail: awp@gmu.edu www.awpwriter.org/

Association of Performing Arts Presenters 112 16th Street, NW, Suite 400, Washington DC, 20036; Tel: 888 820-2787, 202 833-2787; www.artspresenters.org/

AVISO American Association of Museums, 1575 Eye Street, NW, Suite 400, Washington, DC, 20005; 202 289-1818; E-mail: aviso@aa-us.org www.aam-us.org/aviso

California Poets in the Schools, 1333 Balboa St., #3, San Francisco, CA 94118; Tel: 415 221-4201, 877 274-8764; www.cpits.org/

Chamber Music Magazine Chamber Music America, 305 7th Ave., New York, NY 10001; Tel: 212 242-2022; E-mail: info@chamber-music.org www.chamger-music.org

Chronicle Careers The Chronicle of Higher Education, 1255 23rd St., N.W., Suite 700, Washington, D.C. 20037; Tel: 202 466-1000; www.chronicle.com/jobs/

College Art Association of America 275 7th Ave., New York, NY 10001; Tel: 212 691-105; E-mail: newyorkoffice@collegeart.org www.collegeart.org

Employment Opportunities National Guild of Community Schools of the Arts, PO Box 8018, Englewood, NJ 07631; Tel: 201 871-333; E-mail: info@nationalguild.org www.nationalguild.org

History News Dispatch American Association for State and Local History, 530 Church Street, Nashville, TN 37219; Tel: 615 320-3203; E-mail: history@aaslh.org www.aaslh.org

IAAM News International Association of Assembly Managers, 4425 West Airport Freeway, Suite 590, Irving, TX 75062; Tel: 972 255-8020; E-mail: tamml.trull@iam.org www.iaam.org

International Society for the Performing Arts Foundation 17 Purdy Avenue, PO Box 909, Rye, NY 10580; Tel: 914 921-1550; E-mail: info@ispa.org www.ispa.org

The International Ticketing Association Newsletter 250 West 57th Street, Suite 722, New York, NY 10107; Tel: 212 581-0600; E-mail: info@intix.org www.intix.org

Job Contact Bulletin Southeastern Theatre Conference, PO Box 9868, Greensboro, NC 27429; Tel: 336 272-0868; E-mail: staff@setc.org www.setc.org

Mid-Atlantic Arts Organization, MAAF, 22 Light Street, Suite 300, Baltimore, MD 21202; Tel: 410 539-6656; www.artistsandcommunities.org/

National Guild of Community Schools of the Arts E-mail: mayadas@verizon.net; www.nationalguild.org/index.html

National Network for Artist Placement, NNAP 935 W. Avenue 37, Los Angeles, CA 90065; Tel: 323 222-4035; E-mail: NNAPnow@aol.com www.artistplacement.com

New York Foundation for the Arts, NYFA, Current Jobs List New York Foundation for the Arts, 155 Avenue of the Americas, 14th Floor, New York, NY 10013-1507; Tel: 212 366-6900; Fax: 212 366-1778; www.nyfa.org/opportunities.asp?type=Job&id=94&fid=6&sid=17

Online Poetry Classroom
E-mail: webmaster@onlinepoetryclassroom.org
www.onlinepoetryclassroom.org/

Opportunity NOCs The Management Center, 580 California Street, Suite 200, San Francisco, CA 94104-1008; Tel: 415 362-9735; Fax: 415 362-4603; E-mail: tmc@tmcenter.org www.tmcenter.org

Release Print Film Arts Foundation, 346 Ninth Street, 2nd Floor, San Francisco, CA 94103; Tel:415 552-8760; E-mail: innbo@filmarts.org www.filmarts.org

Teachers & Writers Collaborative, 5 Union Square West, New York, NY 10003-3306; Tel: 888 BOOKS-TW, 212-691-6590; Fax: 212 675-0171; email: info@twc.org; www.twc.org/ with links to other sites for teaching in the schools.

United Arts/COMPAS 416 Landmark Center, 75 West 5th Street, St. Paul, MN 55102; Tel: 615 292-3222; E-mail: compass@migizi.org www.compass.org

Variety Michael Stanton, 5700 Wilshire Blvd., Suite 120, Los Angeles, CA 90036; Tel: 323857-6600; www.variety.com/index.asp?layout=classifieds

Virginia Commission for the Arts
www.arts.state.va.us/artsjobs.htm

Art That Pays

Appendix B: Basics Resources

Housing

General

The 100 Best Small Art Towns in America: Where to Discover Creative Communities, Fresh Air, and Affordable Housing by John Villani, John Muir Publications, revised 1996. P.O. Box 613, Santa Fe, NM 87504. With a title that long, do I have to describe it?

Alliance of Artists Communities Arts communities, job opportunities, great links.
www.artistcommunities.org/links-resources.html

If You're Thinking of Living in …All About 115 Great Neighborhoods in and Around New York, Michael Leahy, editor, Three Rivers Press, 1st edition, February 1999. Random House, Inc., 280 Park Avenue, New York, NY 10017; Fax: 212 940-7381. A guidebook for neighborhoods and housing in 115 neighborhoods in New York, drawn from the NY Times column of the same name.
www.randomhouse.com/crown/trp.html

The Live/Work Institute, a not-for-profit founded to advocate, assist and encourage the development of live/work and zero commute housing. Thomas Dolan Architecture, Embarcadero West, 173 Filbert Street, Oakland, California 94607; E-mail: tda@live-work.com
www.live-work.com/

Artist Housing in California

The Brewery A 1990 Harvard study reported The Brewery to be the world's largest artist-in-residence complex. The 23-acre Brewery is an outstanding example of adaptive reuse. In 1982, the abandonedPabst Blue Ribbon brewery was reborn as an artists' community. Today comprising 22 buildings, including a structure from 1888 as well as one of the city's first power stations, the complex is home to more than 500 artists who live and/or work onsite. The waiting list is 2 years long (though not always followed). They accept professional artists, and do not allow pets or children. The cost is from $.60 to $.80 per square foot and the 300 spaces are live/work spaces ranging from 300 to 6000 square feet. 1920 N. Main Street Los Angeles, CA 90031; Tel: 213 694-2911; www.breweryart.org/

Los Angeles Downtown Artist District is a city-designated redevelopment area with 2,500 spaces with 300 to 400 in live/work condition. They rent to the "creative professional," which can be enforced by having a business license. They rent from $.80 to $1.20 per square foot.

A View of the Los Angeles Artist Loft District
lalofts.mine.nu/

 Los Angeles Art and Music Festival _Downtown Artist District, Los Angeles, 300 Santa Fe Ave. to 400 Santa Fe Ave., From 3rd St. to the 4th St. bridge. laamf.org/

Santa Fe Arts Colony is privately owned industrial buildings that have been developed by Marvin Feidler to be a stable productive community of artists. Out of the 57 units approximately 85% of them are live/work lofts and cost anywhere from $.50 to $.80 a square foot. 2401 South Santa Fe Los Angeles, CA 90058;
Tel: 323 587-5513; www.santafeartcolony.com/indexIE.html

ArtShare Los Angeles Owned by artists and arts organization the 30 live and workspaces are between 500 and 2,000 square feet, and cost between $.60 and $.76 per foot. Volunteer participation in youth programs can substitute for rent. East 4th Place, Los Angeles, CA; Tel: 213 687-4art; www.artsharela.org

Artist Housing in Chicago

Acme Artists Community in West Town is an artist-planned and owned community in Chicago. They planned to create 25 affordable live/ work spaces for artists in addition to space for three non-profit organizations. Only working professional artists need apply. Contact Laura Weathered, 2418 W. Bloomingdale, Chicago, IL 60647; Tel: 773 278-7677; Fax: 773 278-8451; email: info@twc.org nnwac@artswire.org

Co-Housing in the Chicago Area A list of housing communities. www.chicagocohousing.net/

Artist Housing in New York

Bretton Hall, Southeast corner of Broadway & 86th Street, New York, NY; Tel: 212 787-7000

Common Ground Community is a subsidized living housing facility. According to a 1993 article there were 80 artists living there. 505 Eighth Ave., 15th floor, New York, NY 10018; Tel: 212-389-9334; Fax: 212-389-9312; email: info@commonground.org www.commonground.org/

Manhattan Plaza, 400 West 43rd Street, New York, NY 10036; Tel: 212 97-0660

New York Coalition for Artist's Housing, Brooklyn Arts Council. Coordinates the development of safe, legal, permanent, secure and affordable artist communities. w w w . b r o o k l y n a r t s c o u n c i l . o r g / indexcfm?fuseaction=organizationdetail&category_id=3&organization_id=225&ts=0422003150217

Westbeth, 463 West Street, New York 10014; Submit an application with references. There are 383 units in this community set in Greenwich Village. You must have been a professional artist and a committee will review your application. Send a SSAE to the above address. There is a waiting list of 7 to 10 years. www.westbeth.org/index.html

Commercial Links for Housing

ApartmentHunterz.com 454 S. Robertson Blvd., Suite B, Beverly Hills, CA 90211; Tel: 310 276-4663; Fax: 310 276-2700; email: info@4rentinla.com   www.apartmenthunterz.com

EasyRoommate.com
Tel: 800 877-2257; www.EasyRoommate.com

LARental.com/Rental Express, 6230 Wilshire Blvd., # 112, Los Angeles, CA 90048; Tel: 310 388-5618; E-mail: info@larental.com www.larental.com

Metro Rent
Tel: 323 848-3490; www.metrorent.com

Rentimes 7901 Melrose Ave., #205, Los Angeles, CA 90046; Tel: 323 653-7368; www.rentimes.com

Roommate Express 3100 S. Rural Road #1, Tempe, AZ 85282; Tel:800 487-8050, 480 966-4121, Fax: 480 966-0483; www.roommateexpress.com

Roommate.com
www.roommate.com

Sublet.com
Tel: 877 367-7368; www.Sublet.com

RoommateAccess.com
Tel: 866 823-2200; www.RoommateAccess.com

Westside Rental Connection
Tel: 310 395-7368, 877 872-6998; www.westsiderentals.com

Telephone Service Providers

Visit these web sites for plans and services available in your area:

SBC:
www.sbc.com/

AT&T:
www.att.com/

MCI:
www.mci.com/

Sprint:
www.sprint.com/

Nextel:
www.nextel.com/

T-mobile:
www.tmobile.com/

Verizon:
www.verizon.com/

Unemployment insurance

The Beehive, a nonprofit, internet-based organization that has helpful information about unemployment insurance and how to apply for unemployment. You can find the agency nearest you and get information about your benefits.
www.thebeehive.org/jobs/contests/unemployment-insurance.asp

US Department of Labor Employment & Training Administration Great information about getting assistance when you are without a job. U.S. Department of Labor, Frances Perkins Building, 200 Constitution Avenue NW, Washington, DC 20210;
Tel: 877 US-2JOBS;
www.workforcesecurity.doleta.gov/unemploy/aboutui.asp

Publicity

Center for Cultural Innovation "Advancing the business of art."
www.cci2002.org/

Fine Artist's Guide to Marketing and Self-Promotion by Julius Vitali, Allworth Press, 1996. 12 East 23 Street, Suite 510, New York, NY 10010. Tel: 212 777-8395. Fax: 212 777-8261; www.allworth.com

Fine Art Publicity: The Complete Guide for Galleries and Artists by Susan Abbott & Barbara Webb, Allworth Press, 1991. 12 East 23 Street, Suite 510, New York, NY 10010. Tel: 212 777-8395. Fax: 212 777-8261; www.allworth.com

Getting the Word Out: An Artist's Guide to Self Promotion, Carolyn Blakeslee, editor, Art Calendar Publishing, Inc., 1995. P.O. Box 2675, Salisbury, MD 21802; www.artcalendar.com

Jean Hester teaches web marketing workshops...this is her cool site. www.divestudio.org/index.php

Publicity, Chicago Artists' Coalition. 11 East Hubbard Street, 7th Floor, Chicago, IL 60611. Part of a series of self-help guides for artists. www.caconline.org.

Stage Directions Guide to Publicity by Stephen Peithman & Neil Offen, Heinemann, 1999. Written particularly for the small theatre. P.O. Box 6926 Portsmouth, NH 03802-6926; Tel: 800 225-5800; Fax: 603 431-2214; www.heinemann.com

Health Facilities, Service Providers and Assisted Health Plans

New York

Bellevue Hospital Center
"Care provided to all, regardless of ability to pay."
462 First Avenue
New York, New York 10016
Tel: 212 562-4141
www.nyc.gov/html/hhc/bellevue/home.html

Family Health Plus
Public health insurance program for those who do not have health insurance but have too high an income to qualify for Medicaid.
Tel: 877 934-7587
www.health.state.ny.us/nysdoh/fhplus/index.htm

Healthy NY Program
Provides affordable health insurance for those who are without. Cost and qualifications vary. Tel: 866 432-5849
www.ins.state.ny.us/healthny.htm

Planned Parenthood of New York City
Women's healthcare and testing, sliding scale fees available. Three locations:

> Boro Hall Center
> 44 Court Street
> (between Remsen and Joralemon Streets)
> Brooklyn, New York 11201
>
> Margaret Sanger Center
> 26 Bleecker Street
> (at Mott Street)
> New York, New York 10012
>
> Bronx Center
> 349 East 149th Street
> (at Courtlandt Avenue)
> Bronx, New York 10451

Tel: 212 965-7000 or 800 230-PLAN
www.ppnyc.org/services/health.html

Prenatal Care Assistance Program
Provides healthcare throughout pregnancy, delivery and at least two months after, plus healthcare for the baby for at least one year after birth. Certain income guidelines apply, though even those with some medical coverage may be eligible. Tel: 800 522-5006; www.health.state.ny.us/nysdoh/pcap/index.htm

Los Angeles

Health Consumer Center
Helps people, particularly low-income, to get needed health care.
13327 Van Nuys Blvd.
Pacoima, CA 91331-3099
Tel:800 896-3203; Fax:818 834-7552
www.healthconsumer.org/LosAngeles.html

LA County-USC Healthcare Network (previously LA County-USC
Medical Center)
Overall health services/acute care hospital available to all regardless
of ability to pay.
1200 N. State St.
Los Angeles, CA 90033
Tel: 323 226-2622
E-mail: webmaster@dhs.co.la.ca.us
dhs.co.la.ca.us/phcommon/public/adrs/
adrsprogdetail.cfm?orgid=118&unit=lacusc&prog=lacusc&ou=dhs

Los Angeles County Department of Health Services
No-Cost or Low-Cost Health Insurance
Listings for:
Community Clinics
Hospitals
PPP Providers (Public/Private Partnership Program
for those less able to
pay.)

313 N. Figueroa Street
Los Angeles, CA 90012
www.ladhs.org/

Art That Pays

The Los Angeles Free Clinic
www.lafreeclinic.org/
Provides health care free of charge and free of judgment. Services include: general healthcare, women's health and wellness, dental care legal services high risk youth program, mental health and social services, prenatal care family planning, education and outreach. They have establishments at the following three locations:

> Beverly Clinic
> 8405 Beverly Blvd.
> Los Angeles, CA 90048
> Tel: 323 653-8622; Fax: 323 658-6773

> Hollywood Center
> 6043 Hollywood Blvd.
> Los Angeles, CA 90028
> Tel: 323 653-8622; Fax: 323 462-6731

> Hollywood Wilshire Health Center
> 5205 Melrose Avenue
> Los Angeles, CA 90038
> Tel: 323 653-8622; Fax: 323 337-1892

National Center of Excellence in Women's Health
Provides a comprehensive listing of UCLA women's health resources, many for low-income patients.
womenshealth.med.ucla.edu/

Clinic:
> Iris Cantor-UCLA Women's Health Center
> 100 UCLA Medical Plaza, Suite 290
> Los Angeles, CA 90095-7075
> Tel: 310 794-9830
> or
> 800 UCLA-MD1

Planned Parenthood
Testing and healthcare for pregnancy- and sex-related issues for women, as well as sexually related healthcare for men. Twelve locations in Los Angeles.
Tel: 800 230-7526 for locations and/or appointments.
www.pplosangeles.org/

Venice Family Clinic
Free health care to the uninsured. The largest free clinic in the US. Four distinct sites.
Primary health care for those with no other access to health care:
> Venice Family Clinic
> 604 Rose Ave.
> Venice, CA 90291
>
> Pico Facility
> 2509 Pico Blvd.
> Santa Monica, CA 90405

Teen Clinic and Women's Clinic:
> Venice Health Center
> 905 Venice Blvd.
> Venice, CA 90291

Social service referrals, individual and family counseling, Medi-Cal, weekly support groups, children's health programs, health programs:
> Frederick R. Weisman Family Center
> 622 Rose Avenue
> Venice, CA 90291

Appointment Line (for all four sites): 310 392-8636;
www.venicefamilyclinic.org/

Westside Women's Health Center
Affordable women's health clinic and health referral service.
1711 Ocean Park Boulevard
Santa Monica, CA 90405
Tel: 310 450-2191
www.wwhcenter.org/

Actors' Fund of America
www.actorsfund.org/

The Actors' Fund of America is a national organization with offices in New York, Los Angeles, and Chicago. Its services are not restricted to actors, but are available to all bona fide professionals working in any capacity as an entertainment professional, including: designers, writers, sound technicians, musicians, dancers, administrators, directors, film editors, stagehands, electricians—as well as actors. In addition to providing emergency grants for essentials such as food, rent and medical care, The Actors' Fund provides: counseling, substance abuse and mental health services, senior and disabled care, nursing home and assisted living care, an AIDS Initiative, The Actors' Work Program, the Phyllis Newman Women's Health Initiative, the Artists' Health Insurance Resource Center, and supportive housing on both coasts.
Services include:

- Financial assistance grants for essential living expenses such as food, rent, utilities, and payment of hospital, medical and dental bills.
- Psychotherapy and counseling focusing on performance anxiety, career problems, drug and alcohol abuse and other topics.
- AIDS Initiative—with services including counseling, support groups, supportive housing, educational seminars, financial assistance and a resource library.

- Educational seminars on a wide variety of subjects including money management, subletting and roommates, the creative personality, reaching 65 as an active professional, and coping with everyday life.
- A Survival Jobs Program (New York) providing entertainment professionals with temporary employment between engagements.
- Blood drives in Chicago, Los Angeles and New York, which provide hundreds of pints annually.
- Funeral arrangements and burials throughout the United States.
- A Conrad Cantzen Shoe Fund and the Mandel Christmas Fund.
- Actors' Fund Home—a nationally renowned retirement residence in Englewood, New Jersey.
- The Aurora—a shared housing residence in Manhattan, for persons with AIDS, seniors and low-income working professionals.
- The Palm View—apartments for persons with AIDS in West Hollywood, CA.
- The Actors' Work Program which offers career counseling and help in developing a second career, plus regular workshops on job search techniques, interviewing and resume writing.
- Nursing and nursing home care, as well as home visitations and home care for those who need special attention.
- Artists' Health Insurance Resource Center—an online database with information to help artist get and keep health insurance, find health care when uninsured and receive financial assistance for medical bills.

The Actors' Fund Locations:

National Headquarters, The Actors' Fund of America
729 Seventh Avenue, 10th Floor, New York, New York
10019; Tel: 212 221-7300; Fax: 212 764-0238

The Aurora Residence:
New York, New York 10019; Tel:212 489-2020
Fax: 212 489-1116

Musician's Assistance Program: A.F.M. Local 802
322 West 48th Street, New York, New York 10036;
Tel:212 397-4802

Midwestern Region: The Actors' Fund of America
203 N. Wabash, Suite 2104, Chicago, Illinois 60601;
Tel: 312 372-0989; Fax: 312 372-0272

Western Region: The Actors' Fund of America
5757 Wilshire Boulevard, Suite 400, Los Angeles, California
90036; Tel: 323 933-9244 Fax: 323 933-7615

Nursing Home and Assisted Living Care Facility:
The Actors' Fund of America Englewood, New Jersey 07631;
Tel: 201 871-8882; Fax: 201 871-9511

The Actors' Work Program—NY
729 Seventh Avenue New York, New York l0019;
Tel: 212 354-5480 Fax: 212 921-4295

The Actors' Work Program—LA
5757 Wilshire Boulevard, Suite 400 Los Angeles, California
90036; Tel: 323 933-9244; Fax: 323 933-7615

The Palm View:
Palm Avenue, West Hollywood, CA
Tel: 323 933-9244

Recovery Program

MAP—Musicians' Assistance Program. "Providing help to members of the music community who seek treatment for drug and alcohol addiction—regardless of their financial condition." Based in Los Angeles, with branches in Akron OH, Atlanta GA, Austin TX, Boston MA, Chicago IL, Reno NV, London England, Miami FL, Minneapolis MN, Nashville TN, New Orleans, New York NY, Seattle WA; Tel LA: 323 993-3197, 888 MAP-MAP1; www.map2000.org/

Art That Pays

Appendix C: Financial Resources

Organizations

Accountants for the Public Interest
(From their website) "Accountants for the Public Interest (API) is a national network of affiliates through which accountants volunteer their time and expertise to non-profit organizations who need but cannot afford professional accounting services. Accounting volunteers provide direct service (assisting with tax preparation, preparing for the annual audit, establishing record-keeping systems and setting up or computerizing accounting systems), advisory service (financial management, budgets, cash flow forecasts, loan applications) and community affairs services (workshops on a variety of financial topics, serving on non-profits' boards of directors, advising local governmental agencies on accounting, tax, budget and other financial issues)."

Contact:
University of Baltimore
Thurnel Business Center, Room 155
1420 North Charles Street
Baltimore, MD 21201
Phone: 410 837-6533
www.geocities.com/api_woods/api/apihome.html

New York State affiliates:
Barbara Gerson, Volunteer Coordinator
The Support Center of New York
API-Accounting Aid Program

305 7th Avenue, 11th Floor
New York, NY 10001
Phone: 212 924-6744
Fax: 212 924-9544

Carlos Icaza
Community Tax Aid, Inc.
P.O. Box 1040, Cathedral Station
New York, NY 10025
Phone: 800 225-0256
ID# 98741

American Institute of Certified Public Accountants They have a great web page describing what to expect from a pro bono CPA and lists of places that will provide free accounting help. www.aicpa.org/pubs/jofa/nov1999/shafer.html

Center for Cultural Innovation (CCI) is in the business of advancing artists. CCI was launched in 2001 as a financial and management support center for self-employed artists, small arts businesses and the nonprofit arts sector. CCI runs moderately priced workshops on varied topics from copyright and contract information to Web design. All the work focuses on the needs of artists and creative entrepreneurs. GREAT resource, founded and run by Judith Luther Wilder. CCI, 8559 Higuera St., Suite A, Culver City, CA 90232; Tel: 310 815-8011; Fax: 310 815-8035; E-mail: info@cci2002.org; www.cci2002.org/

Community Accountants (CA) provides pro bono accounting-related services through volunteers to help nonprofit organizations become self-sufficient.
Contact:
Debra Collligan, Program Director,
3721 Midvale Avenue
Philadelphia, PA 19129
215-951-0330 ext. 125; Fax: 215-951-0342;

www.volunteersolutions.org/volunteerway/volunteer/
agency/one_181104.html

CPAs for the Public Interest
550 W. Jackson, Suite 900
Chicago, IL 60661
Tel: 312 993-0407
www.cpaspi.org/cpaspi/index.htm

How do I Find a Volunteer Accountant?
www.nonprofits.org/npofaq/16/42.html

Other Business Help

Business Volunteers for the Arts Online Business professionals helping not-for-profits improve their business practices. Listings of local and regional offices.
www.artsandbusiness.org/bvahome.htm

Retirement Accounts

American Century A good solid firm that has no-load retirement accounts (meaning you don't pay anything up front.) The web site has a lot of good information.
www.americancentury.com/workshop/articles/faq.jsp

Smart Money.com   Good info. A for-profit site that has a magazine connected to it.
www.smartmoney.com/retirement/ira/
index.cfm?story=taxfree

General Info A list of sites that can help you research retirement accounts:
www.infospot.com/cgi-bin/meta_results.cgi?Terms=pension

Checkbooks, Record Keeping, Spending Plan

Bankrate.com Good article on the difference between a spending plan and a budget. 11811 U.S. Highway 1, North Palm Beach, FL 33408, Tel: 561-630-2400; Fax: 561-625-4540 www.bankrate.com/brm/news/sav/20000905.asp

Debtors Anonymous
General Service Office
PO Box 920888, Needham, MA 02492-0009;
Tel: 781 453-2743; Fax: 781 453-2745;
E-mail: webmaster@debtorsanonymous.org
www.debtorsanonymous.org/default.htm

Mid-Atlantic Debtors Anonymous A 12 Step Recovery program with good information on spending plans. www.midatlanticda.org/Default.htm

Quicken www.quicken.com/

Recordkeeping Kit by Barbara A. Sloan, AKAS II, revised 1999. P.O. Box 123, Hot Springs, AR 71902-0123. Includes bookkeeping basics and completed sample record keeping forms. www.akasii.com

Safeguard Systems has been in business since 1956 and makes commercial checking products. This web site can help you find your local distributor. A reliable product. SAFEGUARD Business Systems, Alexander Business Systems Ltd., #101-771 Vanalman Ave., Victoria, B.C. V8Z 3B8; Tel: 250 727-3699, 800 909-3611; Fax: 250 727-3449; www.gosafeguard.com/

Spending Plan: A Spiritual Tool A personal account by a member of the 12 Step program Debtors Anonymous. www.solvency.org/spendingplan.htm

Tax Information

AKAS II Source for artist tax guides, record keeping kits and tax forms. www.akasii.com

New Tax Guide for Artists of Every Persuasion, The: Actors, Directors, Musicians, Singers, and Other Show Biz Folk Visual Artists and Writers by Peter Jason Riley, Limelight Editions, 2002. 118 East 30th Street, New York, NY 10016; Tel: 212 532-5525; Fax: 212 532-5526; www.limelighteditions.com

The Tax Workbook for Artists and Others by Susan Harvey Dawson, ArtBusiness, Inc., revised annually. 223 North St. Asaph Street, Alexandria, VA 22314.

Tax Forms

1040.com www.1040.com/

California Franchise Tax Board www.ftb.ca.gov/forms/

Federation of Tax Administrators www.taxadmin.org/fta/link/forms.html

Illinois Department of Revenue www.revenue.state.il.us/taxforms/

Internal Revenue Service They have just about everything you need. www.irs.gov/formspubs/

LSU Libraries, Tax Forms www.lib.lsu.edu/govdocs/taxes.html

New York State Department of Tax and Finance www.tax.state.ny.us/forms/

Tax and Accounting Sites Directory. www.taxsites.com/forms.html

Art That Pays

Appendix D: Internet Resources

Free E-mail Providers
angelfire.lycos.com/
email.about.com/cs/freeemail/
mail.yahoo.com
www.hotmail.com/
www.emailaccounts4free.com/
www.emailaddresses.com/email_web.htm
www.fepg.net/
www.freecenter.com/email.html
www.iopus.com/guides/bestpopsmtp.htm
www.mail.com/
www.passtheshareware.com/free_email.htm
www.totallyfreestuff.com/
index.asp?Level1=Email+Accounts
www.your-free-email.com/

Free Internet Access
Open Studio's site for free Internet access.
www.benton.org/openstudio/home.html

Stuff for Your Website
host99.com/freeemail.htm

www.totallyfreestuff.com/

www.webstat.com/

Software Download Sites

download.com.com/

freewebtools.com/

www.cnet.com/

www.freedownloadscenter.com/

www.freewarefiles.com/

www.gnu.org/

www.kazaa.com/

www.limewire.com

www.macromedia.com/downloads/

www.nonags.com/

www.shareware.com/

Website Tools, Templates, Buttons, Help

freesitetemplates.com/

www.aaa-buttons.com/

www.addme.com/tools.htm

www.antibs.com/

www.builderzap.com/

www.comteche.com/data/topsites/index.asp

www.exactpages.com/

www.freebuttons.com/

www.freelayouts.com/

www.freetemplates.co.uk/

www.freewebtemplates.com/

www.inet-toolbox.com/toolbox/tools.html

www.javafile.com/

www.myfreetemplates.com/

www.steves-templates.com/

www.webmastertoolscentral.com/

www.websitegoodies.com/

Web Hosting Sites

geocities.yahoo.com/

members.freewebs.com/

webmasteryellowpages.com/

www.0catch.com/

www.150m.com/

www.bravenet.com/

www.doteasy.com/

www.fortunecity.com/

www.freecenter.com/homepages.html

www.freehomepages.com/

www.freeparking.co.uk/

www.freeservers.com/

www.freewebspace.com/

www.freewebspace.net/

www.homestead.com/

www.netfirms.com/

www.thefreesite.com/Free_Web_Space/

www.webspawner.com/

Something Else

AnyWho Online Directory www.anywho.com/

Babel Fish Translation   Language translation for web pages. world.altavista.com/

Creative Commons A new approach to copyright, based on the anarchy of the web and the belief that creativity is to be shared. Watch the movies. creativecommons.org/

Digital Independence Web portal dedicated to the promotion of independent entertainment and media.
 www.ottawaactivism.com/Index.cfm

Fractured Atlas "provides services, resources, and support to liberate a nation of artists." www.fracturedatlas.org/

The Internet Public Library www.ipl.org/

The Library of Congress "America's Library." loc.gov/

mnftiu.cc A little entertainment in the midst of whatever work you're doing. mnftiu.cc/

Nicenet "is a volunteer, non-profit organization dedicated to providing free services to the Internet community. Nicenet's primary offering, the Internet Classroom Assistant (ICA) is designed to address the pedagogical needs and limited resources of teachers and their students." www.nicenet.org/

Project Gutenberg where you can download full, free versions of classic books no longer under copyright protection. www.promo.net/pg/

Questia, "the world's largest Online Library" www.questia.com/

Rand Corporation Download any of their publications gratis. www.rand.org/

Snopes.com Urban Legends Reference Pages www.snopes.com/

Transom They will show you how to put together your own radio showpiece (i.e., This American Life-style). www.transom.org/

Tzadik Record label founded by John Zorn. www.tzadik.com/

Virtual Religion Index - Rutgers University Dept. of Religion. religion.rutgers.edu/vri/

Zeroland World Arts and Culture Directory Arts on the Web. Lots and lots. www.zeroland.co.nz/

Search Engines

allsearchengines.com www.allsearchengines.com/

alltheweb.com www.alltheweb.com/

AltaVista www.altavista.com/

AnyWho Online Directory www.anywho.com/

AskJeeves www.ask.com/

CompletePlanet www.completeplanet.com/

copernic www.copernic.com/

direct search www.freepint.com/gary/direct.htm

Dogpile www.dogpile.com/

Excite www.excite.com/

Fazzle www.namedroppers.com/

FileWatcher.org filewatcher.org/

fossik.com fossick.com

Ftpsearchengines.com filewatcher.org/

GenieKnows www.genieknows.com/

Google www.google.com/

Guidebeam guidebeam.com/

HotBot www.hotbot.com/

iBoogie www.iboogie.tv/

Ilor.com www.ilor.com/

InfoNetware www.infonetware.com/

ithaki www.ithaki.net/

Ixquick ixquick.com/

Karnak www.karnak.com/

kartoo www.kartoo.com/

killerinfo www.killerinfo.com/

Lycos www.lycos.com/

Mamma www.mamma.com/

Metacrawler www.metacrawler.com/

MetaEureka.com www.metaeureka.com/

MSN search.msn.com/

Open Project dmoz dmoz.org/

Othnet www.oth.net/

ProFusion www.profusion.com/

Query Server www.queryserver.com/

Reference collection (University of Albany Libraries)
library.albany.edu/reference/

Search Engines Worldwide
home.inter.net/takakuwa/search/search.html

Search.com www.search.com/

SearchEdu.com www.searchedu.com/

SurfWax www.surfwax.com/

Teoma www.teoma.com/

Turbo10 www.surfwax.com/

Virtual Learning Resources Center www.virtuallrc.com/

Vivisimo vivisimo.com/

Yahoo www.yahoo.com/

zapmeta www.zapmeta.com/

Appendix E: Legal Resources

Publications

The Artist-Gallery Partnership: A Practical Guide to Consigning Art, Allworth Press. 10 East 23rd Street, Suite 210, New York, NY, 10010; Tel: 212-777-8395, www.allworth.com/

ArtNetwork, P.O. Box 1360, Nevada City, CA 95959. Tel: 800 383-0677, 530 470-0862; Fax: 530 470-0256. ArtNetwork is an online source for several very practical publications, listed below:

> *Art Office: 80+ Business Forms, Charts, Sample Letters, Legal Documents & Business Plans for Fine Artists* by Constance Smith and Sue Viders.
> *Art Marketing 101 - A Handbook for Fine Artists* by Constance Smith.
> *Art Licensing 101 - Publishing and Licensing your Artwork for Profit* by Michael Woodward.
> *Selling Art on the Internet* by Marques Vickers.
> *Selling Art on eBay* by Susan Greaves.
> *New York Contemporary Galleries* compiled by Manhattan Arts International.
> *Artists' Gallery Guide Chicago)* compiled by Chicago Artists Coalition.

artmarketing.com

Business and Legal Forms for Fine Artists/Illustrators/ Photographers by Tad Crawford, New York, Allworth Press, revised 1997. 12 East 23 Street, Suite 510, New York, NY 10010; Tel: 212 777-8395; Fax: 212 777-8261. Ready-to-use forms, instructions, and advice on negotiations. www.allworth.com

Copyright, Chicago Artists' Coalition, 11 East Hubbard Street, 7th Floor, Chicago, IL 60611. One of a series of self-help guides. www.caconline.org

The Copyright Handbook: How to Protect & Use Written Works by Stephen Fishman, att., Nolo Press. 950 Parker Street Berkeley, CA 94710; Tel: 510 549-1976, 800 728- 3555; www.nolo.com/index.cfm

Copyright for Performing, Literary and Visual Artists. Texas Accountants and Lawyers for the Arts. 1540 Sul Ross, Houston, TX 77006. All about just what the title says. www.talarts.org

Get It in Writing: The Musician's Guide to the Music Business by Brian McPherson, Hal Leonard Publishing, 1999. www.halleonard.com

Legal Aspects of the Music Industry: An Insider's View by Richard Schulenberg, Watson-Guptil Publications, 1999. 770 Broadway, New York, NY 10003; Tel: 800 278-8477; www.watsonguptill.com

Legal Guide for the Visual Artist by Tad Crawford, New York, Allworth Press, revised 1999. Covers copyright, sale of art by artist, gallery or agent, licensing, book contracts, taxation and etc. Model contracts included. 12 East 23 Street, Suite 510, New York, NY 10010; Tel: 212 777-8395; Fax: 212 777-8261.www.allworth.com

Making It in the Music Business: A Business & Legal Guide for Songwriters & Performers by Lee Wilson, Allworth Press revised edition, January 2004. 12 East 23 Street, Suite 510, New York, NY 10010; Tel: 212 777-8395; Fax: 212 777-8261. www.allworth.com

Model Agreements for Visual Artists: A Guide to Contracts in the Visual Arts by Paul Sanderson, Canadian Artists' Representation, Ontario, 1982. 401 Richmond Street West, Suite 443, Toronto, Ontario M5V 3A8, Canada. All about Canadian art law, plus model contracts.
www.carfacontario.ca/resources/bpub.html

Music Copyright for the New Millennium by David J. Moser, ArtistPro.com, 2001. ArtistPro.com/

Musician's Business & Legal Guide by Mark E. Halloran, Prentice Hall, 3rd edition, 2001. Pearson Prentice Hall, One Lake Street, Upper Saddle River, NJ 07458; Tel: 800 848-9500; vig.prenhall.com

101 Questions About Copyright Law: Revised Edition by Andrew Alpern, Dover Pubns, 2nd Revised edition, 2003. 31 East 2nd Street, Mineola, NY 11501-3852; store.doverpublications.com/

Visiting Arts…Directory, London, Visiting Arts, 1999. Available from Visiting Arts, Bloomsbury House 74 – 77, Great Russell Street, London WC1B 3DA, England. Directories outlining the arts infrastructure and providing contact information for countries from Norway to Thailand. www.visitingarts.org.uk/home.html

Visual Artist's Business and Legal Guide, Gregory T. Victoroff, Editor, Englewood Cliffs, Prentice Hall, 1995. Business and legal information, plus artists' contracts, with comments by lawyers on negotiable clauses. vig.prenhall.com/

Volunteer Lawyers for the Arts. 1 East 53rd St, 6th floor, New York, NY 10022-4201; Tel: 212-319-2787, ext. 1; Fax: 212-752-6575. www.vlany.org/res_lib.html

Volunteer Lawyers for the Arts Library and Publications, where you will find the following publications:

> *Business and Legal Forms for Authors & Self Publishers*
> *All You Need To Know About the Music Business*
> *Business and Legal Forms for Authors & Self Publishers*
> *Business and Legal Forms for Fine Artists*
> *Business and Legal Forms for Graphic Designers*
> *Business and Legal Forms for Illustrators*
> *Business and Legal Forms for Photographers*
> *The Copyright Handbook*
> *Graphic Artists Guild Handbook: Pricing & Ethical Guidelines*
> *Legal Guide for Visual Artists*
> *Music Law: How to Run Your Band's Business*
> *Screen Writers Legal Guide*
> *The Writer's Legal Guide*

www.vlany.org/res_lib.html

Volunteer Lawyers for the Arts Guide to Copyright for the Performing Arts/VLA Guide to Copyright for the Visual Arts, Volunteer Lawyers for the Arts, revised 1993. 1 East 53rd Street, 6th Floor, New York, NY 10022-4201; www.vlany.org

Volunteer Lawyers for the Arts Most Called List, Volunteer Lawyers for the Arts, revised 1993. 1 East 53rd Street, 6th Floor, New York, NY 10022-4201. Lists the most frequently requested telephone numbers and addresses from the Art Law Hotline. www.vlany.org

The Writer's Legal Guide – an Authors Guild Desk Reference by Tad Crawford and Kay Murray, co-published by the Authors Guild and Allworth Press, 3rd edition, 2002.
12 East 23 Street, Suite 510, New York, NY 10010; Tel: 212 777-8395; Fax: 212 777-8261. Up to date information regarding copyright law, book contracts, agency contracts,

collaboration agreements, Freedom of Information Act, tax laws. Includes many sample forms. www.allworth.com

Legal Links

The Artist-Gallery Partnership: A Practical Guide to Consigning Art, Allworth Press. 10 East 23rd Street, Suite 210, New York, NY, 10010; Tel: 212-777-8395. Sample contract free for the taking, but get their books. www.allworth.com/

Art Law by Ann Avery Andres, Esq. Legal advice for the arts from a California attorney. www.tfaoi.com/articles/andres/aa1.htm

Author's Guild To help you understand your rights, visit their website: www.authorsguild.org/

Burry Man Writer's Center—Contracts Great web site with all kinds of information. www.burryman.com/biz.html#contracts

California Lawyers for the Arts Nonprofit organization providing lawyer referrals, dispute resolution services and a resource library to artists of all disciplines. www.calawyersforthearts.org/

Copyright Office, Library of Congress Copyright application forms available at this site, as well as "how to's" and answers to frequently asked questions. www.loc.gov/copyright/

Copyright for Performing, Literary and Visual Artists, Texas Accountants and Lawyers for the Arts, 1540 Sul Ross, Houston, TX 77006. All about just what the title says. www.talarts.org

The Copyright Website A portal providing real world practical and relevant copyright information. www.benedict.com/

Guide to Artist-Gallery Consignment Contracts Sample contracts and advice to artists, free for the asking, compliments of St. Louis Volunteer Lawyers for the Arts. www.vlaa.org/pdfs/_Artist-Gallery_Agree.pdf

Intellectual Property Watchdog Free source for information on copyright, intellectual property law and etc. www.ipwatchdog.com/

National Writers Union More information on rights. www.nwu.org/

Nolo.com Self-Help Law Center "Everyday law for everyday people." Includes a legal encyclopedia, legal dictionary, research tips, court information, answers to many questions, easy to find subjects and information on legal books and software. A great resource. www.nolo.com/

Publishing Law Center Many articles about all aspects of publishing contracts. www.publaw.com/
and their links page: www.publaw.com/links.html

Springboard for the Arts Great source of advice and information on marketing, career planning, organizational management, contracts, legal, copyright and etc. Check it out. www.rc4arts.org/

Volunteer Lawyers for the Arts

If we haven't been clear enough, check out this organization for free legal help. Below, find free legal help using Volunteer Lawyers for the Arts on a state by state basis. www.vlany.org

California   www.calawyersforthearts.org/
California Lawyers for the Arts (Oakland)
1212 Broadway St., Ste. 834
Oakland, CA 94612
Tel: 510 444-6351
Fax: 510 444-6352

California Lawyers for the Arts (Sacramento)
926 J St., Ste. 811
Sacramento, CA 95814
Tel: 916 442-6210
Fax: 916 442-6281

California Lawyers for the Arts (San Francisco)
Fort Mason Center, Building C, Rm 255
San Francisco, CA 94123
Tel: 415 775-7200
Fax: 415 775-1143
E-mail: cla@sirius.com

California Lawyers for the Arts (Santa Monica)
1641 18th St.
Santa Monica, CA 90404
Tel: 310 998-5590
Fax: 310 998-5594
E-mail: UserCLA@aol.com

San Diego Lawyers for the Arts
c/o Law Offices of Peter H. Karlen
1205 Prospect St., Ste. 400
La Jolla, CA 92037
Tel: 619 454-9696
Fax: 619 454-9777

Colorado
Colorado Lawyers for the Arts
P.O. Box 48148
Denver, CO 80204

Tel: 303 722 7994; Fax: 303 778 0203
E-mail: cola@artstozoo.org
www.coloradoartslawyers.org/

Connecticut
Connecticut Volunteer Lawyers for the Arts
Connecticut Commission on the Arts
One Financial Plaza
755 Main St.
Hartford, CT 06103
Tel: 860 566-4770
Fax: 860 566-6462

District of Columbia
Washington Area Lawyers for the Arts WALA)
1120 Connecticut Avenue, NW, Suite 260
Washington, DC 20036
Tel: 202 429 0960
Fax: 202 429 0965
www.thewala.org

Florida
ArtServe, Inc./ Volunteer Lawyers for the Arts
1350 East Sunrise Blvd.
Ft. Lauderdale FL 33304
Tel: 954 462-9191
Fax: 954 462-9182
E-mail: ArtServeFl@aol.com

Volunteer Lawyers for the Arts of Pinnellas County
400 Pierce Blvd.
Clearwater, FL 33756
Tel: 727 464-4043
Fax: 727 464-4608
E-mail: bkotchey@co.pinellas.fl.us

Georgia
Southeast Volunteer Lawyers for the Arts
Bureau of Cultural Affairs
675 Ponce De Leon Ave. NE, #550
Atlanta, GA 30308
Tel: 404 873-3911
Fax: 404 817 6827
E-mail:gla@glarts.org
www.glarts.org

Illinois
Lawyers for the Creative Arts
213 W. Institute Pl.
Chicago, IL 60610
Tel: 312 944-2727 / 312 944- 2787
Fax: 312 944- 2195

Kansas
American Arts Resources, Inc.
PO Box 363
Lindsborg, KS 67456
Tel: 785 227-2321
Fax: 785 227-3471

Louisiana
Louisiana Volunteer Lawyers for the Arts
225 Baronne Street, Suite 1712
New Orleans, LA 70112
Tel: 504 523-1465

Maine
Maine Volunteer Lawyers for the Arts
43 Pleasant Street
South Portland, ME 04106
Tel: 207 799 9646
Fax: 207 846 1035

Massachusetts
Volunteer Lawyers for the Arts of Massachusetts, Inc.
249 A Street, Studio 14
Boston, MA 02110
Tel: 617 350-7600
TTY: 617 350-7600
Fax: 617 350-7610
E-mail:mail@vlama.org
www.vlama.org

Michigan
Volunteer Lawyers for the Arts & Culture
17515 West Nine Mile Road, Suite 1025
Southfield, MI 48075-4426
Tel: 248 557-8288 x21; Fax: 248 557-8581
E-mail: volunteer@artservemichigan.org
 www.artservemichigan.org/volunteer/vlac/indpr.html

Minnesota
Resources and Counseling for the Arts
308 Prince St.
St. Paul, MN 55101
Tel: 651 292-4381, 800 546-2891 ext. 1
Fax: 651 292-4315
E-mail: info@RC4Arts.org

Missouri
St. Louis Volunteer Lawyers and Accountants for the Arts
3540 Washington
St. Louis, MO 63103
Tel: 314 652-2410; Fax: 314 652-0011
E-mail: vlaa@stlrac.org
www.vlaa.org/

Montana
Montana Arts Council
P.O. Box 202201

Helena, MT 59620-2201
Tel: 406 444 6430; Fax: 406 444 6548
E-mail: mac@state.mt.us
www.art.state.mt.us/

New Hampshire
Lawyers for the Arts/New Hampshire
One Granite Pl.
Concord, NH 03301
Tel: 603 224-8300
Fax: 603 226-2963
E-mail: Joan.Goshgarian@JPFinancial.com

New York
Albany/Schenectady League of Arts Inc.
19 Clinton Ave.
Albany NY 12207
Tel: 518 449-5380
E-mail: artsleague@aol.com

Volunteer Lawyers for the Arts (Manhattan)
1 E. 53rd St., 6th Fl.
New York, NY 10022
Tel: 212 319-2787
Fax: 212 752-6575
E-mail: vlany@vlany.net
www.vlany.org

North Carolina
North Carolina Volunteer Lawyers for the Arts (NCVLA)
PO Box 26513
Raleigh, NC 27611
Tel: 919 788 0506; Fax: 775 255 5286
E-mail: info@ncvla.org
www.ncvla.org/index.htm

Ohio

Volunteer Lawyers and Accountants for the Arts-Cleveland
c/o The Cleveland Bar Association
113 St. Clair Ave., Ste. 100
Cleveland, OH 44114
Tel: 216 696-3525

Toledo Volunteer Lawyers and Accountants for the Arts
608 Madison, Ste. 1523
Toledo, OH 43604
Tel: 419 255-3344
Fax: 419 255-1329

Oklahoma

Oklahoma Accountants and Lawyers for the Arts
c/o Eric King, Gable & Gotwals
One Leadership Sq., 15th Fl.
211 N. Robinson
Oklahoma City, OK 73102
Tel: 405 235-5500
Fax: 405 235-2875
E-mail: eking@gablelaw.com

Oregon

Northwest Lawyers for the Arts
621 SW Morrison Street, Suite 1417
Portland, Oregon 97205
Tel: 503 295 2787
E-mail: artcop@aol.com

Pennsylvania

Philadelphia Volunteer Lawyers for the Arts
251 South 18th St.
Philadelphia, PA 19103
Tel: 215 545-3385; Fax: 215 545-4839
E-mail: pvla@libertynet.org
www.pvla.org/

ProArts
425 Sixth Ave., Ste. 360
Pittsburgh, PA 15219-1819
Tel: 412 391-2060; Fax: 412 394-4280
E-mail: proarts@cmu.edu
proarts-pittsburgh.org/

Rhode Island
Ocean State Lawyers for the Arts
PO Box 19
Saunderstown, RI 02874
Tel: 401 789-5686
E-mail: dspatt@artslaw.org

Texas
Artists' Legal and Accounting Assistance
P.O. Box 2577
Austin, TX 78751
Tel: 512 476 4458

Texas Accountants & Lawyers for the Arts
1540 Sul Ross
Houston, TX 77006
Tel: 713 526-4876; Fax: 713 526-1299
E-mail: info@talarts.org
www.talarts.org/

Utah
Utah Lawyers for the Arts
PO Box 652
Salt Lake City, UT 84110
Tel: 801 482-5373, 801 521-3200

Washington
Washington Lawyers for the Arts
1835 12th Avenue
Seattle, WA 98122

Tel: 206 328 7053
E-mail: director@wa-artlaw.org
 www.wa-artlaw.org/

International

Australia
Ian Collie, Director
Rochina Iannella, Legal Officer
The Gunnery, 43 Cowper Wharf Road
Woolloomooloo, Sydney NSW 2011
ACN 002 706 256
Tel: 02/356 2566 & 008/221 457
Fax: 02/ 358 6475

Canada
Canadian Artists' Representation, Ontario CARO)
1 Yonge Street, Suite 1900
Toronto, Ontarion M5E 1E5
Canada
Tel: 416 340 7791
Fax: 416 360 0781
www.caea.com

Appendix F: Grant Resources

Researching grants

The Grantsmanship Center 650 S. Spring Street, Suite 507, Los Angeles, CA 90015. A large training center which provides grantsmanship workshops all over the country. www.tgci.com/

New York University Libraries, 70 Washington Sq. South, New York, NY 10012-1091; Tel: 212 998-2500. Research assistance and a great place to begin! library.nyu.edu/research/art/grants.html

The Research Library, The Foundation Center, 79 Fifth Avenue/16th Street, New York, NY 10003-3076; Tel: 212 620-4230, 800 424-9836; Fax: 212 807-3677; www.fdncenter.org/

Arts Education Grants

Surdna Arts Teachers Fellowship Program The Surdna Foundation invites arts teachers from specialized, public arts high schools to apply for funding for artistic development through its Arts Teachers Fellowship Program. The program offers teachers the opportunity to immerse themselves in their own creative work, interact with other professional artists, and stay current with new practices. 330 Madison Avenue, 30th Floor, New York, NY 10017; Tel: 212 557-0010; Fax: 212 557-0003; E-mail: request@surdna.org www.surdna.org/programs/arts.html

Grants Links

Arts Deadline List has a monthly newsletter for opportunities: grants, residencies, competitions, scholarships, internships, fellowships, etc. This is a free service, though there is also a paid premium edition at this site. www.artdeadlineslist.com/

The Chronicle of Philanthropy Web site offers the complete contents of the latest issue, an archive of past issues and articles published since October 1997, and two issues' worth of the most recent grant listings—all fully searchable. www.philanthropy.com/

CSC Non-profit Resource Center – Lists over 1,000 sites. www.home.comcast.net/~cscunningham/Foundation.htm

The Grantsmanship Center TGCI has provided grantsmanship training and grant information for over 30 years. P.O. Box 17220, Los Angeles, CA 90017; Tel: 213 482-9860; Fax: 213 482-9863; www.tgci.com/

The Grantsmanship Center Magazine Select issues from this quarterly magazine devoted to fundraising issues in the nonprofit sector are available online. www.tgci.com/magazine/archives.asp

The National Resource Guide for the Placement of Artists, edited by Cheryl Slean. The National Network for Artist Placement, 935 West Avenue 37, Los Angeles, CA 90065. Revised regularly. An annotated guide to arts organizations that provide support to artists. www.artistplacement.com

University of Arizona A web list of grants and fellowships for the arts compiled by Prof. Gayle Wimmer. Well organized and regularly updated. Check it out for niche grant opportunities. Good source. www.library.arizona.edu/users/juarezm/artfun.html

University of Delaware An Internet gateway to beginning research on grant sources. Helpful to begin navigating through the web. www2.lib.udel.edu/subj/foce/internet.htm

University of Maryland A list of grants and awards for visual artists compiled by University Libraries, University of Maryland. www.lib.umd.edu/ART/guides/grants.html/

World Wide Web Arts Source The largest marketplace for contemporary art, international art news, research and gallery portfolios, online since 1995. Cool portal. wwar.com/categories/Agencies/Grants_Related/

Yahoo! Society and Culture: Issues and Causes: Philanthropy This section of Yahoo! provides more than 1,000 links to sites relating to community service, volunteerism, grant making foundations, corporate philanthropy, and public charities. Always updating their information.www.yahoo.com/Society_and_Culture/Issues_and_Causes/Philanthropy

Zuzu's Petals Literary Links: Grant Information www.zuzu.com/granlink.htm

Links to Foundations and Arts Organizations

Alliance of Artists' Communities www.artistcommunities.org/links-resources.html

American Association of Community Theater Arts Organizations www.aact.org/orgs.html

ArtistResource Art Organizations www.artistresource.org/artorgs.htm

ArtScene.org Arts Organizations www.artscene.org/organizations.asp

ArtsEdge (The Kennedy Center) Professional Resources
artsedge.kennedy-center.org/professional_resources/

ArtSeek – Art on the Web
www.artseek.com/institutions/orgs/

Artslynx International Dance, Music Visual, Performance Arts Organizations www.artslynx.org/

Arts Organizations of Color
www.indians.org/color/

British Council—USA.Org
www.britishcouncil-usa.org/arts/index.shtml

Brooklyn Arts Council Directory of Brooklyn Arts Organizations, 195 Cadman Plaza West, Brooklyn, NY 11201;
Tel: 718 625-0080; Fax: 718 625-3294;
E-mail: bac@brooklynartscouncil.org,
www.brooklynartscouncil.org/
index.cfm?fuseaction=organization.level1&category_id=9&ts=10202003124608

Carnegie Library of Pittsburgh International Resources
www.carnegielibrary.org/subject/art/orgs.html

CategoryWeb.com
categoryweb.com/Top/Arts/Organizations

City of Seattle Arts Resource Network
www.artsresourcenetwork.org/opportunities/
competitions_funding/individuals_organizations.asp

Communications Roundtable – Professional Organizations
www.roundtable.org/professional.html

College Art Association www.collegeart.org/

Cultural Policy and the Arts National Data Archive
www.cpanda.org/resources/intlorgs.html

Directory GettyBest.com Arts Organizations
dir.gettybest.com/?categ=22

Directory.Net Arts Organizations
www.directory.net/Arts/Organizations/

DMOZ Open Directory Project
dmoz.org/Arts/Organizations/

Guideall.com Arts Organizations
www.guideall.com/artsorg.htm

Internet Public Library: Fine Arts Internet Public Library,
University of Michigan School of Information, 304 West Hall,
Ann Arbor, MI 48109-1092;
www.ipl.org/div/aon/browse/hum20.00.00/

*Los Angeles County Arts Commission—Grants and
Professional Growth* www.lacountyarts.org/fundingops.html

Manhattan Arts International
www.manhattanarts.com/pages/organizations.htm

Michigan State University, Grants and Related Resources, 100
Library, E. Lansing, MI 48824-1048;
Tel. voice mail: 517 355-6669; Fax: 517 432-8050;
www.lib.msu.edu/harris23/grants/

Nodeworks Directory Arts Organizations
dir.nodeworks.com/Arts/Organizations/

OpenHere.com Arts Organizations
openhere.com/arts/organizations/

Polish Yellow Pages Arts Organizations
www.yellowpages.pl/ca/95633/Arts/Organizations/

Slider.com Arts Organizations
slider-secure.vendercom.com/Arts/Organizations.htm

TopiaSearch Arts Organizations
www.topiasearch.com/Arts/Organizations/

University of Art and Design Helsinki
www2.uiah.fi/library/linkit/organisaatiot.htm

University of Notre Dame Directories: Organizations
University of Notre Dame, Notre Dame, Indiana 46556;
Tel:574-631-6258; lib.nd.edu/refdesk/subjects/
directories:organizations.html

VSA Arts Affiliates www.vsarts.org/affiliates/

World Wide Arts Resources
wwar.com/categories/Agencies/Arts_Councils/

Yahoo Directory Listings dir.yahoo.com/Arts/Organizations/

National Arts Organizations and Foundations
Major resources to which artists can apply for grants and other financial help. Many also offer employment opportunities as well as connection to audience venues.

The Catalog of Federal Domestic Assistance (CFDA) This is an online resource to help you find all Federal programs available to State and local governments. Helpful in how to write grant proposals and what government agencies to apply to. Check it out. www.cfda.gov/public/

The Foundation Center, 79 Fifth Avenue/16th Street, New York, NY 10003-3076 ;Tel: 212 620-4230; Fax: 212 807-3677, 800 424-9836; fdncenter.org/

The Washington Office of the Foundation Center is located at 1001 Connecticut Avenue, NW, Washington, DC 20036-5588; Tel: 202-331-1400. Founded in 1956, The Foundation Center is the nation's leading authority on philanthropy and is dedicated to serving grant seekers, grant makers, researchers, policymakers, the media, and the general public.

Institute of International Education The IIE is the administrator of Fulbright Fellowships for foreign study, teaching, and research. Fellowships available for post-baccalaureate study, post-doctoral study, teaching, and research in most countries friendly to the United States. 809 United Nations Plaza, New York, NY 10017-3580; Tel: 212 984-5330 www.iie.org/fulbright

The John Simon Guggenheim Memorial Foundation Specializing in fellowships for advanced professionals. 90 Park Avenue, New York, NY 10016; www.gf.org

National Assembly of State Arts Organizations (NASAA) 1029 Vermont Avenue, NW, 2nd Floor Washington, DC 20005; Tel: 202-347-6352; Fax: 202-737-0526; www.nasaa-arts.org/

National Endowment for the Arts (NEA) 1100 Pennsylvania Avenue, NW, Washington, DC 20506; Tel:202 682-5400;   arts.endow.gov/

National Endowment for the Humanities 1100 Pennsylvania Ave., N.W., Washington, D.C. 20506; www.neh.fed.us./

National Foundation for the Advancement of the Arts 800 Brickell Avenue, Suite 500, Miami, FL 33131; Tel: 800 970-ARTS; Fax: 305 377-1149; www.nfaa.org/

US Regional and State Arts Organizations and Foundations

Arts Midwest
2908 Hennepin Avenue, Suite 200, Minneapolis, MN 55408-1954; Tel:612 341-0755; Fax: 612 341-0902;
E-mail: general@artsmidwest.org Serves artists throughout Illinois, Indiana, Iowa, Michigan, Minnesota, North Dakota, Ohio, South Dakota, and Wisconsin. www.artsmidwest.org/

Consortium for Pacific Arts & Cultures (AS, CM, GU)
735 Bishop Street, Suite 310, Honolulu, HI 96813-4819;
Tel: 808-946-7381; Fax: 808-955-2722;
E-mail: cpac@pixi.com

District of Columbia (DC) Commission on the Arts and Humanities, 410 Eighth Street, NW, Fifth Floor Washington, DC 20004; Tel: 202-724-5613; Fax: 202-727-4135
E-mail: dcarts@dc.gov dcarts.dc.gov/main.shtm

The Getty Grant Program
1200 Getty Center Drive, Los Angeles, CA 90049–1679;
Tel: 310 440-7300; Funding a diverse range of projects in the history of visual arts and cultural heritage, the Getty Grant Program provides critical support to institutions and individuals worldwide. It consistently searches for collaborative efforts that make significant contributions. www.getty.edu/grants/index.html

Mid-America Arts Alliance
912 Baltimore Avenue, Suite 700, Kansas City, MO 64105;
Tel: 816 421-1388; Fax: 816 421-3918;
E-mail: info@maaa.org Serves artists in Arkansas, Kansas, Missouri, Nebraska, Oklahoma and Texas. www.maaa.org/

Mid-Atlantic Arts Foundation
201 N. Charles Street, Suite 401, Baltimore, MD 21201;
Tel: 410 539-6656; Fax: 410 837-5517;
E-mail; maaf@midatlanticarts.org\ Serves artists throughout Delaware, District of Columbia, Maryland, New Jersey, New York, Pennsylvania, Virginia, U.S. Virgin Islands, and West Virginia. www.charm.net/~midarts/

New England Foundation for the Arts (NEFA)
266 Summer Street, 2nd Floor, Boston, MA 02210;
Tel:617 951-0010; E-mail: info@nefa.org NEFA was created through collaboration between the six state arts agencies of New England and including Connecticut, Maine, Massachusetts, New Hampshire, Rhode Island, and Vermont. www.nefa.org/

San Francisco Arts Commission (SFAC)
San Francisco Arts Commission, 25 Van Ness Ave, Ste. 240 San Francisco CA 94102; Fax: 415 252-2595;
TTY: 800 735-2929; SFAC is a city agency that supports the arts in San Francisco. The SFAC programs integrate the arts into all aspects of City life. The Commission was established by charter in 1932. www.sfgov.org/sfac/

San Francisco Foundation
225 Bush Street, Suite 500, San Francisco, CA 94104;
Tel: 415 733-8500; Fax: 415 477-2783; www.sff.org/

Southern Arts Federation
1800 Peachtree Street NW, Suite 808, Atlanta, Georgia 30309;
Tel:404 874-7244; Fax: 404 873-2148; E-mail: saf@southarts.org The organization works in partnership with the state arts agencies of Alabama, Florida, Georgia, Kentucky, Louisiana, Mississippi, North Carolina, South Carolina and Tennessee.
www.southarts.org/

Western States Arts Federation (WESTAF)
1743 Wazee Street, Suite 300, Denver, CO 80202;
Tel: 888 562-7232, 303 629-1166; Fax: 303 629-9717;
E-mail: staff@westaf.org   WESTAF is supported by the art agencies of Alaska, Arizona, California, Colorado, Idaho, Montana, Nevada, New Mexico, Oregon, Utah, Washington, and Wyoming www.westaf.org/

The States

Alabama State Council on the Arts
201 Monroe Street, Montgomery, AL 36130-1800;
Tel: 334-242-4076; Fax: 334-240-3269; www.arts.state.al.us/

Alaska State Council on the Arts
411 West 4th Avenue, Suite 1E, Anchorage, AK 99501-2343;
Tel: 907 269-6610; Fax: 907 269-6601;
www.eed.state.ak.us/aksca/

Arkansas Arts Council
1500 Tower Building, 323 Center Street, Little Rock, AR 72201; Tel: 501 324-9766; Fax: 501 324-9207;
E-mail: info@arkansasarts.com www.arkansasarts.com/

Arizona Commission on the Arts
417 West Roosevelt Street, Phoenix, AZ 85003;
Tel: 602-255-5882; Fax: 602-256-0282;
E-mail: general@arizonaarts.org www.arizonaArts.org/

California Arts Council
1300 I Street, Suite 930, Sacramento, CA 95814;
Tel: 916 322-6555 or 800-201-6201; Fax: 916 322-6575;
www.cac.ca.gov/

Colorado State Council on the Arts
1380 Lawrence Street, Suite 1200, Denver, CO 80204;
Tel: 303 866-2723; Fax: 303 866-4266; E-mail:
coloarts@state.co.us www.coloarts.state.co.us/default.asp

Connecticut Commission on the Arts
One Financial Plaza, 755 Main Street, Hartford, CT 06103;
Tel: 860 566-4770, outside Hartford: 800 411-1312;
TDD: 860566-6460; Fax: 860566-6462;
E-mail: artsinfo@ctarts.org www.ctarts.org/Index.htm

Delaware Division of the Arts
Carvel State Office Building, 820 North French Street, 4th
Floor, Wilmington, DE 19801; Tel: 302 577-8278;
Fax: 302 577-6561; E-mail: delarts@state.de.us
www.artsdel.org/default.shtml

Florida Division of Cultural Affairs
Department of State, The Capitol, 1001 DeSoto Park Drive,
Tallahassee, FL 32301; Tel: 850-245-6470;
Fax: 850-245-6492;
E-mail: culturalAffairs@mail.dos.state.fl.us
www.florida-arts.org/index.asp

Georgia Council for the Arts
260 14th Street, NW, Suite 401, Atlanta, GA 30318;
Tel: 404 685-2787; Fax: 404 685 2788;
E-mail: gaarts@gaarts.org www.gaarts.org/

State Foundation on Culture and the Arts (Hawaii)
250 South Hotel Street, 2nd Floor, Honolulu, HI 96813;
Tel: 808-586-0300; Fax: 808-586-0308;
E-mail: sfca@sfca.state.hi.us www.state.hi.us/sfca/

Idaho Commission on the Arts
PO Box 83720, 2410 North Old Penitentiary Road,
Boise, ID 83712-0008; Tel: 208 334-2119; Fax: 208 334-2488;
E-mail: info@ica.state.id.us www2.state.id.us/arts/

Illinois Arts Council
100 West Randolph Street, Suite 10-500, Chicago, IL 60601;
Tel: 312 814-6750; Fax: 312 814-1471;
E-mail: info@arts.state.il.us www.state.il.us/agency/iac/

Indiana Arts Commission
150 W. Market Street, Suite 618, Indianapolis, IN 46204;
Tel: 317 232-1268; Fax: 317 232-5595;
E-mail: arts@state.in.us www.IN.gov/arts/

Iowa Arts Council
Capitol Complex, 600 E. Locust, Des Moines, IA 50319-0290;
Tel: 515 281-4451; Fax: 515 242-6498;
www.iowaartscouncil.org/

Kansas Arts Commission
Jayhawk Tower, 700 SW Jackson, Suite 1004, Topeka, KS
66603-3761; Tel: 785 296-3335; Fax: 785 296-4989;
E-mail: KAC@arts.state.ks.us arts.state.ks.us/

Kentucky Arts Council
Old Capitol Annex, 300 West Broadway, Frankfort, KY 40601;
Tel: 502 564-3757 or 888 833-2787;
E-mail: kyarts@ky.gov www.kyarts.org/

Louisiana Division of the Arts
PO Box 44247, Baton Rouge, LA 70804;
Tel: 225 342-8180; Fax: 225 342-8173;
E-mail: arts@crt.state.la.us www.crt.state.la.us/arts/

Maine Arts Commission
193 State Street, 25 State House Station
Augusta, Maine 04333-0025; Tel: 207 287-2724;
Fax: 207 287-2725; E-mail: mac.info@maine.gov
www.mainearts.com/index.shtml

Maryland State Arts Council
175 W. Ostend Street, Suite E, Baltimore, MD 21230;
Tel: 410 767-6555; Fax: 410 333-1062;
TDD: 410 333-4519;
E-mail: marylandstateartscouncil@msac.org
www.msac.org/

Massachusetts Cultural Council
10 St. James Street, 3rd Floor, Boston, MA 02116;
Tel: 617 727-3668; Fax: 617 727-0044;
E-mail: web@art.state.ma.us   www.massculturalcouncil.org/

Michigan Council for Arts and Cultural Affairs
702 W. Kalamazoo, PO Box 30705, Lansing, MI 48909;
Tel: 517 241-4011; Fax: 517 241-3979;
E-mail: artsinfo@michigan.gov
www.michigan.gov/hal/0,1607,7-160-17445_19272—
,00.html

Minnesota State Arts Board
Park Square Court, 400 Sibley Street, Suite 200,
St. Paul, MN 55101; Tel: 651 215-1600 or 800-8MN-ARTS;
Fax: 651-215-1602;   E-mail: msab@arts.state.mn.us
www.arts.state.mn.us/

Missouri Arts Council
111 North 7th Street, Suite 105, St. Louis, MO 63101-2188;
Tel: 314 340-6845; Fax: 314 340-7215;
E-mail:moarts@ded.state.mo.us
www.missouriartscouncil.org/

Mississippi Arts Commission
239 North Lamar Street, 2nd Floor, Jackson, MS 39201;
Tel: 601 359-6030 or 6040; Fax: 601 359-6008;
www.arts.state.ms.us/

Montana Arts Council
City County Building, 316 North Park Avenue, Suite 252,
P.O. Box 202201, Helena, MT 59620-2201;
Tel: 406 444-6430; Fax: 406 444-6548;
E-mail: mac@state.mt.us www.art.state.mt.us/

Nebraska Arts Council
Joslyn Carriage House, 3838 Davenport Street,
Omaha, NE 68131-2329; Tel: 402 595-2122;
Fax: 402 595-2334; www.nebraskaartscouncil.org/

Nevada Arts Council
716 North Carson Street, Suite A, Carson City, NV 89701;
Tel: 775-687-6680; Fax: 775-687-6688;
E-mail: cjnemani@clan.lib.nv.us
dmla.clan.lib.nv.us/docs/arts/

New Hampshire State Council on the Arts
2 1/2 Beacon Street, 2nd Floor, Concord, NH 03301-4974;
Tel: 603 271-2789; TTY/TDD: 800 735-2964;
Fax: 603 271-3584; www.state.nh.us/nharts/

New Jersey State Council on the Arts
225 West State Street, P.O. Box 306, Trenton, NJ 08625-0306;
Tel: 609 292-6130; Fax: 609 989-1440;
www.njartscouncil.org/

New Mexico Arts
228 East Palace Avenue, Santa Fe, NM 87501;
Tel: 505 827-6490; Fax: 505 827-6043;
www.nmarts.org/

New York State Council on the Arts
175 Varick Street, 3rd Floor, New York, NY 10014;
Tel: 212 627-4455; Fax: 212 620-5911;
www.nysca.org/public/home.cfm

North Carolina Arts Council
Department of Cultural Resources, Jenkins House,
221 East Lane Street, Raleigh, NC 27699-4632;
Tel: 919 733-2821; Fax: 919 733-4834; www.ncarts.org/

North Dakota Council on the Arts
1600 East Century Avenue, Suite 6, Bismarck, ND 58503;
Tel: 701 328-7590; Fax: 701 328-7595;
E-mail: comserv@state.nd.us   www.state.nd.us/arts/

Ohio Arts Council
727 East Main Street, Columbus, OH 43205;
Tel: 614 466-2613; Fax: 614 466-4494;
www.oac.state.oh.us/

Oklahoma Arts Council
Jim Thorpe Building, PO Box 52001-2001,
Oklahoma City, OK 73152-2001; Tel: 405 521-2931;
Fax: 405 521-6418; E-mail: okarts@arts.state.ok.us
www.oklaosf.state.ok.us/~arts/

Oregon Arts Commission
775 Summer Street NE, Suite 200, Salem, OR 97301-1284;
Tel: 503 986-0082; Fax: 503 986-0260;
E-mail: Oregon.ArtsComm@State.OR.US
www.oregonartscommission.org/main.php

Pennsylvania Council on the Arts
216 Finance Building, Harrisburg, PA 17120;
Tel: 717 787-6883; Fax: 717 783-2538;
www.artsnet.org/pca/

Rhode Island State Council on the Arts
83 Park Street, 6th Floor, Providence, RI 02903;
Tel:401 222-3880; Fax: 401 222-3018;
TDD: 401 222-7828; E-mail: info@risca.state.ri.us
www.arts.ri.gov/

South Carolina Arts Commission
1800 Gervais Street, Columbia, SC 29201; Tel: 803 734-8696;
Fax: 803 734-8526; www.state.sc.us/arts/

South Dakota Arts Council
Office of the Arts, 800 Governors Drive,
Pierre, SD 57501-2294; Tel: 605 773-3131;
Fax: 605 773-6962; E-mail: sdac@stlib.state.sd.us
www.state.sd.us/deca/sdarts/index.htm

Tennessee Arts Commission
Citizens Plaza, 401 Charlotte Avenue,
Nashville, TN 37243-0780; Tel: 615 741-1701;
Fax: 615 741-8559; www.arts.state.tn.us/

Texas Commission on the Arts
PO Box 13406, Capitol Station, Austin, TX 78711;
Tel: 512 463-5535; Fax: 512 475-2699;
E-mail: front.desk@arts.state.tx.us
www.arts.state.tx.us/

Utah Arts Council
617 E. South Temple Street, Salt Lake City, UT 84102;
Tel: 801 236-7555; Fax: 801 236-7556;
arts.utah.gov/index.html

Vermont Arts Council
136 State Street, Drawer 33, Montpelier, VT 05633-6001;
Phone: 802 828-3291; Fax: 802 828-3363;

E-mail: info@vermontartscouncil.org
www.vermontartscouncil.org/

Virginia Commission for the Arts
223 Governor Street, 2nd Floor, Richmond, VA 23219;
Tel: 804 225-3132; Fax: 804 225-4327;
E-mail: vacomm@artswire.org
www.arts.state.va.us/index.html

Washington State Arts Commission
234 8th Avenue SE, P.O. Box 42675, Olympia, WA 98504-2675; Tel: 360 753-3860; Fax: 360 586-5351;
www.arts.wa.gov/

West Virginia Commission on the Arts
1900 Kanawha Boulevard East, Charleston, WV 25305;
Tel: 304 558-0240; Fax: 304 558-2779;
www.wvculture.org/arts/index.html

Wisconsin Arts Board
101 East Wilson Street, 1st Floor, Madison, WI 53702;
Tel: 608 266-0190; Fax: 608 267-0380; arts.state.wi.us/static/

Wyoming Arts Council
2320 Capitol Avenue, Cheyenne, WY 82002;
Tel: 307 777-7742; Fax: 307 777-5499
E-mail: wyoarts@artswire.org wyoarts.state.wy.us/

International Arts Organizations

American Samoa Council on Culture, Arts and Humanities
P.O. Box 1540, Office of the Governor, Pago Pago, AS 96799;
Tel: 684 633-4347; Fax: 684 633-2059

Arts International (AI)
251 Park Avenue South, 5th Floor, New York, NY 10010-7302;
Tel:212 674-9744; Fax:212 674-9092;
AI is devoted solely to the development and support of global exchange of art. www.artsinternational.org/

Commonwealth Council for Arts and Culture (Northern Mariana Islands)
PO Box 5553, CHRB Saipan, MP 96950; Tel: 670 322-9982 or 9983; Fax:: 670 322-9028; E-mail: galaidi@gtepacifica.net

Guam Council on the Arts & Humanities Agency
P.O. Box 2950, Hagatna, Guam 96932;
Tel: 671 475-4226/0220; Fax: 671 475-4227;
E-mail: Kaha1@kuentos.guam.net
www.guam.net/gov/kaha/

International Drama/Theater and Education Association (IDEA) educ.queensu.ca/%7Eidea/index.htm

International Society for Education Through Art (INSEA)
cspace.unb.ca/insea/

International Society for Music Education (ISME)
ISME International Office P.O. Box 909 Nedlands 6909, WA Australia; Tel: ++61-(08-9386 2654;
Fax: ++61-(08-9386-2658; www.isme.org/

Institute of Puerto Rican Culture
P.O. Box 9024184, San Juan, PR 00902-4184;
Tel: 787 724-0700; Fax: 787 724-8393; icp.gobierno.pr/

The United States Center for the International Association of Theater for Children and Young People (ASSITEJ/USA)
724 Second Avenue South, Nashville, TN 37210; Tel: 615 254-5719; Fax: 615 254-3255; www.assitej-usa.org/

Virgin Island Council on the Arts
P.O. Box 103, St. Thomas, VI 00802; Tel: 340 774-5984;
Fax: 340 774-6206; E-mail: vicouncil@islands.vi

Bridge Loans

Nonprofit Finance Fund
For more information, or to receive Bridge Loan Program
guidelines and an application, contact Ruth Rosenberg, SMAC
Arts Stabilization Consultant, Tel: 916 448-3017;
E-mail: rurosenberg@yahoo.com
www.nonprofitfinancefund.org/details.asp?autoId=5

Associated Grant Makers (AGM)
AGM is the regional association of grant makers in
Massachusetts, New Hampshire and Rhode Island supporting
foundations, corporate giving programs and other organized
donor institutions, AGM also supports nonprofit organizations
engaged in corporate and foundation fundraising.
www.agmconnect.org/agmwebmanager.nsf/hf/lib-Res-
Techasst
AGM has a great page of resources for those of you wanting
to better manage your nonprofit organization. Check it out at:
www.agmconnect.org/agmwebmanager.nsf/hf/lib-Res-
Techasst

Publications on Grant Writing

American Art Directory, R.R. Bowker Publishing. 630 Central
Ave., New Providence, NJ 07974; Tel: 888 269-5372: E-mail:
info@bowker.com   www.bowker.com

Annual Artists' Resource Directory (The Most Comprehensive Desk Reference for the Visual Artist) by Barbara L. Dougherty and Jefferson Boyer, ed., Art Calendar. P. O. Box 2675, Salisbury, MD 21802; Tel: 866 427-8225: Fax: 410 749-9626; www.artcalendar.com

Art & Design Scholarships: A Complete Guide by Conway Greene, Conway Greene Co., 1995.

Directory of Grants in the Humanities, 17th Edition, Oryx Press, 2003 (Latest edition in *Reference*). Greenwood Publishing, 88 Post Road West, Westport, CT; Tel: 800 225-5800; Fax: 603 431-2214; www.greenwood.com

Dramatists Sourcebook: Complete Opportunities for Playwrights, Translators, Composers, Lyricists and Librettists by Gillian Richards and Ray Sweatman, Theater Communications Group, New York, 1988/89. 520 Eighth Ave., 24th Fl, New York, NY 10018-4156; Tel: 212 609-5900; Fax: 212 609-5901; E-mail: tcg@tcg.org   www.tcg.org

Dollars for College - Art, Music, Drama, Garrett Park Press, Garrett Park, Maryland, 1997. PO Box 190, Garrett Park, MD 20896; Tel: 301 946-2553

Free Money for People in the Arts by Laurie Blum, Collier Books, 1991. Macmillan Publishing Company, 201 West 103rd Street, Indianapolis, IN 46290; Tel: 800 257-5755; E-mail: orders@mcp.com   www.mcp.com/

GrantFinder, Arts and Humanities, New York, St. Martin's Press, 2000. 175 Fifth Avenue, New York, NY 10010; Tel: 212 674-5151; www.stmartins.com/

Grants for Arts, Culture, and the Humanities, Foundation Center, New York, 1998. 79 Fifth Avenue/16th Street, New York, NY 10003-3076 ;Tel: 212 620-4230; Fax: 212 807-3677, 800 424-9836; fdncenter.org/

How to Find a Scholarship Online by Shannon R. Turlington McGraw-Hill, New York, 2001. P.O. Box 182604, Columbus, OH 43272; Tel: 877 833-5524; Fax: 614 759-3759; E-mail: customer.service@mcgraw-hill.com www.mcgraw-hill.com

Making Art Pay by Bernard Denvir and Howard Gray, Phaidon, 1989. AOL Time Warner Books, Three Center Plaza, Boston, MA 02108; Tel: 800 759-0190; www.phaidon.com

Money for Artists: A Guide to Grants and Awards for Individual Artists, Laura R. Green, ed., American Council for the Arts Books, New York, 1987.

Money for Film and Video Artists by Douglas Oxenhorn, ACA Books (American Council for the Arts), Allworth Press, New York, 1993. 1023 East 23 Street, Suite 510, New York, NY 10010; Tel: 212 777-8395: Fax: 212 777-8261; E-mail: PUB@allworth.com www.allworth.com

Money for Visual Artists, American Council for the Arts, New York,1993.

*Money to Work II: Funding for Visual Artists,*by Helen M. Brunner and Donald H. Russell with Grant E. Samuelsen, 1st Edition, Art Resources International, Washington, DC, 1992

National Directory of Arts Internships 2003/3004 Edition, Warren Christensen and Ron Clawges, ed., National Network for Artist Placement, NNAP, 935 West Avenue 37, Los Angeles, CA 90065; Tel: 323 222-4035; www.artistplacement.com/intern.htm

National Guide to Funding in Arts and Culture by Stan Olson, Ruth Kovacs and Suzanne Haile, 4th edition, Foundation

Center, New York, June 1996. Foundation Center, 79 Fifth Avenue, Department XL, New York, NY 10003-3076; Tel: 800 424-9836 or 212 620-4230; fdncenter.org

The National Directory of Grants and Aid to Individuals in the Arts, International, Washington International Arts Letter, Washington, DC.

Money Business: Grants and Awards for Creative Artists by Rita K. Roosevelt, Artists Foundation, Boston, 1982. www.artistsfoundation.org

Promoting Fine Art: Baltimore and Maryland: A Guide to Art Agencies, Organizations, and Galleries by Nannette Clapman Blinchikoff, N.C. Blinchikoff, Baltimore, 1997. NCB Enterprises, 8240 Streamwood Dr., Baltimore, MD 21208; Tel: 410 484-6434.

Corporate Grant Directories

Guide to Corporate Giving in the Arts 2 by Robert Porter, New York, ACA Books, American Council for the Arts, 1981.

The National Directory of Arts and Education Support by Business Corporations, 2 by Daniel Millsaps, Washington International Arts Letter, Washington, DC, 1982.

Publications On Government Grants

Cultural Directory II: Federal Funds and Services for the Arts and Humanities, Smithsonian Institution Press, Washington, DC, 1980. 750 Ninth Street, NW, Suite 4300, Washington, DC 20560-0950; Tel: (202) 275-2300; www.sipress.si.edu/

Guide to the National Endowment for the Arts 1992-93,
National Endowment for the Arts, Washington, DC, 1991.
www.nea.gov/pub/
Visual Arts Fellowships: Application Guidelines 1991-92.
National Endowment for the Arts, Washington, DC, 1991.
www.nea.gov/pub/

Publications on Foundation Grants

The Foundation Directory, Foundation Center, New York,
1960-. 79 Fifth Avenue, Department XL, New York, NY
10003-3076; Tel: 800 424-9836 or 212 620-4230;
fconline.fdncenter.org/

The Foundation Grants Index, Foundation Center, New York,
1970-. 79 Fifth Avenue, Department XL, New York, NY
10003-3076. Tel: 800 424-9836 or 212 620-4230;
fdncenter.org

Foundation Grants to Individuals, Foundation Center, New
York, 1999. 79 Fifth Avenue, Department XL, New York, NY
10003-3076. Tel: 800 424-9836 or 212 620-4230;
gtionline.fdncenter.org/

National Directory of Arts Support by Private Foundations
by Daniel Millsaps, Washington International Arts Letter,
Washington, DC, 1983.

Art That Pays

Appendix G: Community Resources

MFA Programs in the Arts, Links

Acting Depot links, theatre arts schools.
www.actingdepot.com/dramaticarts.htm

America's Best Graduate Schools 2004, U.S.News Rankings of over 1000 graduate programs, school directory featuring admissions statistics, financial aid information, and student body demographics, articles on how to choose the right school. Free online edition or premium edition (online or hard copy) for about ten bucks.
www.usnews.com/usnews/edu/grad/rankings/arts/artsindex_brief.php

American University This graduate program specializes in Visual Media. 4400 Massachusetts Avenue, NW, Washington, D.C. 20016; Tel: 202 885-2060; Fax: 202 885-2019; E-mail: communication@american.edu
www.soc.american.edu/main.cfm?pageid=65

Antioch University Master of Fine Arts in Creative Writing (MFA) "...the preeminent low-residency MFA degree program on the West Coast." Antioch University Los Angeles, Admissions Office, 13274 Fiji Way, Marina del Rey, CA 90292; E-mail: admissions@antiochla.edu
www.antiochla.edu/programs_mfa.shtml

California Institute for the Arts, CALArts grants graduate and undergraduate degrees in both visual and the performing arts. 24700 McBean Parkway, Valencia, CA 91355-2397; Tel: 661 255-1050; www.calarts.edu/

Columbia University School of the Arts
63.151.45.66/index.cfm?fuseaction=arts.main

Cooper Union The Cooper Union for the Advancement of Science and Art, established in 1859, is among the nation's oldest and most distinguished institutions of higher learning. The college, the legacy of Peter Cooper, occupies a special place in the history of American education. It is the only private, full-scholarship college in the United States dedicated exclusively to preparing students for the professions of art, architecture and engineering. Tel: 212 353-4000. The Cooper Union for the Advancement of Science and Art, Cooper Square, New York, NY 10003-7120; www.cooper.edu/

Film School Confidential by Karin Kelly and Tom Edgar, Perigee, 1997. This book contains objective and subjective information about schools that offer M.F.A. degrees in film production. These are links to MFA schools' websites. www.lather.com/fsc/fsc4.html

Gradschool.com Fine Arts Graduate School Programs REALLY a lot of information here, domestic and international. www.gradschools.com/listings/menus/art_fine_menu.html

Randy Miller compiled a great list of MFA's for creative writing programs. Many of these programs also offer an MFA in other disciplines as well. Miller makes the following caveat to the links he has chosen, "The links lead to pages primarily designed for those who want to do the kind of writing that shows up in most academic creative writing journals; the kind that outside of academe is usually called 'literary.' There aren't many resources for genre writing (mystery, romance, science fiction, and so on), though you'll find a few here and there. We have nothing against genre fiction, but by and large it's a separate market." www.sc.edu/library/science/mfa.html

Rhode Island School of Design, RISD A well-known graduate program in several visual arts disciplines. Tel: 401 454-6700; E-mail: gstudies@risd.edu. www.risd.edu/

Screensite on Film/TV/Video College Programs - a great portal informational site for people interested in studying film making. www.tcf.ua.edu/ScreenSite/teach/schools/filmTV.htm

The School of the Art Institute of Chicago 37 South Wabash Avenue, Chicago, IL 60603; Tel: 312 899-5219; E-mail: admiss@artic.edu
www.artic.edu/saic/programs/depts/graduate/index.html

School of Film and Television at Chapman University Robert Bassett, Dean, Cecil B. DeMille Hall, One University Drive, Orange, California 92866; Tel: 714 997-6765; Fax: 714 997-6700; E-mail: ftvinfo@chapman.edu ftv.chapman.edu/

UCLArts Contact: Caron Cronin, Student Advisor, UCLA Department of Art, 11000 Kinross Ave., Suite 245, Box 951615, Los Angeles, CA 90095; Tel: 310 206-7363; E-mail: artinfo@arts.ucla.edu
www.art.ucla.edu/graduate/degree_programs/
degree_programs.htm

University of California, Berkeley does not offer a graduate program in Creative Writing, but they provide links. learning.berkeley.edu/creative/page8.html

University of Idaho compiled this comprehensive list of graduate schools (addresses and telephone numbers) to which artists can apply to do graduate work in the arts. www.class.uidaho.edu/uisculpture/mfaschools.htm

Yahoo Directory We reviewed this list and it is a good list of schools to apply to for an MFA in writing. dir.yahoo.com/Arts/ Humanities/Literature/Creative_Writing/Education/ MFA_Programs/ And then there's this one:

Yahoo Directory Arts Graduate Programs dir.yahoo.com/Arts/Education/College_and_University/ Departments_and_Programs/Graduate_Programs/

World Wide Arts Resources, absolutearts.com—Academic Arts section listings on all areas of art education from classes for children to the graduate level, continuing education programs, art therapy, summer camps and programs, outreach programs and more. Can be browsed by interest or alphabetically. wwar.com/categories/Academic/

Yale University School of Art Administrative Offices Holcombe T. Green, Jr. Hall, 1156 Chapel Street, New Haven CT 06520-833; Tel: 800 282-1550, Directory Assistance: 203°432-4771; www.yale.edu/art/

Community Links

Suite 101.com Online community for all types. www.suite101.com/

Conferences and Colonies for Artists & Writers

Association of Writers and Writing Programs, AWP with listings of conferences, writing programs, contests state by state and international.

Contact:

George Mason University

Mailstop 1E3

Fairfax, VA 22030-4444

Tel: 703 993-4301; E-mail: awp@gmu.edu

Google Directory of Writer's Conferences www.google.com/search?hl=en&lr=&ie=UTF-8&oe=UTF-8&newwindow=1&safe=off&q=writing+conferences&sa=N&tab=wd&cat=gwd%2FTop

Shaw Guide to Writing Conferences is a great site with reliable information about a great variety of conferences. writing.shawguides.com/

Conferences from this list include:

The Algonkian Writer Workshops Advice on the best way to learn the craft of the novel, how to find an agent in these "Agent-Editor" workshops, plus poetry and short story workshops. webdelsol.com/Algonkian/

Aspen Summer Words Writing Retreat & Literary Festival A conference set in among Aspen's mountains with award-winning and bestselling authors and intensive workshops, readings, presentations, panel discussions, professional consultations, and social networking. www.aspenwriters.org

Jack London Writers Conference One-day conference featuring keynote luncheon speaker as well as workshops and panels by distinguished writers, editors, agents and publishers. www.peninsulawriter.com

Poets & Writers has a *Speakeasy*, which is an online chat room where you can get up-to-date advice and help from other writers who have been to a conference. The best way to get information about colonies or conferences is to talk to the people who have been there. Here is one opportunity: www.pw.org/speak.htm

Proprioceptive Writing® In Ireland They teach a form of writing for finding your authentic voice at Anam Cara, an Irish Retreat overlooking Coulagh Bay, Beara Peninsula, West Cork. www.contemplativewriting.com

Sewanee Writers' Conferences A twelve-day conference where you can talk to and learn from some of America's best working writers. www.sewaneewriters.org

Under the Volcano Professional writing workshops in Mexican village. Weeklong retreats January & August. The Volcano says, "No hype, just today's best literary writers teaching what you need to learn." www.underthevolcano.org

Wesleyan Writers Conference Seminars, workshops, and manuscript consultations with noted faculty, designed to give you new perspectives and introduce you to other writers who share your interests.
www.wesleyan.edu/writing/conferen.html

Whidbey Island Writers Conference Presenters specifically selected for their talent, passion for writing, and desire to teach. www.writeonwhidbey.org

The Writers Studio "The most personal program," NY Times. Beginning & Advanced Classes in NYC & online. Founded by Philip Schultz. Alumni include Walter Mosley, Martha McPhee, Jennifer Egan. Tutorials available. www.writerstudio.com

The Writing Mill: Windmill Writing Workshop Two 8-day workshops led by award-winning writers. Work on your novel, short story, play or screenplay on a mountain in Majorca. www.thewritingmill.org

Yahoo.com For another group of links to various artists' residency programs, see:d4.dir.scd.yahoo.com/arts/ organizations/artists__retreats_and_colonies/

The Zuzu's Petals Literary Resource U.S. Regional Writers' Conferences, Colonies and Centers, by State and Country. www.zuzu.com/worklink.htm

Colonies & Writer's Programs Publications

Artists & Writers Colonies: Retreat, Residencies and Respites for the Creative Mind by Gail Hellund Bowler, Poets & Writers, Blue Heron Pub., Portland, OR, 2000.

Artists Communities: A Directory of Residencies in the United States That Offer Time and Space for Creativity, 2nd Ed. Allworth Press, New York, 2000. 10 East 23rd Street, Suite 210, New York, NY, 10010; Tel: 212-777-8395; www.allworth.com

Artist's Resource: The Watson-Guptill Guide to Academic Programs, Artists' Colonies and Artist-in-Residence Programs, Conferences, Workshops by Karen Chambers, Watson-Guptill Publications, New York, 1999. 770 Broadway, New York, NY 10003; Tel: 800 278-8477; Fax 646-654-5487; watson-guptill.com

Colonies

Act I Creativity Center, #1201 c/o Plotsky, 4550 Warwick Blvd., Kansas City, MO 64111; Tel: 816 753-0208

Anam Cara Writer's and Artist's Retreat, Eyeries, Beara, West Cork, Ireland; Tel: 353 (0)27 74441 Fax: 353 (0)27 74448; E-mail: anamcararetreat@eircom.net www.ugr.com/anamcararetreat/

Atlantic Center for the Arts, 1414 Art Center Avenue, New Smyrna Beach FL 32168; Tel: 904 427-6975

Bellagio Study and Conference Center, Rockefeller Foundation, 1133 Avenue of the Americas, New York, NY 10036; Tel: 212 869-8500

Blue Mountain Center, Blue Mountain Lake, New York, NY 12812; Tel: 518 325-7391

Centrum Artist-In-Residence, P.O. Box 1158, Port Townsend, WA 98368; Tel:206 385-3102

The Clearing, P.O. Box 65, Ellison Bay, WI 54210; Tel: 414 854-4088

Cottages at Hedgebrook, 2197 E. Millman Rd., Langley, WA 98260; Tel: 206 321-4786

Curry Hill Plantation Writer's Retreat, 404 Cresmont Ave., Hattiesburg, MS 39401; Tel: 601 264-7034

Djerassi Foundation, 2325 Bear Gulch Rd., Woodside, CA 94062; Tel: 415 851-8395

Dorland Mountain Arts Colony, P.O. Box 6, Temecula, CA 92593; Tel: 714 676-5039

Dorset Colony House for Writers, P.O. Box 519, Dorset, VT 05251; Tel: 802 867-2223

Edward Albee Foundation, 14 Harrison Street, New York, NY 10013; Tel: 212 226-2020

Fine Arts Work Center, 24 Pearl Street, P.O. Box 565, Provincetown, MA 02657; Tel: 508 487-9960

The Hambridge Center, P.O. Box 339, Rabun Gap, GA 30568

Kalani Honua, R.R. 2, Box 4500, Pahoa, HI 96778; Tel: 808 965-7828

The MacDowell Colony, 100 High St., Peterborough, NH 03458; Tel: 603 924-3886, 212 966-4860

Mantalvo Center for the Arts, P.O. Box 158, Saratoga, CA 95071; Tel: 408 741-3421

Mary Anderson Center, #1201, c/o Sarah Yates, 101 St. Francis Drive, Mt. St. Francis, IN 47146; Tel: 812 923-8602; Fax: 812 923-3200; E-mail: sry847@aol.com

Mesa Refuge, c/o Common Counsel Foundation, 1221 Preservation Park Way, Oakland, CA 94612; Tel:510 834-2995

Millay Colony for the Arts, Steepletop, P.O. Box 3, Austerlitz, NY 12017-0003; Tel: 518 392-3103

Niaguna Colony, Route 1, Stoutland, MO 65567 (No Phone)

Northwood Institute Creativity Center, 3225 Cook Rd., Midland, MI 48640-2398; Tel: 517 837-4478

Oregon Writers Colony House, P.O. Box 15200, Portland, OR 97215; Tel: 513 771-0428

Palenville Interarts Colony, P.O. Box 59, Palenville, NY 12463; Tel: 518 678-3332

Potash Arts, 9 Frazier Lane, Cummington, MA 01026; Tel: 413 634-2172

Ragdale Foundation, 1260 N. Green Bay Rd., Lake Forest, IL 60045; Tel: 708 234-1063

The Saint James Colony, P.O. Box 71, Saint James, MI 49782; (No Telephone)

The Syvenna Foundation Writers-In-Residence, Route 1, Box 193, Linden, TX 75563; Tel: 903 835-8252

Ucross Foundation, 2836 U.S. Highway 14-16 East, Clearmont, WY 82835; Tel: 307 737-2291

Vermont Studio Center, P.O. Box 613, Johnson, VT 05656, Tel: 802 635-2727

Virginia Center for the Creative Arts, Box VCCA, Sweet Briar, VA 24595 Tel: 804 946-7236

The Woodstock Guild's Byrdcliffe Arts Colony, 34 Tinker St., Woodstock, NY 12498 Tel: 914 679-2079

The Writer's Place, Cliffs of Moher, County Clare, Ireland info@salmonpoetry.com (+) 353 65 7081941.
The Writers' Colony at Dairy Hollow, 515 Spring Street, Eureka Springs, AR 72632; Tel: 501-253-7444 fax: 501-253-9859; email: director@writerscolony.org
www.writerscolony.org

Helene Wurlitzer Foundation, P.O. Box 545, Taos, NM 87571, Tel: 505 758-2413

Yaddo, P.O. Box 395, Saratoga Springs, NY 12866-3095 Tel: 518 548-0746

Yosemite Renaissance Artists-in-Residence Program, PO Box 1430, Mariposa, CA 95338; Tel: 209-946-4808.
Open to artists with established reputations within the arts community working in any visual art medium.° Free housing for up to one month in Yosemite National Park.° Must participate in one community event with local artists. www.yosemiteart.org/prod2.htm

∞

Art That Pays

Appendix H: Overseas Resources

Links

anweb.co.uk   Great source of contact information for artists in the UK and Europe. www.anweb.co.uk/

Art Diary International Giancarlo Politi Editor, Via Carlo Farini 68, 20159 Milano, Italy - Tel: +39 02 6887341; Fax: +39 02 66801290. Up-to-date contact information for artists, galleries, designers, photographers and arts services. www.flashartonline.com/sections/international/artdiary_int.asp

Arts International Search Engine for festivals, events and other international organizations. www.artsinternational.org/knowledge_base/database_newer/search_database.asp?entity=org

Arts International a non-profit solely devoted to "the development and support of global interchange in the arts." Tel: 212 674-9744; www.artsinternational.org/

Artslynx International Arts jobs information. www.artslynx.org/jobs.htm

International Theatre Institute
- World Theatre Day
- International Dance Day
- Theatre of the Nations
- Radio Play Competition
- International One Man Show Festival

- Workshop for Young Directors
- And more

iti.unesco.org/index.html

Canada Council for the Arts Information on programs available to Canadians, or in Canada. Great links page for international arts councils and organizations. Tel: 800 263-5588 (Canada only) or 613 566-4414;
www.canadacouncil.ca/artsinfo/

Ecomonist.com
Briefings and information about countries and cities around the world and all articles from The Economist magazine. Extensive site.
The Economist
25 St James's Street
London, SW1A 1HG
United Kingdom
Fax: +44 20 7839 2968/9;
E-mail: letters@economist.com
www.economist.com/countries/

Edinburgh Festival Fringe The Fringe was founded on the principal of open access for all performers. On the site you will find information on and applications for working at the Fringe and trading & performing on "the Royal Mile" during the festival. Plus stories from those who have been there.
Contact:
Edinburgh Festival Fringe
180 High Street
Edinburgh, EH1 1QS, Scotland
Tel: +44 (0)131 226 0026
E-mail: admin@edfringe.com
www.edfringe.com/

Idealist.org "Find Organizations" Searchable database of nonprofit and community organizations from around the world. www.idealist.org/ip/orgSearch?MODULE=ORG

Lonely Planet Excerpts from the travel guides of Lonely Planet Publications, plus what are probably the best guidebooks available. www.lonelyplanet.com/
Contact:

In Australia
Lonely Planet Publications
ABN 36 005 607 983
Locked Bag 1
Footscray
Victoria 3011
talk2us@lonelyplanet.com.au
Tel: +61 3 8379 8000
Fax: +61 3 8379 8111

In the US
Lonely Planet Publications
150 Linden Street
Oakland CA 94607
info@lonelyplanet.com
Tel: 510.893.8555
Fax: 510.893.8563

In the UK
Lonely Planet Publications
72-82 Rosebery Avenue
Clerkenwell, London, EC1R 4RW, ENGLAND
go@lonelyplanet.co.uk
Tel: 44 20 7841 9000
Fax: 44 20 7841 9001

In France
Lonely Planet Publications
1 rue du Dahomey
75011 Paris
bip@lonelyplanet.fr
Tel: 01 55 25 33 00
Fax: 01 55 25 33 01

Online real-time bulletin board postings for advice from others, the Thorn Tree. thorntree.lonelyplanet.com/

Money for International Exchange in the Arts by Jane Gullong, Noreen Tomassi, and Anna Rubin. New York: American Council for the Arts, published in cooperation with Arts International, revised 2000. Available from Arts International, Institute of International Education, 809 United Nations Plaza, New York, NY 10017-3850. Information on grants, fellowships and awards for travel and work abroad, international artists' residencies and etc. www.artsinternational.org

Musica Mundi Sponsors of a series of international choir competitions & festivals, organised by the INTERKULTUR Foundation. www.musica-mundi.com/mc_en/index.html

OANDA.com Currency Converter, multi-lingual and up-to-date. Find out how much you're *really* being paid. www.oanda.com/converter/classic

RawArtLink.com/Links International festivals and fairs, galleries, exhibitions, foundations and charities. www.rawartlink.com/html/links.html

Study Abroad Links A searchable web guide for opportunities to study abroad. www.studyabroadlinks.com/index.htm

TCAEP.co.UK The constants and equations page for science, maths and astronomy (in case you need to estimate the Doppler Effect of the taxi passing you by or you're stuck for something clever to say to your new Romanian girlfriend).
tcaep.co.uk/

Travel Warnings & Consular Information Sheets from U.S. Department of State Bureau of Consular Affairs American Citizens Services   In addition to travel warnings (terrorist related and other-wise) this site furnishes Consular Information Sheets which "are available for every country of the world. They include such information as location of the U.S. Embassy or Consulate in the subject country, unusual immigration practices, health conditions, minor political disturbances, unusual currency and entry regulations, crime and security information, and drug penalties."
travel.state.gov/travel_warnings.html

University of Colorado at Boulder   Grants information and places to study the arts overseas. www.colorado.edu/ocg/arts_hum/

VirtualTourist.com   A directory of all the WWW servers worldwide. www.virtualtourist.com/vt/

Visiting Arts...Directory, London. Visiting Arts, 1999. Available from Visiting Arts, Bloomsbury House 74–77, Great Russell Street, London WC1B 3DA, England. Directories outlining the arts infrastructure and providing contact information for countries from Norway to Thailand. www.visitingarts.org.uk/home.html

World Anthem Database - browsable collection of national anthems from around the world (just in case your stuck for an encore number and want to impress the locals). www.geocities.com/CollegePark/Library/9897/

Zeroland New Zealand-based integrated, well-organized and searchable website directory of arts and cultures of the world. Many listings and portals for international film, arts, music and dance festivals, plus much more. Updated monthly. Well worth a visit. Adrian Hart, Director, Zeroland, 17A Garmons Way, Milford, Auckland, New Zealand;
Tel or Fax: 64 410 0785; E-mail: ahart@zeroland.co.nz
www.zeroland.co.nz/index.html

Publications

The CIA World FactBook "The World Factbook 2003 printed version provides a 'snapshot' of the world as of 1 January 2003. The online Factbook is updated regularly - generally weekly - throughout the year.
www.odci.gov/cia/publications/factbook/

Purchasing information: www.odci.gov/cia/publications/factbook/docs/purchase_info.html
Superintendent of Documents
P. O. Box 371954
Pittsburgh, PA 15250-7954
Tel: 202 512-1800, 866 512-1800
Fax: 202 512-2250.

or:

National Technical Information Service
5285 Port Royal Road
Springfield, VA 22161
Tel: 800 553-6847 (only in the US),
703 605-6000 (for outside US)
Fax: 703 605-6900
www.ntis.gov/

"The *Factbook* is in the public domain. Accordingly, it may be copied freely without permission of the Central Intelligence Agency (CIA). (The official seal of the CIA, however, may NOT be copied without permission as required by the CIA Act of 1949. Misuse of the official seal of the CIA could result in civil and criminal penalties.)"
Available for hardcopy purchase or Internet download.

Overseas Americans: The Essential Guide To Living And Working Abroad by William Beaver, Paladin Press, illustrated edition, July 2001; Gunbarrel Tech Center, 7077 Winchester Circle, Boulder, Colorado 80301; Tel: 303 443-7250; Fax: 303 442-8741; E-mail: service@paladin-press.com
www.paladin-press.com/

Travel Warnings & Consular Information Sheets from U.S. Department of State Bureau of Consular Affairs American Citizens Services In addition to travel warnings (terrorist related and other-wise) this site furnishes Consular Information Sheets which "are available for every country of the world. They include such information as location of the U.S. Embassy or Consulate in the subject country, unusual immigration practices, health conditions, minor political disturbances, unusual currency and entry regulations, crime and security information, and drug penalties."
travel.state.gov/travel_warnings.html

The Travel Writer's Handbook, 5th Ed: How to Write and Sell Your Own Travel Experiences by Louise Purwin Zobel, Surrey Books, 5th edition, July 2002; 230 East Ohio Street, Suite 120, Chicago, Illinois 60611; Tel: 312 751-7330; Fax: 312 751-7334; surreybooks.com/

VirtualTourist.com   A directory of all the WWW servers worldwide. www.virtualtourist.com/vt/

World Anthem Database - browsable collection of national anthems from around the world (just in case your stuck for an encore number and want to impress the locals). www.geocities.com/CollegePark/Library/9897/

Free Internet Access

Open Studio's sites for free Internet access. www.benton.org/openstudio/home.html

Appendix I: Acting Resources

Publications on Acting

Acting Instruction

Acting: The First Six Lessons by Richard Boleslavski, Routledge, 1st edition, 2003. 10650 Toebben Drive, Independence, KY 4105; Tel: 800 634-7064; www.routledge-ny.com It's old, it's short, it's brilliant.

Actors Guide to qualified Acting Coaches: New York by Larry Silverberg, Smith and Kraus Books, 1996. One Main Street., P.O. Box 127, Lyme, NH 03768; Tel: 800 895-4331.

An Actor Prepares by Constantine Stanislavski, et al., Theatre Arts Books, reprint edition 2002.

Audition: Everything an Actor Needs to Know to Get the Part by Michael Shurtleff, Bob Fosse, Bantam Dell Pub., 1986. Still the definitive book on auditioning. www.randomhouse.com/bantamdell/

The Fervent Years: The Group Theatre and the Thirties by Harold Clurman, DaCapo Press, 1988. Perseus Books Group, 11 Cambridge Center, Cambridge, MA 02142; Tel: 617 252-5200; www.dacapopress.com

Monologues for Young Actors, Lorraine Cohen, Editor, Avon, 1994. HarperCollins Publishers, 10 East 53rd Street, New York, NY 10022; Tel: 212 207-7000; www.harpercollins.com/

On the Technique of Acting by Michael Chekhov, Harper Resource, 1993. HarperCollins Publishers, 10 East 53rd Street, New York, NY 10022, Tel: 212 207-7000; www.harpercollins.com

Sanford Meisner on Acting by Sanford Meisner, et al., Random House/Vintage Books, 1st edition, 1987. 745 Broadway, 15-3, New York, NY 10019; One of the best books on acting. www.randomhouse.com/vintage/

Stella Adler: The Art of Acting by Stella Adler, Applause Books, 2000. 151 West 46th Street, 8th Floor, New York, NY 10036; Tel: 212 575-9265; www.applausepub.com

To the Actor by Michael Chekhov, Routledge, 2002. 10650 Toebben Drive, Independence, KY 41051, Tel: 800 634-7064; www.routledge-ny.com

Where to Train, Silver Screen Publishing, 2001. 1438 N. Gower St., #39, Hollywood, CA 90028.

Agents/Casting Directors

The Actor's Encyclopedia of Casting Directors: Conversations with Over 100 Casting Directors on How to Get the Job by Karen Kondazian, et al., Lone Eagle Publishing Company, 2000. Hollywood Creative Directory, C/O IFILM Publishing, 1024 N. Orange Dr., Hollywood, CA 90038; Tel: 323 308-3490 or 800 815-0503; Fax: 323-308-3493. Interviews with casting directors, plus their mailing addresses. www.hcdonline.com/

The Agencies —What the Actor Needs to Know (New York edition and Hollywood edition) by Lawrence Parke, Acting World Books. P.O. Box 3899 Hollywood, CA 90028; published monthly. www.actingworldbooks.org/

The Agency Guide: The Official Guide to Talent Agencies in Los Angeles, Breakdown Services, Ltd. 2140 Cotner Avenue Los Angeles, CA 90025. Published bi-annually.

Agents on Actors: Over Sixty Professionals Share Their Secrets on Finding Work on the Stage and Screen by Hettie Lynne Hurtes, et al. Back Stage Books, First Edition, 2000. Watson-Guptill Publications, 1515 Broadway, New York, NY 10036; www.watsonguptill.com

Agents, Managers & Casting Directors 411, Published by 411 Publishing/Variety, this directory is updated twice a year, so its claim of "up-to-date listings of agents, managers and casting directors for the film and television industry" seems to be fairly accurate. Information for Los Angeles, New York, Chicago and for some other U.S. cities. 411 Publishing Company, 5700 Wilshire Blvd., Suite 120, Los Angeles, CA 90036-5804; Tel: 323 965-2020, 800 545-2411; www.411publishing.com

The Backstage Guide to Casting Directors by Hettie Lynne Hurts, Back Stage Books, 1998. Watson-Guptill Publications, 1515 Broadway, New York, NY 10036; www.watsonguptill.com

The C.D. Directory, a quarterly address book available through Breakdown Services, Ltd. In Los Angeles: 1120 S. Robertson, Third Floor, Los Angeles, CA 90035; 310 276-9166. In New York: 212 869-2003; www.breakdownservices.com

Casting Director Guide, 2003, L.A. Actors Online, 60 E. Magnolia Blvd., Burbank, CA 91502. Tel: 818 841-7165; www.laactorsonline.com/

The Casting Directors and the Casting Process by Keith Wolfe, Silver Screen Publishing, 2001. 1438 N. Gower St., #39, Hollywood, CA 90028.

From Agent to Actor: An Unsentimental Education or What the Other Half Knows by Adgar & Edgar Small, Samuel French Trade, First Edition, 1991. 7623 Sunset Blvd., Hollywood, CA 90046; Tel: 323 876-0570; Fax: 323 876-6822. Good stuff. www.samuelfrench.com/

Getting the Part: Thirty-Three Professional Casting Directors Tell You How to Get Work in Theater, Films, Commercials, and TV by Judith Searle, et al. Limelight Editions, 3rd Edition, 1999. 118 East 30 Street, New York, NY 10016; Tel: 212 532-5525; Fax: 212-532-5526; www.limelighteditions.com/

The Hollywood Edition of the Agencies, What the Actor Needs to Know, 2003. Acting World Books P.O. Box 3899 Hollywood, CA 90078; Tel: 818 905-1345.

How to Agent Your Agent by Nancy Rainford, et al; Lone Eagle Publishing Company, First Edition 2002.Hollywood Creative Directory, C/O IFILM Publishing, 1024 N. Orange Dr., Hollywood, CA 90038; Tel: 323 308-3490 or 800 815-0503; Fax: 323-308-3493; www.hcdonline.com/

Los Angeles Agents Book,The, by K. Callan, Sweden Press, 2001. Box 1612, Studio City, CA 91614; Tel: 818 995-4250; Fax: 818 995-4399; www.swedenpress.com/NY.htm

Movie Extra Work for Rocket Scientists: The Original Hollywood Movie Extra Casting Agency Directory, Back To One Publications, 2003 Edition. P.O. Box 753, Hollywood, CA 90078; www.backtoone.net

New York Agent Book: Get the Agent You Need and the Career You Want by K. Callan, Kristi Nolte, Editor, SCB International, 6th edition, 2000. The best of its kind for the New York scene. Sweden Press, Inc., Box 1612, Studio City, CA 91614; Tel: 818 995-4250; Fax: 818 995-4399; www.swedenpress.com/NY.htm

Business

Acting as a Business: Strategies for Success by Brian O'Neil, Lisa Barnett, editor, et al. Heinemann, 1st Edition, 1999. Heinemann, P.O. Box 6926, Portsmouth, NH 03802-6926; Tel: 800 225-5800; Fax: 603 431-2214; e-mail: ustserv@heinemann.com www.heinemanndrama.com

The Business of Acting by Brad Lemack, Ingenuity Press, 2002. P.O. Box 69822; Los Angeles, CA 90069; www.ingenuitypressusa.com

Make Acting Work: The Practical Path to a Successful Career, by Chrys Salt, et al., Methuen Publishing Limited, 2nd Edition, 2001. 215 Vauxhall Bridge Road, London SWIW IEj; Tel: +44 20 7798 160; Fax: +44 20 7828 2098 or 7233 9827; www.methuen.co.uk

Promoting Your Acting Career by Glenn Alterman, Allworth Press, 1998. 10 East 23rd St., New York, NY 10010; Tel: 212 777-8395; www.allworth.com

Self Promotion, Self Publicizing, Self Advertising for Actors, Acting World Books 1984/1999. P.O. Box 3044, Hollywood, CA 90078; www.actingworldbooks.org

Your Film Acting Career: How to Break Into the Movies & TV & Survive in Hollywood by M.K. Lewis, Rosemary R. Lewis, et al. Gorham House Publishing, 4th edition, 1998. 2118 Wilshire Blvd., Suite 777, Santa Monica, CA 90403. All about the business of acting.

Hollywood

Actor's Guide, An – Your First Year in Hollywood by Michael Saint Nicholas, Allworth Press, revised edition. 10 East 23 Street, Suite 510 New York, NY 10010. Tel: 212 777-8395; www.allworth.com/

The Agency Guide - The Official Guide to Talent Agencies in Los Angeles, Winter/Spring 2003, Breakdown Services Ltd. In Los Angeles: 1120 S. Robertson, Third Floor, Los Angeles, CA 90035; 310 276-9166. In New York: 212 869-2003; www.breakdownservices.com

The Hollywood Edition of the Agencies, What the Actor Needs to Know, 2003. Acting World Books P.O. Box 3899 Hollywood, CA 90078; Tel: 818 905-1345.

The Los Angeles Agents Book by K. Callan. Sweden Press, 2001. Box 1612, Studio City, CA 91614; Tel: 818 995-4250; Fax: 818 995-4399; www.swedenpress.com/NY.htm

New York

An Actor's Guide: Making it In New York City by Glenn Alterman, et al. Allworth Press, First Edition, 2002. 10 East 23 Street, Suite 510, New York, NY 10010; Tel: 212 777-8395; www.allworth.com/

An Actor's Guide – Your First Year in New York by Michael Saint Nicholas, Allworth Press, revised edition. 10 East 23 Street, Suite 510, New York, NY 10010; Tel: 212 777-8395; www.allworth.com/

New York Agent Book: Get the Agent You Need and the Career You Want, by K. Callan, Kristi Nolte, Editor, SCB International, 6th edition, 2000. Sweden Press, Inc., Box 1612, Studio City, CA 91614; Tel: 818 995-4250; Fax: 818 995-4399; www.swedenpress.com/NY.htm

Specialty Age Groups

Acting in Prime Time: The Mature Person's Guide to Breaking Into Show Business by Terry Chayefsky, et al. Heinemann,

1st Edition, 1996. P.O. Box 6926, Portsmouth, NH 03802-6926; Tel: 800 225-5800; Fax: 603 431-2214; e-mail: ustserv@heinemann.com   www.heinemanndrama.com

Monologues for Young Actor, Lorraine Cohen, Editor. Avon, HarperCollins Publishers, 1994. 10 East 53rd Street, New York, NY 10022; Tel: 212 207-7000; www.harpercollins.com

Stars in Your Eyes, Feet on the Ground: A Practical Guide for Teenage Actors (and Their Parents) by Annie Jay with Lu Anne Feik, et al. American Theatre Works, Inc., 1st Edition, 1999. 173 Church St., P.O. Box 510, Dorset, VT 05251-0510; www.theatredirectories.com

Miscellaneous

Acting In Chicago: How to Break Into Theatre, Film, and Television, by Belinda Bremner, et al. Act 1 Bookstore, 3rd Edition, 2002. 2540 N. Lincoln, Chicago, IL 60614.

The Actor's Guide to the Internet: The Definitive Reference Guide for Actors Who Wish to Explore the Countless Opportunities Awaiting Them in Cyberspace by Rob Kozlowski, book and CD-ROM edition, Heinemann, 1999. P.O. Box 6926, Portsmouth, NH 03802-6926; Tel: 800 225-5800; Fax: 603 431-2214; e-mail: ustserv@heinemann.com www.heinemanndrama.com

Career Opportunities in Theater and the Performing Arts, 2nd edition, by Shelly Field, Checkmark Books. Facts On File, Inc., 11 Penn Plaza, New York, NY 10001; www.factsonfile.com

Not for Tourists Web Directory for New York, Chicago and Los Angeles Great general info as well as specific to all areas of the arts. www.notfortourists.com/

Samuel French Books Every play you could want.
New York: Samuel French, Inc., 45 West 25th Street, New York, NY 10010; Tel: 212 206-8990; Fax: 212 206-1429; *Los Angeles:* Samuel French, Inc., 7623 Sunset Blvd., Hollywood, CA 90046; Tel: 323 876-0570; Fax: 323 876-6822 *Studio City:* Samuel French Bookstore, 11963 Ventura Blvd., Studio City, CA 91604; Tel: 818 762-0535; *Canada:* Samuel French (Canada) Ltd. 100 Lombard Street, Toronto, Ont., Canada M5C 1M3; Tel: 416 363-3536; Fax: 416 363-1108

Smart Actors, Foolish Choices: A Self-Help Guide to Coping with the Emotional Stresses of the Business by Katherine Mayfield, et al. Back Stage Books,1st Edition, 1996. Watson-Guptill Publications, 1515 Broadway, New York, NY 10036; www.watsonguptill.com

Survival Jobs by Deborah Jacobson, Broadway Books, 1998. 1540 Broadway, New York, NY 10036; www.randomhouse.com/broadway

Theater Sources Dot Com: A Complete Guide to Online Theatre and Dance Resources by Louis E. Catron, et al., 1st Edition, 2001. Heinemann, 361 Hanover St., Portsmouth, NH 03801-3912. www.heinemanndrama.com

Acting Links

Academy Players Directory Database actually used by casting people. Membership fee. www.acadpd.org/index.html

Actingbiz.com Articles, resources, book reviews… www.actingbiz.com

Acting Insane Site for actors, playwrights and etc. Directories and resources, including free website tools. www.dvshop.ca/dvcafe/film/actinsane.htm

The Acting Page Young actress, Leslie Wolos, gives surprisingly insightful guidance to young actors, plus links. start.at/theactingpage

Acting Resources Good links, including connections for South Asian and Aboriginal performers. www.dvshop.ca/dvcafe/film/actres.htm

Acting Resources for New York City from the NY Public Library for the Performing Arts www.nypl.org/research/lpa/internet/acting.htm

ActorSite A lot of free information, including help designing and building your own website. actorsite.com/community/

Actor's Post Pay site, but with free portals for casting directors, talent agencies, headshot photographers, casting notices, etc. Listings for all states. www.actorspost.com/

ActorsSource Homepage, the "most extensive acting related homepage on the internet." For whatever that's worth. www.actorsource.com/

Actors Workout Studio, Fran Montano teaching the Meisner Technique as taught by the late Edward Kaye-Martin. 4735 Lankershim Blvd., North Hollywood, CA 91602; Tel: (818) 766-2171; e-mail: info@actorsworkout.com www.actorsworkout.com/

Allworth Press Publishers of business and self-help books for artists, writers, designers, film and performing artists. www.allworth.com/

The American Musical Theatre Reference Library More extensive than you could possibly imagine. www.americanmusicals.com/Links_htm.htm

ArtsLynx Library of on-line theatre resources.
www.artslynx.org/theatre/acting.htm

AWOL: Acting Workshop On-Line Free lessons and pithy advice for actors. Lots of links. Fun to checkout.
www.redbirdstudio.com/AWOL/acting2.html

Backstage/Backstage West "The Complete Online Performing Arts Resource." www.backstage.com

Brooklyn Arts Council Well maintained and informative web site.
www.brooklynartscouncil.org/index.cfm?ts=04222003150344

California Arts Advocates Links
www.calartsadvocates.org/MEMBERSHIP/links.html

Candace Silvers Studios Silvers teaches how to live in possibility, no hedging. Acting coach, life coach. Free sessions each Friday, noon to 1:00. 12215 Ventura Blvd. Suite 207 Studio City CA 91604; Tel: 818 755-4609; e-mail: CandaceSilversStudios@aol.com; www.candacesilvers.com/

Caryn.com Cited in Backstage West as one of the most useful career resources online. Actors, especially you relative newcomers, should check it out. www.caryn.com/acting/

Circle in the Square Theatre School Information and programs for all the arts, education, job opportunities, etc.
www.circlesquare.org/arts_education.html

DMOZ Open Directory Project Free resource guide for the aspiring. dmoz.org/Arts/Performing_Arts/Acting/

DoNotPay.org Please, actors, visit this site. Hear what Mr. DaMota has to say. www.donotpay.org/

East LA College Acting Resources Good stuff.
www.perspicacity.com/elactheatre/library/acting.htm

Getty Multicultural Undergraduate Internships at Los Angeles Arts Organizations
www.getty.edu/grants/funding/leadership/internships/la.html

Google Directory Very helpful.
directory.google.com/Top/Arts/Performing_Arts/Acting/

The Internet Theatre Index More than a thousand links for the theatrically minded. www.dramaturgy.net/index/?src=store

Larry Edmunds Bookshop On-line source for acting books.
www.larryedmunds.com/

Los Angeles County Arts Internship Program for nonprofit "performing, presenting, literary and municipal arts organizations." lacountyarts.co.la.ca.us/internship.html

New York Play Development Theatre Resource Links Abundant links for companies, playwriting resources and etc. nyplaydevelopment.home.pipeline.com/Links.htm

New York Theatre Development Fund Listing of New York theatres and acting schools.
www.tdf.org/services/tktsplus/nyc.html

The New York Theatre Experience, Inc. Theatre resources, companies both in and out of NY, plus link to "Lego Hamlet." How could you pass that up?
www.nytheatre.com/nytheatre/links.htm

Not for Tourists Web Directory for New York, Chicago and Los Angeles Great general info as well as specific to all areas of the arts. www.notfortourists.com/

NYCastings.com Acting news, casting news, agents, casting directors, etc. www.nycastings.com/acting

The Open Directory Project "the largest, most comprehensive human-edited directory on the Web." Great links. Spend some time surfing. dmoz.org/Arts/

Performance Studies International A professional association founded to promote international communication between performers and scholars of performing arts. www.psi-web.org/mission.html

Performing Arts Online Links section with over 15,000 performing arts related websites for all disciplines. Plus they will help you, gratis, to build your own website. performingarts.net/index.html

Questia—The World's Largest Online Library Great source for readings, plays, monologues—free. www.questia.com

UCLA Shakespeare Group Links Festivals, companies, online theatre resources. www.uclashakespeare.org/sklinks.htm

University of Massachusetts Theatre Links Dept. of Theater, Fine Arts Center 112, University of Massachusetts, 151 Presidents Drive, Amherst, MA 01003; www.umass.edu/theater/links.html

University of Tennessee Theatre Resources Links Steven R. Harris, Librarian for Theatre, 145 Hodges Library, Tel: 865 974-8693; Fax: 865 974-9242; www.lib.utk.edu/refs/theatre/

The VoiceWorks, "an up-to-date listing of individuals already working in the industry, and a vital reference site for those embarking on their careers." Good resource for television, radio and music performers. www.thevoiceworks.com/contact.htm

The WWW Virtual Library Theatre and Drama Free virtual library of all things theatrical. vl-theatre.com/

Yahoo Theatre Directory Wonderful source of all links theatrical: acting, plays, directing, playwriting and on and on... dir.yahoo.com/Arts/Performing_Arts/Theater/

Acting Unions

Actor's Equity

National Headquarters:
165 West 46th Street, New York, NY 10036;
Tel: 212 869-8530; Fax: 212 719-9815

The Eastern Region:
New York
165 West 46th Street, New York, NY 10036;
Tel: 212-869-8530; Fax: 212-719-9815
Orlando
10319 Orangewood Boulevard, Orlando, Florida 32821;
Tel: 407-345-8600; Fax: 407-345-1522

The Central Region:
Chicago
125 S. Clark Street, Suite 1500, Chicago, Illinois 60603;
Tel: 312 641-0393; Fax: 312 641-6365; Auditions: 312 641-0418

The Western Region:
Los Angeles
Museum Square, 5757 Wilshire Boulevard, Suite One, Los Angeles, CA 90036; Tel: 323-634-1750; Fax: 323-634-1777

San Francisco
350 Sansome Street, Suite 900, San Francisco, CA 94104;
Tel: 415-391-3838;
Fax: 415-391-0102

Online, news and casting info for actors:
www.actorsequity.org/home.html

AFTRA

American Federation of Television & Radio Artists
National Headquarters
260 Madison Ave., 7th Floor
New York, NY 100116-2401
Tel: 212 532-0800

5757 Wilshire Blvd., 9th Floor
Los Angeles, CA 90036-3689
Tel: 323 634-8100; www.aftra.org

SAG

Screen Actors Guild
Hollywood:
5757 Wilshire Blvd.
Los Angeles, CA 90036-3600
Tel: 323 954-1600

New York
360 Madison Avenue, 12th Floor
New York, New York 10017; Tel: 212 944-1030

On the website, information for beginning actors and a complete list of SAG-franchised agents and much more. www.sag.org/

Appendix J: Dance Resources

Dance Organizations

The American Dance Guild ADG is a non-profit membership organization concerned with promoting the art of dance. Since 1956 the ADG has been serving the needs of performers, choreographers, teachers and students through all stages of their development and careers. www.americandanceguild.org/

American Dance Therapy Association (ADTA) National organization for Dance/Movement therapists who couple movement therapy with counseling, psychotherapy and/or rehabilitation. Tel: 410 997-4040; Fax: 410 997-4048; www.adta.org/

American Guild of Music Artists AGMA is a National Union, without a system of locals. However, AGMA does have an area structure for representation to the Board of Governors and a level of area administration. Many areas have an Area Executive Committee and an Area Chairperson. Members are encouraged to attend area meetings and other functions during the course of the year. A member's area is determined by their primary address on record at AGMA. In some cases where an artist lives in one area but perhaps has most of his or her employment in another area, that artist may designate a different area as their area. Mailings such as audition notices, meetings, and other important information is often based by areas. The composition of the Board of Governors is based on a formula of members in good standing (paid to date) for each of the following categories: Soloist, Chorister, Dancer/

Choreographer, Stage Manager/Stage Director. www.musicalartists.org/HomePage.htm

Dance /USA: 1156 15th Street NW, Suite 820, Washington, DC 20005; Tel: 202-833-1717; www.danceusa.org/

National Dance Education Organization, Bethesda, MD. Telephone: 301-657-2880; www.ndeo.org/

National Dance Project sponsored by New England Foundation for the Arts. Through the dedicated efforts of dance presenters across the country, NDP helps audiences connect with the rich and varied talents of choreographers and their companies. www.nefa.org/grantprog/ndp/index.html

Dance Companies

Alvin Ailey American Dance Theatre Alvin Ailey Dance Foundation, Inc. 211 West 1st Street, 3rd Floor New York, NY 10023; Tel: (212) 767-0590; Fax: (212) 767-0625; www.alvinailey.org/

American Repertory Ballet, Cranbury Studio, 29 North Main, St. Cranbury, NJ 08512; Tel: 609 921-7758; *New Brunswick Studio,* 80 Albany St. 2nd Floor, New Brunswick, NJ 08901; Tel: 732 249-1254: Fax: 732 249-8475; *Princeton Studio,* 301 North Harrison Street, Princeton, NJ 08540; Tel: 609-921-7758; Fax: 609-921-3249; www.arballet.org/

Art of the Matter Deborah Slater Dance Theatre 3288 21st Street, #PMB71, San Francisco, CA 94110. Tel: 415-267-7687; Fax: 415-332-7171; artofthematter.org/dsdt.html

Ballet Chicago 218 South Wabash Ave. 3rd Fl. Chicago, IL 60604; Tel: (312) 251-8838; www.balletchicago.org/

Houston Metropolitan Dance Company 1202 Calumet @ SanJacinto Houston TX 77004; Mailing Address: P. O. Box 980457, Houston TX 77098; Tel: 713-522-6375; www.houstonmetdance.com/proco.html

Hubbard Street Dance Chicago 1147 W. Jackson Blvd. Chicago, IL 60607; Tel: 312-850-9744; Fax: 312-455-8240; www.hubbardstreetdance.org/

Joffrey Ballet School 434 Avenue of the Americas, New York, NY, 10011; Tel: 212 254-8520; Fax: 212 614-0148: www.joffreyballetschool.com/

Lula Washington Dance Theatre 5041 West Pico Blvd., Los Angeles, CA 90019; Tel: 323-936-6591 Fax: 310-671-4572. Founded in 1980, the Lula Washington Dance Theatre is one of the most admired African-American dance institutions in California. It is known for great, energetic dance and wonderful residencies. www.lulawashington.com/history.htm

Malashock Dance Company. Company founded in 1988 by John Malashock, former principal with the Twyla Tharp Company, "one of California's premiere dance companies, providing performances, educational programs, outreach projects, and classes to thousands of people each year." Malashock Dance 3103 Falcon Street, Suite J, San Diego, CA 92103; Tel: 619 260-1622; Fax: 619 260-1621; www.malashockdance.org/

Merce Cunningham Studio 55 Bethune St., New York, NY 10014; Tel: 212 691-9715 ext. 30; www.merce.org/

Mid America Dance Company 502 Mistletoe, St. Louis, MO 63122; Tel/Fax: (314) 821-0660; www.midamericadance.com/

National Ballet School/L'Ecole Nationale de Ballet, Canada
105 Maitland Toronto, Ontario Canada M4Y 1E4; Tel: 416 964-3780; Fax: 416 964-5133; www.nationalballetschool.org/

Zenon Dance Company Performance and teaching company based in Minneapolis/St. Paul. Zenon Dance Company and School, Inc., 528 Hennepin Ave., #400, Minneapolis, MN 55403; Tel: 612 338-1101; Fax: 612 338-2479; www.zenondance.org/

Links

American Musical Theatre Reference Library, The. More extensive than you could possibly imagine. www.americanmusicals.com/Links_htm.htm

DanceArt.com. Not sure what it does, but there are links. www.danceart.com/

Artslynx International Dance Resources. Brilliant, well-maintained, thoughtful site. Lists 2,000 dance companies worldwide. www.artslynx.org/dance/index.htm

BalletCompanies.com National and International list of dance companies on the web. Great resource. www.balletcompanies.com/Countries/USAd.shtml

The Bridge Dance Theatre. Interesting dance company, great dance links. home.earthlink.net/~thebridgednc/bridge.html

Canadian Society of Professional Agents (CSPA) Dance School List "The dance schools listed below are known to be legitimate and honest in their dealings with actors. The CSPA feels that a new actor should be training with any of those listed." www.infosite.ca/schoolsd.htm

DanceArt.com. Not sure what it does, but there are links. www.danceart.com/

Dance Collective Online source for dancers with university guide, listings for auditions, dance school directory, searchable data-base of dancers and more.
Contact:
Creative Edge, Inc.
P.O. Box 557
Mercer Island, WA 98040
Tel: 888 726-9016;
E-mail: webmaster@dancecollective.com
www.dancecollective.com/gw2.htm

Dancer.com Online catalogue for the Gaynor Minden Dance Boutique in Chelsea with much information and many links. www.dancemagazine.com/

Dance Magazine
333 Seventh Avenue, 11th Floor,
New York, NY 10001
Tel: 212 979.4803
Fax: 646 674.0102
www.dancemagazine.com/

Dance Spirit Magazine Online version of magazine plus resources, store, other info. www.dancespirit.com/

Dance Spirit Directory of Dance Schools
Contact:
Dance Directory
c/o Russell Johns Associates, Ltd.

P.O. Box 1510
Clearwater, FL 33757-1510
Tel: 800 237-9851, 727 443-7666;
Fax: 727 445-9380;
E-mail: dd@rja-ads.com
www.rja-ads.com/dancedirectory/

Dance USA National service organization for professional dance. An online community for dancers. www.danceusa.org/

Dancewear.com Recommended Dance School Web Sites
e-dancewear.com/Dance_Schools.html

DMOZ Open Directory Project – Dance
dmoz.org/Arts/Performing_Arts/Dance/

GaramChai.com Indian Dance and Music Schools of North America   www.garamchai.com/danceschools.htm

National Guild of Community Schools of the Arts Complete List of 81 Dance Schools "The Guild is the national service organization for a diverse constituency of non-profit, non-degree granting institutions located in urban, inner-city, suburban and rural communities throughout the United States. [Its mission is] to foster and promote broad access to high quality arts education designed to meet community needs. To that end it provides service, advocacy and leadership for community arts education organizations."
www.nationalguild.org/dance0.htm

Performing Arts Online links.
performingarts.net/Links/dance.html

Southern California Dance and Directory, plus links.
www.usc.edu/dept/dance/

Strickler, Fred Biography University of Riverside – Dance Department www.dance.ucr.edu/people/strickler.html

Studio of Dance.com Dance Studio Directory A collection of websites, plus help in building your own (if you happen to have a dance school). www.studioofdance.com/studios.htm

Voice of Dance Online dance resource. www.voiceofdance.org/

Art That Pays

Appendix K: Music Resources

Professional Musicians Union

American Federation of Musicians (AFM) www.afm.org/
Local musician's unions are affiliated with the AFM, as well as the AFL-CIO, and can use the power of these larger associations for collective bargaining and to purchase insurance and pension plans at much reduced costs.

There is no audition for joining the union. You simply fill out an application (available at the local office, by mail, or, in some cases, from the local's website.)

Every local in the AFM sets its own annual membership and work dues rates, however the average cost to join is between $250 and $300, with approximately $100 of that as an initiation fee and the rest in the form of yearly dues, which can be prorated. Youths under the age of 21 are generally excused from paying the initiation fee.

Benefits:
- Earned credit in pension plan.
- Musician's Network, a non-fee referral service.
- Access to the Musician's Credit Union
- Legal Assistance and Arbitration
- Low cost rehearsal rooms
- Equipment insurance

- Musician's Assistance Program (MAP), for help with drug and alcohol dependency
- Medical, dental and life insurance (with enough work)

To find the local in your area, you can visit the AFM site and follow the links, either "How to Join the AFM", or "List of AFM Locals", to any area in Canada or the U.S. Below are a few of the major market contacts:

Los Angeles:
Professional Musicians, Local 47
Membership Department
817 Vine St., Hollywood, CA 90038
Tel: 323 993-3116.
www.promusic47.org/

New York:
Local 802
322 West 48th Street
New York, NY 10036
Tel: 212 245-4802
www.local802afm.org

Nashville:
Nashville Association of Musicians
11 Music Circle North
P.O. Box 120399
Nashville, TN 37212
Tel: 615 244-9514
www.afm257.org

Chicago:
Chicago Federation of Musicians
Local 10-208, AFM
175 W. Washington St.

Chicago, IL 60602
Tel: 312 782-0063
www.livemusichicago.com

Austin:
Austin Federation of Musicians
Local 433, AFM
P.O. Box 161480
Austin, TX 78716
Tel: 512 440-1414
www.afm.org/433

San Francisco:
Musicians' Union
Local 6, AFM
116 Ninth St.
San Francisco, CA 94103
Tel: 415 575-0777
www.afm6.org

Las Vegas:
Musicians' Union of Las Vegas
Local 369, AFM
P.O. Box 7467
Las Vegas, NV 89125
Tel: 702 647-3690
www.musicianslasvegas369.com

Performing Rights Organizations

ASCAP—The American Society of Composers, Authors and Publishers
One of the two major performing rights organizations. Many workshops and events for musicians/songwriters.
www.ascap.com/

ASCAP Member Services, Tel: 800 95-ASCAP

ASCAP Offices:

ASCAP - New York
One Lincoln Plaza
New York, NY 10023
Tel: 212 621-6000
Fax: 212 724-9064

ASCAP - Los Angeles
7920 W. Sunset Boulevard, Third Floor
Los Angeles, CA 90046
Tel: 323 883-1000
Fax: 323 883-1049

ASCAP - London
8 Cork Street
London W1X1PB
Tel: 011-44-207-439-0909
Fax: 011-44-207-434-0073

ASCAP - Nashville
Two Music Square West
Nashville, TN 37203
Tel: 615 742-5000
Fax: 615 742-5020

ASCAP - Miami
420 Lincoln Rd, Suite 385
Miami Beach, FL 33139
Tel: 305 673-3446
Fax: 305 673-2446

ASCAP - Chicago
1608 N Milwaukee
Suite 1007
Chicago, IL 60647
Tel: 773 394-4286
Fax: 773 394-5639

ASCAP - Puerto Rico
654 Ave. Muñoz Rivera
IBM Plaza Ste. 1101 B
Hato Rey, PR 00918
Tel: 787 281-0782
Fax: 787 767-2805

ASCAP Membership - Atlanta
PMB 400
541 Tenth Street NW
Atlanta, GA 30318
Tel: 404 351-1224
Fax: 404 351-1252

ASCAP Licensing - Atlanta
2690 Cumberland Parkway, Suite 490
Atlanta, GA 30339
Tel: 800 505-4052

BMI—Broadcast Music Incorporated. The other big one.
Check them out, compare, do the research. Many services
available aside from collecting your pay. bmi.com/home2.asp

New York
320 West 57th Street
New York, NY 10019-3790
Tel: 212 586-2000

Nashville
10 Music Square East
Nashville, TN 37203-4399
Tel: 615 401-2000

Los Angeles
8730 Sunset Blvd.
3rd Flr West
West Hollywood, CA 90069-2211
Tel: 310 659-9109

London
84 Harley House
Marylebone Rd
London NW1 5HN, ENGLAND
Tel: 011-0044 207486 2036

Miami
5201 Blue Lagoon Drive
Suite 310
Miami, FL 33126
Tel: 305 266-3636

Atlanta
P.O. Box 19199
Atlanta, GA 31126
Tel: 404 261-5151

Puerto Rico
255 Ponce de Leon
East Wing, Suite A-262
BankTrust Plaza
Hato Rey, Puerto Rico 00917
Tel: 787 754-6490

SESAC And one more. The acronym once stood for "Society of European Stage Authors and Composers," but now it's just a name, in that the company, which once handled only European and gospel music, is now diversified to include all types of music. A smaller company than the other two, SESAC prides itself on having personal relationships with its clients as well as being more selective in the copyrights represented. sesac.com/

Contact:

SESAC (headquarters)
  55 Music Square East
  Nashville, TN 37203
  Tel: 615-320-0055
  Fax: 615-329-9627

SESAC New York
  152 West 57th ST
  57th Floor
  New York, NY 10019
  Tel: 212-586-3450
  Fax: 212-489-5699

SESAC Los Angeles
  501 Santa Monica Blvd
  Suite 450
  Santa Monica, CA 90401-2430
  Tel: 310-393-9671
  Fax: 310-393-6497

SESAC International
  6 Kenrick Place
  London W1H 3FF

Tel: 020 7486 9994
Fax: 020 7486 9929

SGA—Songwriters Guild of America. The largest and oldest songwriters organization, offering contract review, royalty collection, access to group medical and much more. www.songwriters.org/

Los Angeles Office:
6430 Sunset Boulevard
Suite #705
Hollywood, CA 90028
Tel: 323 462-1108
Fax: 323 462-5430
E-mail: LASGA@aol.com

Nashville Office:
1222 16th Avenue South
Suite #25
Nashville, TN 37212
Tel: 615 329-1782
Fax: 615 329-2623
E-mail: SGANash@aol.com

New York Office:
1560 Broadway
Suite #1306
New York, NY 10036
Tel: 212 768-7902
Fax: 212 768-9048
E-mail: SongNews@aol.com

Songwriter Organizations

American Composers Forum Committed to supporting composers and helping to develop new markets for their music. National community, support, connections. 332 Minnesota Street, Suite E-145, St. Paul, MN 55101; Tel: 651 228-1407; Fax: 651 291-7978; www.composersforum.org/

ISA (International Songwriters Association) For professionals and non-professionals, members in more than 50 countries. The site offers news, interviews, contests and information about publishers, labels and much more. www.songwriter.co.uk/

Jazz Composers Collective Non-profit based in New York and dedicated to advancing the music of "forward-thinking composers." www.jazzcollective.com/

L.A. Songwriters Network A network of songwriters, musicians and music business professionals offering support and community. www.songnet.org/

Science Songwriters Association Promoting the writing of songs about science and the use of music in teaching science. Who knew?
E-mail: sciencesongs-subscribe@yahoogroups.com
www.tranquility.net/~scimusic/SSA/

SongwriterUniverse.com For a link to regional and nationwide songwriter associations: SongwriterUniverse, 11684 Ventura Blvd., # 975, Studio City, CA 91604;
www.songwriteruniverse.com/songwriterassociations.html

VOCAL - The Virginia Organization of Composers And Lyricists A not-for-profit organization for all levels of songwriter. Contests, showcases, support. VOCAL, P.O. Box 34606, Richmond, VA 23225; Tel: 804 342-0550; www.vocalsongwriter.org

Publications for Musicians

101 Music Business Contracts, by Platinum Millennium, R. Williams, Williams Publishing, June, 2001. www.theindustryyellowpages.com/

2004 Songwriter's Market: 700+ Places to Market Your Songs (Songwriter's Market, 2004) Writers Digest Books, 2003. F&W Publications, 4700 E. Galbraith Rd., Cincinnati, OH 45236; Tel: 513 531-2690, ext. 1483; www.writersdigest.com

All You Need to Know About the Music Business: Revised and Updated for the 21st Century by Donald S. Passman, Simon & Schuster, revised and updated edition, October, 2000. 1230 Avenue of the Americas, New York, NY 10020; Tel: 212 698-7000; www.simonandschuster.com

And Then I Wrote: The Songwriter Speaks by Tom Russell, editor, Arsenal Pulp Press, 1996. Consortium Book Sales, 1045 Westgate Drive, Suite 90, St Paul, MN 55114; Tel: 800 283-3572, 651 221-9035; Fax: 651 221-0124; www.arsenalpulp.com/

Billboard Musician's Guide to Touring and Promotion, The, city by city listing of clubs, radio stations, record stores, press; A&R directory to major and independent labels; music conference showcase contacts; directory of agents, managers, attorneys; musician website listings; directory of music publications; tape and disc services directory; Hardcopy or on disk at: Tel: 800 407-6874; www.musiciansguide.com/musicianmag/index.jsp

Bottom Line is Money, The: A Comprehensive Guide to Songwriting and the Nashville Music Industry, Jennifer Ember Pierce, A. Miccinello (editor), Bold Strummer Ltd, 1993. 110C Imperial Circle, P.O. Box 2037, Westport, CT 06880-2037; Tel: 800 375-3786, 203 227-8588; www.boldstrummerltd.com/

Complete Handbook of Songwriting, The: An Insider's Guide to Making It in the Music Industry by Mark Liggett et al; New York, Plume, 2nd edition, 1993.

Confessions of a Record Producer, 2 Ed: How to Survive the Scams and Shams of the Music Business by Moses Avalon, Backbeat Books, 2nd edition, February, 2002. 600 Harrison Street, San Francisco, CA 94107; Tel: 415 947-6615; www.backbeatbooks.com/

The Craft and Business of Songwriting by John Braheny, Writers Digest Books, 2nd edition, 2001. F&W Publications, 4700 E. Galbraith Rd., Cincinnati, OH 45236; Tel: 513 531-2690, ext. 1483 www.writersdigest.com

The Craft of Lyric Writing by Sheila Davis, Writer's Digest Books, 1985. F&W Publications, 4700 E. Galbraith Rd., Cincinnati, OH 45236 Tel: 513 531-2690, ext. 1483; www.writersdigest.com

Creating Melodies: A Songwriter's Guide to Understanding, Writing and Polishing Melodies by Dick Weissman, Writer's Digest Books, 1994. F&W Publications, 4700 E. Galbraith Rd., Cincinnati, OH 45236; Tel: 513 531-2690, ext. 1483; www.writersdigest.com

How I Make $100,000/Year in the Music Business (Without a Record Label, Manager, or Booking Agent) by David Hooper, Lee Kennedy, Kathode Ray Music, January, 2002. www.kathoderaymusic.com/

How to Be a Working Musician: A Practical Guide to Earning Money in the Music Business by Mike Levine, Billboard Books, 1997. Watson-Guptill, 770 Broadway, New York, NY 10003; Tel: 800 278-8477; Fax: 646 654-5487; commonsense, like our book is meant to be. Recommended. www.watsonguptill.com/

How to Make & Sell Your Own Recording: The Complete Guide to Independent Recording by Diane Sward Rapaport, Jerome Hedlands/Prentice-Hall, 5th Edition, 1999. Pearson Education One Lake Street, Upper Saddle River, NJ 07458; vig.prenhall.com/

In Cold Sweat – Interviews with Really Scary Musicians by Thomas Wictor, Limelight Editions. 118 East 30th Street, New York, NY 10016; Tel: 212 532-5525; Fax: 212 532-5526; www.limelighteditions.com/

The Indie Bible "The PREMIERE Directory for Independent Recording Artists" (their words, not ours), Big Meteor Publishing, PO Box 6043, Ottawa J, Ontario K2A 1T1 Canada; Tel: 613 596-4996; www.indiebible.com/

The Industry Yellow Pages, Volume 6: The Complete Major & Independent Record Label Music Business Directory, 2002-2003 International Edition by Platinum Millennium, June 2002. www.theindustryyellowpages.com/

Music Business Primer by Diane Sward Rapaport, Prentice Hall, 2002. Pearson Education, One Lake Street, Upper Saddle River, NJ 07458; vig.prenhall.com/

Music Law: How to Run Your Band's Business by Richard Stim, Nolo Press, 1998. Nolo, 950 Parker Street, Berkeley, CA 94710; Tel: 510 549-1976, 800 728- 3555. Like all the Nolo Press books, this one is good. www.nolo.com/index.cfm

Musician's Atlas, The, available in print or on CD-Rom. Music business contacts in more than 25 categories, including major and indie label A&R departments, commercial and college radio program directors, managers, agents, distributors, radio promoters, publishers, film & TV music supervisors, cd manufacturers, and more. CD-Rom version features email and URL connections, mailing lists, spreadsheets and invoices for business income and expenses. The Musician's Atlas, P.O. Box 682, Nyack, NY 10960; www.musiciansatlas.com

Music Publishing: A Songwriter's Guide by Randy Poe, Writer's Digest Books, revised 1997. F&W Publications, 4700 E. Galbraith Rd., Cincinnati, OH 45236; Tel: 513 531-2690, ext. 1483; www.writersdigest.com

The Songwriter's Handbook by Tom T. Hall, Rutledge Hill Press, 2001. Nelson Ministry Services, PO Box 140300, Nashville, TN 37214-0300; Tel: 800 441-0511; www.rutledgehillpress.com/

The Songwriter's Market Guide to Song & Demo Submission Formats, Donna Collingwood, Editor, Writers Digest Books, 1994. F&W Publications, 4700 E. Galbraith Rd., Cincinnati, OH 45236; Tel: 513 531-2690, ext. 1483; www.writersdigest.com

Songwriting: A Complete Guide to the Craft by Stephen Citron, Limelight Editions, 1990. 118 East 30th Street, New York, NY 10016; Tel: 212 532-5525; Fax: 212 532-5526; www.limelighteditions.com/

This Business of Music Marketing and Promotion by Tad Lathrop and Jim Pettigrew, Billboard Books, 2nd edition, March, 1999. Watson-Guptill, 770 Broadway, New York, NY 10003; Tel: 800 278-8477; Fax: 646 654-5487; www.watsonguptill.com/

This Business of Music: The Definitive Guide to the Music Industry by M. William Krasilovsky, et al., Watson-Guptill Pubns; 9th edition, May 2003. Watson-Guptill, 770 Broadway, New York, NY 10003; Tel: 800 278-8477; Fax: 646 654-5487; www.watsonguptill.com/

What They'll Never Tell You About the Music Business: The Myths, Secrets, Lies (& a Few Truths) by Peter M. Thall, Watson-Guptill Publications, June 2002. 770 Broadway, New York, NY 10003; Tel: 800 278-8477; Fax: 646 654-5487; www.watsonguptill.com/

The Young Musician's Survival Guide: Tips from Teens & Pros by Amy Nathan, Oxford University Press Children's Books, July, 2000. 198 Madison Avenue, New York, NY 10016; Tel: 212 726-6000; www.oup-usa.org/

Songwriting Contests

Ago/ECS Publishing Award in Choral Position
www.agohq.org/organize/index.html

Billboard Song Contest
www.billboard.com/bb/songcontest/index.jsp

Composers Commissioning Program 332 Minnesota Street, Suite E-145, St. Paul, MN 55101-1300; Tel: 651 228-1407; Fax: 651 291-7978; www.composersforum.org

Dallas Songwriters Assoc www.dallassongwriters.org

Great American Song Contest www.greatamericansong.com

Holkamp-AGO Award in Organ Composition 2940 South Quaker Avenue, Tulsa, OK 74114-5310; Tel: 918 743-0024; Fax: 918 592-3635; www.agohq.org/organize/index.html

International Songwriting Competition 211 Seventh Avenue North, Suite LL-20, Nashville, TN 37219; Tel: 615 251-4441; Fax: 615 251-4442; www.songwritingcompetition.com

The John Lennon Songwriting Contest
www.jlsc.com

McAllister Awards for Opera Singers
www.members.iquest.net/~opera

NACUSA Young Composers Competition
www.music-usa.org/nacusa

New Folk Concerts for Emerging Songwriters PO Box 291466, Kerrville, Texas 78029;
www.kerrville-music.com/newfolk.htm

Portland Songwriters Assoc. Annual Songwriting Competition P.O Box 16985, Portland, Oregon 97292-0985; Tel: 503 914-1000; www.pdxsongwriters.org

Pulitzer Prize in Music www.pulitzer.org/Entry_Forms

Rome Prize Fellowship in Musical Composition www.aarome.org/prize.htm

Songs Inspired By Literature Songwriting Comp The SIBL Project, 2601 Mariposa Street, 2nd floor, San Francisco, CA 94110; Tel: 415 553-3330; www.siblproject.org/competition.html

Thelonious Monk Institute Int'l Jazz Composers Competition www.monkinstitute.com/index5.html

Unisong International Song Contest www.unisong.com/uisc/index.html

USA Songwriting Competition www.songwriting.net

Songwriting Contest Portals:

1NetCommunications 1netcommunications.com/dir/Arts/Music/Songwriting/Contests/

AnsMe Directory directory.ansme.com/arts/200635.html

Arts, Entertainment & Recreation www.arts-entertainment-recreation.com/Arts/Music/Songwriting/Contests/

ASCAP Resource Guide www.ascap.com/resource/resource-10.html

dmoz open directory project
dmoz.org/Arts/Music/Songwriting/Contests/

Excite UK –Directory
www.excite.co.uk/directory/Arts/Music/Songwriting/Contests

Humanux.comIndex search.humanux.com/index/Arts/Music/
Songwriting/Contests/

International Songwriter's Association
www.songwriter.co.uk/page3.html
The Living Web
www.thelivingweb.net/contests.html

The Muse's Muse
www.musesmuse.com/contests.html

Nashville Songwriter's Association – Greeneville, SC
www.nsaigreenville.com/Resources/Contests.asp

Open Here
www.openhere.com/music/songwriting/contests/

Songwriting Contest AZ
www.asai.org.au/downloads/Contests%20List.doc

Target Studios
www.targetstudios.com/contests.html

The Songwriting Education Resource
www.craftofsongwriting.com/contests.htm

The VGP www.thevgp.com/index.php/Arts/Music/
Songwriting/Contests/

Links for Musicians

All About Jazz Musician Directory If you are a jazz musician, they will carry your website as a listing. www.allaboutjazz.com/

The American Musical Theatre Reference Library More extensive than you could possibly imagine. www.americanmusicals.com/Links_htm.htm

The American Music Center 30 West 26 Street, Suite 1001, New York, NY 10010 Tel: 212-366-5260; Fax: 212-366-5265; AMC is a national service and information center for new American music. Great web site! www.amc.net/

ArtLex Art Dictionary. Free, full, fascinating. Get lost for a while searching out your favorite artists and anything remotely to do with them. www.artlex.com/

Association of Professional Orchestra Leaders. Chicago-based not-for-profit founded to give bandleaders a place to exchange information, ideas and mutual support. www.bandleaders.org/

The Bold Strummer Ltd. Interesting publishing company. Many books on guitar and music in general. Also, "...the leading American source for books on Flamenco, Romani and Gypsy culture." www.boldstrummerltd.com/

Choral Net Portal for choral music online resources and communication. www.choralnet.org/

EastCoastBookings.com If you can deal with the pop-ups, this site may be of help to you. www.eastcoastbookings.com/

ElectricEarl.com   Kinda goofy, kinda cool. Great links and info on the LA music scene, plus weather, smog and traffic reports and live web cam from the hills of Silverlake. Fun. www.electricearl.com/

Fractured Atlas   Artists' community on the web. With membership there is access to help with medical insurance, accounting, grant writing. Without member ship, you can browse their links which, "…contain links to just about every arts-related website in existence." www.fracturedatlas.org/

Goodnight Kiss Music   Source of community and info for songwriters. Good links. www.goodnightkiss.com/

Hit Quarters A membership service with contact information for A&R, managers, publishing, production and radio stations. Not that expensive. www.hitquarters.com

Hollywood Bowl links   Links to just about every classical music/symphony/chamber group site you could want, plus a few jazz and world sites as well. www.hollywoodbowl.org/about/links.cfm

International Music Resources from Artslynx Brilliant, well-maintained, thoughtful site. www.artslynx.org/music/

Jazz Institute of Chicago   Jazz magazine online. jazzinstituteofchicago.org/

Kathode Ray Music Music promotion and artist development company in Nashville. Good info, books, links. www.kathoderaymusic.com/

Li'l Hank's Guide For Songwriters A somewhat faux-folksy web site that contains tons of information for singer/

songwriters and performers. Continually updated schedules of open mic nights and showcases, articles on protecting copyright and credit, legal advice for musicians and advice for performers, plus many useful links. Definitely worth checking out. www.halsguide.com

MAP—Musicians' Assistance Program "Providing help to members of the music community who seek treatment for drug and alcohol addiction—regardless of their financial condition." Based in Los Angeles, with branches in Akron OH, Atlanta GA, Austin TX, Boston MA, Chicago IL, Reno NV, London England, Miami FL, Minneapolis MN, Nashville TN, New Orleans LA, New York NY, Seattle WA; Tel: (LA): 323 993-3197, 888 MAP-MAP1; www.map2000.org/

MosesAvalon.com Pseudonymous author of *Confessions of a Record Producer,* he tells us "what record companies don't want you to know." Interesting. www.mosesavalon.com/

Musica International International database of choral repertoire. www.musicanet.org/

MusicContracts.com Pay site. They don't guarantee the contracts, so that could be a sticking point, but perhaps worth checking out. www.musiccontracts.com/

Music Performance Trust Fund Affiliated with the American Federation of Musicians, the MPTF sponsors over 25,000 free musical events each year. www.mptf.org/

The Musician's Source The best placed to search for published music on the web. Everything from Hal Leonard and Berklee Press to Miller Freeman/Backbeat Books. Rock, classical, religious. Brass, guitar, organ, vocal. Brass band scores, full opera scores. Books for all types and levels of musical performers. And a free bulletin board to buy and sell instruments. www.musiciansource.com/

Musicians Contact Service Pay site. Just what it says: listings of jobs, listings of the jobless. Check it out. Been around for quite a while, since 1969. At the very least, they have a fine selection of links. Tel: 818 888-7879; www.musicianscontact.com

NYC Music Places Searchable database of available rehearsal and performance spaces for instrumental and vocal musicians. Great links, too. www.nycmusicplaces.org/

The Open Directory Project "The largest, most comprehensive human-edited directory on the Web." Great links. Spend some time surfing. dmoz.org/Arts/Music/

Oregon Festival of American Music/The American Music Institute E. Broadway & High Street, PO Box 1497, Eugene OR 97440; Tel. 541-687-6526, 800 248 1615; www.ofam2.org/

Percussive Arts Society A music service organization. Community for drummers. www.pas.org/

Performing Arts Online Links. performingarts.net/Links/music.html

Pro Tools Free www.digidesign.com/ptfree/

The Singers Workshop Online info and community for pop singers. www.thesingersworkshop.com/

Songwriter.com A collective for songwriters to combine marketing and promotional efforts. You must have an independently and professionally produced CD in order to join. They (a loose "they") will listen to what you send in and decide if you fit, and then, for about $100 per year, you are a member. They will help you to set up your own website, if you don't already have one, and link it to their website and the major search engines. One way to find community. Submissions may be sent to: songwriter.com c/o 5 Happiness Webmaster, 9148 Skyline Blvd., Oakland, CA 94611; www.songwriter.com/

Songwriter's Directory Another place to find community on the web. Resources, classifieds, advice, a way to get your songs possibly heard. Links to contests, resources for the songwriter. No audition necessary, and as of this writing, membership is free. www.songwritersdirectory.com

Songwriters Resource Network
www.SongwritersResourceNetwork.com/

Vocal Area Network Site dedicated to the advancement of vocal ensemble music in the New York City area. www.van.org/

The Vocal Jazz Resource Community on the web for, you guessed it, jazz vocalists. www.jazzvocal.com/

The Young New Yorkers' Choru, For amateur, student and professional musicians. www.youngnewyorkerschorus.org/

Recovery Program

MAP—Musicians' Assistance Program. "Providing help to members of the music community who seek treatment for drug and alcohol addiction—regardless of their financial condition." Based in Los Angeles, with branches in Akron OH, Atlanta GA, Austin TX, Boston MA, Chicago IL, Reno NV, London England, Miami FL, Minneapolis MN, Nashville TN, New Orleans, New York NY, Seattle WA; Tel (LA): 323 993-3197, 888 MAP-MAP1; www.map2000.org/

Appendix L: Visual Arts Resources

Fine Arts Publications

Art Diary International Giancarlo Politi, Editor. Via Carlo Farini 68, 20159 Milano, Italy - Tel. +39 02 6887341 Fax +39 02 66801290. Up-to-date contact information for artists, galleries, designers, photographers and arts services. www.flashartonline.com/sections/international/ artdiary_int.asp

The Artist-Gallery Partnership: A Practical Guide to Consigning Art by Tad Crawford and Susan Mellon, Allworth Press, revised edition, 1998. 10 East 23rd Street, Suite 210, New York, NY, 10010; Tel: 212 777-8395. Sample contract free for the taking, but get their books. www.allworth.com/

Artists' Housing Manual: A Guide to Living in New York City. Volunteer Lawyers for the Arts, 1 East 53rd Street, 6th Floor, New York, NY 10022-420. Information on housing and workspace and loft space in NYC, for both tenants and landlords. www.vlany.org/

Business and Legal Forms for Fine Artists/Illustrators/ Photographers by Tad Crawford et al, Allworth Press, various dates. Ready-to-use forms, instructions, and advice on negotiations. 10 East 23rd Street, Suite 210, New York, NY, 10010; Tel: 212 777-8395 www.allworth.com/

Copyright for Performing, Literary and Visual Artists, Texas Accountants and Lawyers for the Arts, 1540 Sul Ross, Houston, TX 77006. All about just what the title says. www.talarts.org

How to Survive and Prosper As an Artist: Selling Yourself Without Selling Your Soul by Caroll Michels, Owl Books, December 2001. Henry Holt and Company, Inc., 115 West 18th Street, New York, NY 10011, Tel: 212 886-9200; Fax: 212 633-0748; publicity@hholt.com www.henryholt.com/owlbooks.htm

Model Agreements for Visual Artists: A Guide to Contracts in the Visual Arts by Paul Sanderson, Canadian Artists' Representation, Ontario (CARO), 1982. 401 Richmond Street West, Suite 443, Toronto, Ontario M5V 3A8, Canada. All about Canadian art law, plus model contracts. www.carfacontario.ca/resources/bpub.html

National Resource Guide for the Placement of Artists, Cheryl Slean, Editor, The National Network for Artist Placement, revised regularly. 935 West Avenue, Suite 37, Los Angeles, CA 90065. An annotated guide to arts organizations that provide support to artists. www.artistplacement.com

Taking the Leap: Building a Career As a Visual Artist by Cay Lang, Chronicle Books, April 1998. 85 Second St., Sixth Floor, San Francisco, CA 94105; Tel: 415 537-4200, 800 722-6657; Fax: 415 537-4460; mailto:frontdesk@chroniclebooks.com www.chroniclebooks.com/

Visiting Arts.....Directory, Visiting Arts, London, 1999. Available from Visiting Arts, Bloomsbury House 74 – 77, Great Russell Street, London WC1B 3DA, England. Directories outlining the arts infrastructure and providing contact information for countries from Norway to Thailand. www.visitingarts.org.uk/home.html

Visual Arts Links

About.com Painting. painting.about.com/

AbsoluteArts.com. The largest marketplace for contemporary art, international art news, art research and marketing tools, online since 1995. ww.absolutearts.com/

Artforum. 350 Seventh Avenue, New York, NY 10001, Tel: 212 475-4000; Fax: 212 529-1257; www.artforum.com/

Artnet Magazine with galleries, links, extensive directories. 61 Broadway, 23rd Floor New York, NY 10006-2701; Tel: 212 497-9700; Fax: 212 497-9707; www.artnet.com/

Artnews Online Read the magazine, search back issues, great links. www.artnewsonline.com/

ArtsiteGuide.com Art and art history information source, links to art supplies resources. www.artsiteguide.com/artsupplies.html

Artslynx Visual arts resources. Brilliant, well-maintained, thoughtful site. www.artslynx.org/vis/index.htm

Juxtapoz Art magazine online for the slightly bent. www.juxtapoz.com

Modern Painters Magazine 3rd Floor,52 Bermondsey Street, London SE1 3UD; Tel: 44 (0) 20 7407 9247; www.modernpainters.co.uk/

Nita Leland's International Art School Links www.nitaleland.com/links/schoolsinternatllinks.htm

Nita Leland's U.S. Art School Links www.nitaleland.com/links/schoolslinks.htm

Open Directory Art Supplies Listings dmoz.org/Shopping/Visual_Arts/Supplies/

World Wide Arts Resources Some interesting links.
wwar.com/index4.html

Business Links for Visual Artists

Accountants for the Public Interest A non-profit organization which can assist those artists and small business owners unable to afford it with their tax preparation, record keeping, setting up or computerizing an accounting system; they can also advise on financial management, budgets and loan applications.
www.geocities.com/api_woods/api/apihome.html

AKAS II Source for artist tax guides, record keeping kits and tax forms. www.akasii.com

Allworth Press Publishers of business and self-help books for artists, writers, designers, film and performing artists. 10 East 23 Street, Suite 510, New York, NY 10010; Tel: 212-777-8395; Fax: 212-777-8261; E-mail: PUB@allworth.com
www.allworth.com/

Artist Resource, Northern California and Beyond. For visual artists and writers. Listings of arts organizations, links, classes, shows, classifieds; help with web site design and etc.
www.artistresource.org/

ArtLex Art Dictionary Free, full, fascinating. Get lost for a while searching out your favorite artists and anything remotely to do with them. www.artlex.com/

Alliance of Artists Communities Arts communities, job opportunities, great links. 255 South Main Street, Providence, RI 02903; Tel: 401 351-4320; Fax: 401 351-4507; E-mail: aac@artistcommunities.org
www.artistcommunities.org/links-resources.html

Brooklyn Arts Council Very well maintained and informative web site. 195 Cadman Plaza West, Brooklyn, NY 11201; Tel: 718 625-0080; Fax: 718 625-3294; E-mail: bac@brooklynartscouncil.org
www.brooklynartscouncil.org/index.cfm?ts=04222003150344

The Business Center for the Arts Sponsors workshops and provides information on grant and proposal writing and other career-related topics. www.bcadc.org/

Business Volunteers for the Arts Online Business professionals helping not-for-profits improve their business practices. Listings of local and regional offices. www.artsandbusiness.org/bvahome.htm

Schools, Internships and Jobs for Visual Artists—Links

Circle in the Square Theatre School Information and programs for all the arts, education, job opportunities, etc. www.circlesquare.org/arts_education.html

Gardner's Guides to Internships, Washington, DC. Contact: Anthony Mason, Marketing Director; Tel: 703 793-8604; Fax: 703 793-8830; E-mail: anthony@ggcinc.com www.gogardner.com/

The Live/Work Institute, a not-for-profit founded to advocate, assist and encourage the development of live/work and zero commute housing. Thomas Dolan Architecture Embarcadero West, 173 Filbert Street, Oakland, California 94607; www.live-work.com/

Los Angeles County Arts Internship Program for nonprofit "performing, presenting, literary and municipal arts organizations." lacountyarts.co.la.ca.us/internship.html

National Endowment for the Arts Sponsors grants and various programs designed to nurture and support the arts. 1100 Pennsylvania Ave., NW, Washington, DC 20506; Tel: 202 682-5400; E-mail: webmgr@arts.endow.gov, www.arts.endow.gov

New York Foundation for the Arts Service organization for artists that provides this free national information resource for artists in all disciplines. 155 Avenue of the Americas, 14th Floor, New York, NY 10013-1507; Tel: 212 366-6900; Fax: 212 366-1778; www.nyfa.org/

Not for Tourists Web Directory for New York, Chicago and *Los Angeles.* Great general info as well as specific to all areas of the arts. www.notfortourists.com/

Performance Studies International, a professional association founded to promote international communication between performers and scholars of performing arts. PSI, Department of Drama, Stanford University, Stanford, CA 94305-5010; E-mail: admin-mail@psi-web.org
www.psi-web.org/mission.html

Performing Arts Online Links section with over 15,000 performing arts related websites, plus they will help you, gratis, to build your own website. performingarts.net/index.html

Graphic Arts Publications

Business and Legal Forms for Graphic Designers, by Tad Crawford and Eva Doman Bruck, Allworth Press, revised edition. 10 East 23rd Street, Suite 210, New York, NY, 10010; Tel: 212 777-8395; www.allworth.com/

The Business Side of Creativity: The Complete Guide for Running A Graphic Design or Communications Business by Cameron S. Foote, Mark Bellerose (illustrator), W. W. Norton & Company, Inc., 500 Fifth Avenue, New York, NY 10110; Tel: 212 354-5500; www.wwnorton.com/

Communication Arts Magazine for designers.
Tel: 800 688-1971; www.commarts.com/

Graphic Artists Guild Handbook: Pricing & Ethical Guidelines, 11th edition, Graphic Artists Guild. 90 John Street, Suite 403, New York, NY 10038-32-2; Tel: 212 791-3400; www.gag.org/

The Graphic Designer's Guide to Creative Marketing: Finding & Keeping Your Best Clients by Linda Cooper Bowen, Wiley Publishing. Corporate Headquarters, 111 River Street, Hoboken, NJ 07030; Tel: 201 748-6000; Fax: 201 748-6088; www.wiley.com/

Graphic Designer's Guide to Pricing, Estimating & Budgeting by Theo Stephan Williams, Brenner Books. Brenner Information Group, P.O. Box 721000, San Diego, CA 92172-1000; Tel: 858 538-0093; www.brennerbooks.com/

Graphic Designer's Ultimate Resource Directory by Poppy Evans, Cincinnati, North Light Books, 1999.

Graphic Arts Links

American Institute of Graphic Arts (AIGA), 164 Fifth Avenue, New York, NY 10010; Tel: 212 807 1990; www.aiga.org/

Corbis License-free images. www.corbis.com/

The Desktop Graphic artists website. Up to date and informative. Desktop Graphics, Post Office Box 66456, Los Angeles, CA 90066-6456; Tel: 877 391-9696, 310 391-5275; Fax: 310 391-9865; www.thedesktop.com/

DesignStore/01 All the design books you could ever want. www.designstore01.com/store/books/1829/9/1/

Flash Kit Online community of Flash developers. Tutorials etc. www.flashkit.com/index.shtml

FontHaus www.fonthaus.com/

Fonts.com Fonts from Agfa. Agfa Monotype Corporation Attn: Customer Care, 200 Ballardvale Street, Wilmington, MA 01887-1069; www.fonts.com/

Getty Images "The world's leading provider of imagery, film and digital services." creative.gettyimages.com/

Gif.com Online art specialists. www.gif.com/

Graphic Artists Guild a national union of illustrators, designers, web creators, production artists, and others. 90 John Street, Suite 403, New York, NY 10038-3202; Tel: 212-791-3400; www.gag.org/

HTML Goodies Tutorials for developers. www.htmlgoodies.com/

Icon Factory www.iconfactory.com/

Graphic Designers Paradise Good links. www.desktoppublishing.com/design.html

Virtual Graphic Artist. Perhaps a bit simplistic, but... www.deluxacademy.com/

Society of American Graphic Artists (SAGA) Service organization for fine art printmakers. Graphic Artists, Inc., PO Box 7869, Marietta, Georgia 30065; Tel: 404 641-7388, Cell/Office: 770 637-5366; E-mail: Info@graphicartistsinc.com www.graphicartistsinc.com/

LA Graphic Artists/Designers www.at-la.com/biz/@la-graph.htm

Suite 101.com Articles for artists. www.suite101.com/welcome.cfm/graphic_artists_retired

Webdeveloper.com Tips and info. www.webdeveloper.com/

Appendix M: Writer's Resources

Publications and Periodicals for Writers

Agents and Publishing

2003 Guide to Literary Agents, Rachel Vater, ed. Writer's Digest Books. F&W Publications, Inc., Corporate Office, 4700 E. Galbraith Road, Cincinnati, Ohio 45236; Tel: 513 531-2222; E-mail: writersdig@fwpubs.com www.writersdigest.com/store/books.asp

2003 Novel & Short Story Writer's Market, Anne Bowling, ed., Writer's Digest Books. F&W Publications, Inc., Corporate Office, 4700 E. Galbraith Road, Cincinnati, Ohio 45236; Tel: 513 531-2222; E-mail: writersdig@fwpubs.com www.writersdigest.com/store/books.asp

2004 Writer's Market, Kathryn S. Brogan, Robert Lee Brewer ed., Writer's Digest Books. F&W Publications, Inc., Corporate Office, 4700 E. Galbraith Road, Cincinnati, Ohio 45236; Tel: 513 531-2222; E-mail: writersdig@fwpubs.com www.writersdigest.com/store/books.asp

Jeff Herman's Guide to Book Publishers, Editors, and Literary Agents, 2004 Edition, by Jeff Herman, Kalmbach Publishing Co. 21027 Crossroads Circle, P.O. Box 1612, Waukesha, WI 53187-1612; Tel: 800 533-6644; Fax: 262-796-1615; www.kalmbach.com/

Literary Agents: The Essential Guide for Writers, Debby Mayer, ed., revised edition, Penguin Books, 1998. Penguin Group (USA) Inc., 405 Murray Hill Parkway East, Rutherford, NJ 07073; Tel: 800 788-6262; us.penguingroup.com/

Literary Market Place™ 2004, The Directory of the American Book Publishing Industry, Information Today, Inc. Books. 143 Old Marlton Pike, Medford, NJ 08055-8750; Tel: 609 654-6266; Fax: 609 654-4309; www.literarymarketplace.com/lmp/us/index_us.asp

Writers' and Artist's Yearbook 2003, A&C Black Ltd., 2003. 37 Soho Square, London W1D 3QZ; Tel: 0207 758 0200; E-mail: wayb@acblack.com   www.acblack.com

The Writer's Handbook 2004, Kalmbach Publishing Co. 21027 Crossroads Circle, P.O. Box 1612, Waukesha, WI 53187-1612; Tel: 800 533-6644; Fax: 262-796-1615; www.kalmbach.com/

Write the Perfect Book Proposal: 10 That Sold and Why, 2ⁿᵈ Edition by Jeff Herman and Deborah Levine Herman, John Wiley & Sons, 2001. 10475 Crosspoint Blvd., Indianapolis, IN 46256; Tel: 877 762-2974; Fax: 800 597-3299; E-mail: consumers@wiley.com   www.wiley.com

Freelance Writing

The ASJA Guide to Freelance Writing:A Professional Guide to the Business, for Nonfiction Writers of All Experience Levels, Timothy Harper, editor. St. Martin's Griffin, September, 2003. St. Martin's Press, 175 Fifth Avenue, New York, NY 10010; Tel: 212 674-5151; www.stmartins.com/

The Copyright Permission and Libel Handbook: A Step-by-Step Guide for Writers, Editors, and Publishers by Lloyd J.

Jassin & Steven C. Schechter, John Wiley & Sons, 1998. 10475 Crosspoint Blvd., Indianapolis, IN 46256; Tel: 877 762-2974; Fax: 800 597-3299; E-mail: consumers@wiley.com   www.wiley.com

The Freelance Success Book: Insider Secrets For Selling Every Word You Write by David Taylor & Bob Teufel, Peak Writing Press, 2003. Peak Writing, LLC, 37 W. Fairmont Avenue, Bldg. 2, Suite 202, Savannah, GA 31406; Tel: 912 398-2987; Fax: 912 921-1065; E-mail: info@peakwriting.com   www.peakwriting.com

Freelance Writing for Magazines and Newspapers by Marcia Yudkin, Harper Collins, 1993. HarperCollins Publishers, 10 East 53rd Street, New York, NY 10022; Tel: 212 207-7000; www.harpercollins.com/hc/home.asp

Links for Writers

Artslynx online links to writing sources
www.artslynx.org/writing/index.htm

Bard's Ink. Writing-related links, resources, market and guideline information, writer's block, poetry, writer's critique groups. www.iprimus.ca/%7epjduane

Beginning Writers. Resource for beginning writers,
www.beginningwriters.com

BloomsburyMagazine.com. Practical advice, regular updates from the book business, a calendar of literary dates and links to other sites.
www.bloomsburymagazine.com/WritersArea/default.asp

The Burry Man Writers Center, a worldwide community of writers. There's a plethora of sources including freelance job links, stuff for fiction and nonfiction writers, as well as workingprofessionals and beginners, with particular support for writers interested in Scotland. Too fascinating to pass up. www.burryman.com

Carnegie Mellon Playwriting, screenwriting resources gathered by the good folks at Carnegie Mellon. zeeb.library.cmu.edu/bySubject/Drama/dramplay.html

The Eclectic Writer Resources.
www.eclectics.com/writing/writing.html

HerCorner Resources, inspiration and support. HerPlanet Inc., PO Box 745, New Market, MD 21774; www.hercorner.com

Indispensable Writing Resources Site. Source for writing-related books and web sites. Reference sites, writing sites, writing job sites. www.quintcareers.com/writing

LA Press Club Links Great research portal.
www.lapressclub.org/site/links.shtml

Mindspring.com Playwriting resources.
www.mindspring.com/~splatterson/playwritingresources.html

Net Author Online community and reference source for writers www.netauthor.org

Online Resources for Writers Maintained by peer tutors at the University of Maine Writing Center.
www.ume.maine.edu/~wcenter/resources.html

Pegasus Writers Stable An organization of professional freelance writers. A good place to connect. www.pegasus-writers-stable.com/sys-tmpl/door

Resources for Writers Reviews of books, software and websites about writing. Articles with tips and resources. www.suite101.com/welcome.cfm/writers

Scribe & Quill Resources. www.scribequill.com

Writers Associations and Organizations A great portal site that will take you to many organizations for journalists, screenwriters, technical writing, business industry writing and general writers organizations. www.writerswrite.com/org.htm

WritersDigest.com Online guide to "the writing life." www.writersdigest.com

Writer Gazette Writing resources, tips, techniques . www.writergazette.com

Writers Exchange Writing resources. www.writers-exchange.com

The Writers Home Contains links to websites of interest to writers, a comprehensive instruction section, book reviews, links to author websites, links to publisher websites, and interviews with authors. www.writershome.com

WritersMarket.com is your wired key to publishing success, providing the most comprehensive—and always up-to-date—market contact info available, with electronic tools you won't find anywhere else. www.WritersMarket.com/

Writers Web Resources.
www.swiftsite.com/writersweb/contents.htm

Writing-World.com Writing articles and resources. Tips about how to become a better writer, get published and find writing markets. From Moira Allen. www.writing-world.com

Service Organizations for Writers

The Academy of American Poets 588 Broadway, Suite 604, New York, NY 10012-3210; Tel: 212 274-0343; Fax: 212 274-9427. Founded in 1934 The Academy of American Poets helps support American poets as well as develops American's appreciation of contemporary poetry. One of the oldest and largest organizations in the country dedicated to promoting poetry. www.poets.org/index.cfm

American Society for Journalists and Authors (ASJA), 1501 Broadway, Suite 302, New York, NY 10036; Tel: 212 997-0947. ASJA, a national organization of independent nonfiction writers, supports excellence in nonfiction writing. They offer a myriad of services, including employer-member referral service, an annual nonfiction writers conference focusing on marketing trends, financial assistance for incapacitated writers and a monthly newsletter. www.asja.org/

The Association of Authors' Representatives, Inc. (AAR), a not-for-profit organization of independent literary and dramatic agents. www.aar-online.org/index.html

The Association of Writers and Writing Programs (AWP) is the place for writers to go to find a college level teaching job as a writing instructor. There is a yearly job market conference sponsored by *AWP.* www.awpwriter.org/

The Council of Literary Magazines and Presses, 154 Christopher Street, Suite 3C, New York, NY 10014-9110; Tel: 212 741-9110; Fax: 212 741-9112; www.clmp.org/

The Dramatists Guild of America, Inc., 1501 Broadway, Suite 701, New York, NY 10036; Tel: 212 398-9366; Fax: 212 944-0402. A professional association for playwrights, composers, and lyricists. www.dramaguild.com

International Women's Writing Guild, P.O. Box 810, Gracie Station, New York, NY 10028-0082; Tel: 212 737-7536; Fax: 212 737-9469; www.iwwg.com/

National Writers Union, NWU, 113 University Pl. 6th Fl., New York, NY 10003. Trade union for freelance writers of all genres. Seventeen local chapters throughout the country. www.nwu.org/

PEN American Center, 568 Broadway, Suite 401, New York, NY 10012; Fax: 212 334-2181. A fellowship of writers in existence for more than seventy-five years. PEN helps to advance literature, promote a culture of reading, and defends freedom of expression. www.pen.org/

Poetry Society of America 15 Gramercy Park, New York, NY 10003; Tel: 212 254-9628. The Poetry Society of America sponsors readings, seminars and competitions intended to inspire individuals to write, listen to and read poetry. www.poetrysociety.org/

Poets & Writers, National Office: Poets & Writers, Inc., 72 Spring Street, Suite 301, New York, NY 10012; Tel: 212 226-3586; Fax: 212 226-3963.

California Office: Poets & Writers, Inc., 2035 Westwood Blvd., Suite 211, Los Angeles, CA 90025; Tel: 310 481-7195; Fax: 310 481-7193. Poets & Writers have many programs that support all kinds of creative writers. They have a monthly magazine and a variety of publications designed to help poets and writers with practical ways to advance their careers. www.pw.org

Teachers & Writers Collaborative, 5 Union Square West, New York, NY 10003-3306; Tel: 212 691-6590; Fax: 212 675-0171. T&W was founded in 1967 by noted writers and educatorswho envisioned writers changing the way writing was taught. T&W provides workshops in public and private schools in the New York tri-state region as well as publishing many books and a monthly magazine about the teaching of creative writing. www.twc.org/

Writers Guild of America, 7000 West Third Street, Los Angeles, CA 90048; Tel: 323 951-4000 or 800 548-4532; Fax: 323 782-4800. *Writers Guild of America, East,* 555 West 57th Street, Suite 1230, New York, NY 10019; Tel: 212 767-7800; Fax: 212 582-1909. www.wga.org/

Writer's Groups

Writers' groups an excellent portal to writers groups all over the US. E-mail: Callie@writepage.com
www.writepage.com/groups.htm

Writers' Groups, a list of groups that meet to talk on specific topics for example there are AWS groups writers who have survived abuse who meet to talk about surviving and about writing. www.writerswrite.com/groups.htm

Writers.com A. J. Levinson hosts free writers' groups for fiction writers, nonfiction writers, and poets. Participation in the groups helps build a friendly place where writers can gather for inspiration and support, exchanging critiques, keeping in touch with fellow class members, etc.
E-mail: writers@writers.com www.writers.com/groups

Small Press Publishers

Arcade Publishing They have published more than 500 authors over the past twelve years. www.arcadepub.com/

Avocet Press Inc. A small, independent press, they publish everything from poetry to mysteries and historical fiction. Avocet Press Inc, 19 Paul Court, Pearl River, NY 10965-1539; Tel: 845 620-0986, 877 4-AVOCET; Fax: 845 735-6807; avocetpress.com/

Black Amber Books "The definitive website for British and European Black and Asian writers." All-around publishers but with a focus in 2nd and 3rd generation immigrant Black- and Asian-themed work. BlackAmber Books, 3 Queen Square, London WC1N 3AU; Tel: +00 44 0207 278 2488; Fax: +00 44 0207 278 8864; www.blackamber.com

Black Heron Press Literary press located in Seattle publishing all genres. mav.net/blackheron/

Coffee House Press Award winning non-profit literary publisher. 27 N. 4th St., #400, Minneapolis, MN 55401; Tel: 612 338-0125; Fax: 612 338-4004; Submissions to be sent to Christopher Fischbach, Senior Editor, at the above address. www.coffeehousepress.org/

Cumulus Press Poetry and fiction. PO Box 5205, Station B, Montreal (Quebec) Canada H3B 4B5; Tel.: 514 522-5404; Fax:: 514 522-7324; www.cumuluspress.com

dustbooks.com Small press source. P.O. Box 100, Paradise, CA 95967; Tel: 530 877-6110; Fax: 530 877-0222; Orders: 800 477-6110; E-mail: publisher@dustbooks.com www.dustbooks.com

Fiction Collective Two an "author-run, not-for-profit publisher of artistically adventurous, non-traditional fiction." Submissions can be sent, along with $10, to: FC2 Production Manager, Publications Unit, Campus Box 4241, Illinois State University, Normal, Illinois 61790-4241; distribution is by Northwestern University Press, 625 Colfax Street, Evanston, Illinois 60208-4210;
Tel: 800 621-2736; fc2.org/

Glimmer Train Press, Inc. Publishers of a quarterly journal of short fiction, dedicated to the publishing of new authors. These people love writers. Glimmer Train Press, Inc.
1211 NW Glisan Street, Suite 207, Portland, OR 97209; Tel: 503 221-0836; Fax: 503 221-0837; Questions: eds@glimmertrain.com www.glimmertrain.com/

The International Directory of Little Magazines & Small Presses, Len Fulton, editor. Dustbooks, 2003. The best source of none mainstream presses and magazines. It is updated every year and at this writing it lists nearly 5,000 book and magazine publishers of literary, avant garde, cutting-edge contemporary, left wing, right wing and radical chic fiction to non-fiction essays, reviews, artwork, music, satire, criticism, commentary, letters, parts of novels, long poems, concrete art, collages, plays, and more. P.O. Box 100, Paradise, CA 95967; Tel: 530-877-6110; Fax: 530-877-0222; www.dustbooks.com/

New Hope International: Links to Publishers & Small Presses
www.nhi.clara.net/pslinks.htm

No Exit Press Independent publisher of crime fiction. Submissions may be sent to: Editorial Department, No Exit Press, 18 Coleswood Road, Harpenden, Herts, AL5 1EQ UK. www.noexit.co.uk/

The Paper Journey Press An emerging small literary press in North Carolina publishing fiction and historical narratives. The Paper Journey Press, P.O. Box 1575, Wake Forest, NC 27588; Tel: 919570-0728; submissions: Contact: Wanda G. Wade, Editor - Wanda@thepaperjourney.com thepaperjourney.com/

Shoelace Publishing Inc. Eclectic but somewhat safe publishers, they do accept submissions. Shoelace Publishing Inc. P.O. Box 530849, Henderson, Nevada 89053-0849; www.shoelacepublishing.com/

Small Presses Owned and Operated by People of Color: Publishers of Children's Books Cooperative Children's Book Center, School of Education, University of Wisconsin-Madison www.soemadison.wisc.edu/ccbc/pclist.htm#apctop

Small Publishers Association of North America (SPAN) P.O.Box 1306, Buena Vista, CO 81211; Fax: 719 395-8374; www.spannet.org/

Wildside Press, LLC Publishers of crime, science fiction and romance. P.O. Box 301, Holicong, PA 18928-0301; Tel: 215 345-5645; E-mail: wildsidepress@yahoo.com www.wildsidepress.com

Art That Pays

Yahoo Directory, Literary Small Press
Literary_Small_Press/

Awards and Prizes for Writers

There are many prizes for which you must be nominated by
your publisher. Some of these include:

- *The Betty Trask Awards* (first novel)
- *National Play Award*, National Repertory Theatre
- *Commonwealth Writers Prize* (fiction)
- *Crime Writers' Association Awards*
- *National Book Awards*
- *National Book Critics Circle Awards*
- *Nobel Prize for Literature*
- *PEN/Faulkner Award for fiction*
- *The Pulitzer Prizes.*

Awards you can apply for on your own

Academy of American Poets have several awards that are given
out yearly. Check out these different awards at their web site
www.poets.org/awards/academy.cfm

Alice James Books has three different awards they give out
yearly which include New England/New York Competition,
the Beatrice Hawley Award, and the Jane Kenyon Chapbook
Competition. www.alicejamesbooks.org/submission.html

American Antiquarian Society
www.americanantiquarian.org/artistfellowship.htm

Associated Writers Programs Contests, a variety of contests
for the aspiring writer, students and publisher.
www.awpwriter.org/contests/

The Gift of Freedom Award from A Room Of Her Own which will give $50,000 to a woman writer. www.aroomofherownfoundation.org/awards.htm

National Endowment for the Arts gives money every other year to poets and fiction writers, check out this site for guidelines: www.arts.gov/grants/apply/index.html

National Play Award, National Repertory Theatre Foundation, P.O Box 286, Hollywood, CA 90078; Tel: 323 465-9517; Fax: 323 417-4722

National Poetry Series Open Competition publishes your book and gives you $1,000. Here are the guidelines: www.nationalpoetryseries.org/

National Society of Arts and Letters gives an award to recognize gifted young American Artists, for guidelines go to: www.arts-nsal.org/awards.html

Poets & Writers comprehensive list of small awards and prizes across the United States. Go browse here: www.pw.org/links_pages/Grants_and_Awards/

Sawtooth Poetry Prize Competition from Ahsahta Press www.boisestate.edu/english/ahsahta/contest.htm

Sergel Drama Prize, Court Theatre, 5706 E. Ellis Avenue, Chicago, IL 60637; Tel:312 753-4472.

∞

About the Authors

Adele Slaughter has written for various publications including *USAToday.com*, *Ms. Magazine* and *Written By*. In 2003 she was awarded a national journalism prize for her coverage of multiple sclerosis. In 1993 the White House Commission on Presidential Scholars named her a Distinguished Teacher. She received her M.F.A. in poetry from Columbia University. Slaughter's first book of poems, *What The Body Remembers,* was published by Story Line Press in 1994.

Jeff Kober has appeared extensively on stage, in films and on television. Most recently he was seen in *Defying Gravity* at the Rubicon Theatre in Ventura, California. Kober worked with John Ritter and Jenny Sullivan for several years helping to develop Jenny Sullivan's autobiographical play, *J for J*. His film credits include *A Man Apart* with Vin Diesel, *Enough*, directed by Michael Apted, *Elmore Leonard's Gold Coast* and *The First Power*. Kober was a regular on the series *China Beach,* and has guest starred on many TV shows, most recently *ER* and *The Guardian.* Kober was a student of the late Ed Kaye-Martin and is currently studying acting with Candace Silvers. This is his first book.

∞